The Theory and Practice of Change Management

The Theory and Practice of Change Management

John Hayes

palgrave

First published 2002 by
PALGRAVE
Houndmills, Basingstoke, Hampshire RG21 6XS and
175 Fifth Avenue, New York, N.Y. 10010
Companies and representatives throughout the world

PALGRAVE is the new global academic imprint of
St. Martin's Press LLC Scholarly and Reference Division and
Palgrave Publishers Ltd (formerly Macmillan Press Ltd).

ISBN 0–333–98796–9 hardback
ISBN 0–333–98797–7 paperback

This book is printed on paper suitable for recycling and
made from fully managed and sustained forest sources.

A catalogue record for this book is available
from the British Library.

Library of Congress Cataloging-in-Publication Data
Hayes, John, 1943–
    The theory and practice of change management / John Hayes
        p. cm.
    Includes bibliographical references and index.
    ISBN 0–333–98796–9—ISBN 0–333–98797–7 (pbk.)
    1. Organizational change. 2. Organizational effectiveness. I. Title
    HD58.8 .H39 2002
    658.4′06—dc21   2001058770

Copy-edited and typeset by Povey–Edmondson
Tavistock and Rochdale, England

10   9   8   7   6   5   4   3   2   1
11   10   09   08   07   06   05   04   03   02

Printed and bound in Great Britain by
Antony Rowe Ltd
Chippenham, Wiltshire

To
Helen, Jonathan
Isabel and Miranda

Contents

List of tables   ix

List of figures   x

Preface   xii

Acknowledgements   xiv

Part I   Core concepts   **1**

1   The nature of change: what's all the hype about?   3
2   Organisational effectiveness and the role of change management   11
3   Systems models, congruency and the concept of 'fit'   23
4   Organisational learning and organisational effectiveness   36
5   Process models of change   47

Part II   Recognising and diagnosing the need for change   **61**

6   Recognising the need for change and starting the change process   63
7   Diagnostic models   71
8   Gathering and interpreting information for diagnosis   89

Part III   Managing the people issues   **101**

9   Power, leadership and stakeholder management   105
10   Communicating   114
11   Training and development   122
12   Motivating others to change   128
13   Managing personal transitions   144

**Part IV   Shaping implementation strategies and managing
             the transition**   **159**

14   Shaping the implementation strategy   161
15   Maintaining control during the change   166

Part V   Interventions   **173**

16   Types of intervention   175
17   Selecting interventions   187

Part VI   Keeping the change on track   **199**

18   Managing, reviewing and sustaining change   201

Author index   211
Subject index   214

List of tables

3.1	Mechanistic and organic organisation forms	25
3.2	Examples of element states that do and do not facilitate system adaptation	29
5.1	Possible actions	48
7.1	Examples of the kind of information that might be attended to	73
7.2	Interdependencies between elements	76
7.3	An example of a matrix of interdependencies	76
8.1	Examples of questions asked in the 1993 BBC staff survey	91
13.1	The Social Readjustment Rating Scale	147

List of figures

1.1	Pattern of industry/product category evaluation	6
1.2	Intensity of change over time	6
1.3	Types of organisational change	8
2.1	Examples of functional misalignment	13
3.1	The organisation as an open system	24
3.2	Kotter's (1980) integrative model of organisational dynamics	26
3.3	Nadler and Tushman's (1980) congruence model	31
4.1	Individual and collective learning in organisations	39
5.1	Steps in the change process	54
5.2	The relationship between Chapters 6–18 and the generic process model of change	58
6.1	The trap of success	64
7.1	The causal map of a diagnostic model	77
7.2	Strebel's (1996) cycle of competitive behaviour	79
7.3	Weisbord's (1978) six-box model	81
7.4	Kotter's (1980) integrative model of organisational dynamics	82
7.5	Nadler and Tushman's (1980) congruence model	83
7.6	The Burke–Litwin (1992) causal model of organisational performance and change	84
7.7	The transformational factors	86
8.1	A force-field	96
8.2	Results of the 1993 BBC staff survey	98
9.1	Classification of key stakeholders	107
10.1	An oversimplified model of the interview	117
10.2	The interaction between change agents and organisational members	118
12.1	The expectancy model of motivation	132
12.2	An expectancy model of the motivation to support or resist change	133
13.1	Bridges' (1991) model of transition	150
13.2	Transition phases	151
14.1	A continuum of intervention strategies	162

15.1 A matrix organisation structure   170
16.1 Developments in type of intervention over the last century   176
16.2 Cummings and Worley's (2001) typology of interventions based on
      focal issue   182
17.1 A three-dimensional model to aid choice of interventions   190
17.2 Examples of human-process interventions   191
17.3 Examples of techno-structural interventions   191
17.4 Examples of human-resource interventions   192
17.5 Examples of strategic interventions   192
18.1 The Balanced Scorecard as a framework for change management   206
18.2 Cause and effect relationships in the service–profit chain   208

Preface

This book, *The Theory and Practice of Change Management*, is designed to help you:

- develop your investigative and diagnostic skills so that you will be more effective in assessing what is going on in organisations;
- extend your ability to manage issues arising from internally planned and externally imposed organisational changes;
- improve your awareness of how people can facilitate or resist change and extend your ability to manage the human resource in the context of change.

The book is also distinctive in at least three respects:

- Part I – core concepts – reviews some of the main theoretical perspectives on organisational change. This provides a robust conceptual framework for a more detailed consideration of the practice of change management that is presented in Parts II through VI.
- At several points throughout the book you will be presented with exercises designed to help you articulate and critically examine your own implicit theories of change and change management. You will then be invited to compare your own theories with those presented in the literature and, where appropriate, revise your own theories.
- In order to help you consider how you might apply theory to improve your practice of change management you will also be presented with a series of exercises designed to help you relate theory to your own experience. This will help you reflect on the practical utility of the ideas presented in each chapter.

This book has been written for practising managers and for MBA students and others studying for professional qualifications. The content of the book is organised into 18 chapters. This structure reflects some of the theoretical and practical issues that have been important in my experience consulting with a wide variety of clients on a range of change-related issues. Most university courses on change management, however, tend to be designed around 11 or 12 units. One way of relating the 18 Chapters to an 11–unit course is presented below:

Unit 1 The nature of change (Chapter 1)

Unit 2 Organisational effectiveness and the role of change management (Chapter 2)

Unit 3 System models, congruency and the concept of 'fit' (Chapter 3)

Unit 4 Organisational learning and organisational effectiveness (Chapter 4)

Unit 5 Process models of change (Chapter 5)

Unit 6 Recognising and diagnosing the need for change (Chapters 6, 7, 8)

Unit 7 Managing the people issues (1) Stakeholder management, communication, training and development (Chapters 9, 10, 11)

Unit 8 Managing the people issues (2) Motivating others to change and managing personal transitions (Chapters 12, 13)

Unit 9 Shaping implementation strategies and managing the transition (Chapters 14, 15)

Unit 10 Interventions (Chapters 16, 17)

Unit 11 Managing, reviewing and sustaining change (Chapter 18)

If there is space for a twelfth unit this might involve students reviewing the course and reflecting on what they have learned and to what extent theory can make a positive contribution to the practice of change management.

JOHN HAYES

Acknowledgements

The author and publishers wish to thank the following for permission to reproduce copyright material: Peter Hyde, who co-devised Figure 5.1 with John Hayes; Perseus Books, from *Organizational Diagnosis: A Framework of Theory and Practice* by Marvin R. Weisbord, copyright © 1978 by Marvin R. Weisbord, reprinted by permission of Perseus Books, a member of Perseus Books LLC, and from *Managing Transitions* by William Bridges, copyright © 1991 by William Bridges and Associates Inc., reprinted by permission of Perseus Books, a member of Perseus Books LLC; Elsevier Science, from the *Journal of Psychosomatic Research*, vol. 11, 1967, p. 215, Holmes *et al.*, 'The Social Readjustment Rating Scale'; Pearson Education Ltd for an illustration from *Mastering Management*; Thomson Learning, from Cummings and Worley, *Organization Development and Change*, 7th edn, 2001; Harvard Business School Publishing, for a figure on page 76 of Kaplan and Norton, 'Using the Balanced Scorecard as a Strategic Management System', *Harvard Business Review*, Jan–Feb 1996; John Wiley & Sons, from Nadler, Shaw and Walton, *Discontinuous Change*, figures on pp. 11, 20 and 24; reproduced by permission of Jossey-Bass Inc., a subsidiary of John Wiley & Sons Inc.; the Southern Management Association from the *Journal of Management*, 1992, 18(3), pp. 528, 530. Every effort has been made to contact all the copyright-holders, but if any have been inadvertently omitted the publishers will be pleased to make the necessary arrangement at the earliest opportunity.

Part I

Core concepts

In this part we review some of the main theoretical perspectives on the management of organisational change and provide a robust conceptual foundation for a more detailed consideration of the practice of change management in Parts II–VI.

Chapter 1   The nature of change: what's all the hype about?

This chapter considers the nature of change and the challenges it poses for managers. After reading this chapter you will be asked to reflect on the nature of the changes confronting your organisation and/or your department/unit in the organisation.

Chapter 2   Organisational effectiveness and the role of change management

Change management is about modifying or transforming organisations in order to maintain or improve their effectiveness. This chapter considers:

- alternative definitions of organisational effectiveness; and
- the degree to which managers can intervene to affect the way organisations respond to change – change agency.

Before reading this chapter you will be asked to list the indicators of effectiveness that you believe are used to assess the effectiveness of your organisation *and* your department/unit within the organisation. Partway through the chapter you will be asked to consider whether these indicators/criteria of effectiveness need to be revised (the measurement of organisational performance will also be considered in Chapter 18).

At the end of the chapter you will also be asked to reflect on beliefs about change agency in your organisation and how they affect the way change is managed.

Chapter 3   Systems models, congruency and the concept of 'fit'

This chapter makes a distinction between component and total system models of organisational functioning and goes on to consider organisations from an open-systems perspective. Particular attention is given to the organisation's alignment with the wider environment and the alignment of the organisation's internal elements. After reading this chapter you will be invited to:

- think about your department in terms of a process that transforms inputs into outputs;
- analyse the quality of 'fit' between your department and:
  - (a) those departments (or other constituencies) that supply your department with inputs;
  - (b) those departments or other customers who receive the outputs produced by your department.

Chapter 4   Organisational learning and organisational effectiveness

This chapter provides a brief overview of strategic change management (where the focus is on finding the best fit between the organisation and the wider environment) and the contribution that individual and organisational learning can make to ensuring that the organisation survives and grows. After reading this chapter you will be invited to assess the quality of organisational (collective) learning within your department or the organisation as a whole. A series of questions will provide a framework for this assessment.

Chapter 5   Process models of change

This chapter explores some of the issues and choices involved in developing an approach to managing organisational change. Before reading this chapter you will be presented with a case that involves managing a merger. The case is presented at the start of this unit in order to help you think about and articulate your implicit model of how change should be managed before you are exposed to some of the most widely cited process models of change.

1

The nature of change: what's all the hype about?

In the first section we briefly consider some of the ideas advanced by Toffler (1970), a futurologist, in one of his early books, *Future Shock*. The second section moves on to consider some of the careful empirical work undertaken by Tushman and his colleagues at Columbia University that examines some of the aspects of the changes that confront organisations today. The third section brings these two sets of ideas together to help us understand the consequences of change for individuals and organisations. The final section introduces the dimension of time pressure and builds on the work of Tushman to present a typology for classifying different types of change.

Exercise 1.1 Is the nature of change changing?

There appears to be a growing concern that the management of change is becoming more difficult. Is this concern justified or is it simply the result of hype?

Ask yourself whether the nature of change that confronts society today is any different from the nature of change that confronted our grandparents and their grandparents before them? If you believe that the nature of change has changed, make a list of some of the differences.

PRESSURES FOR GREATER ADAPTABILITY

Toffler (1970) argues that, in many respects, 'future shock' is similar to culture shock, but with one very important difference – there is no going back. If people find it difficult to adapt to a new culture there is often the alternative of returning to the familiar culture they left. For example, if emigrants fail to settle in a new country (national culture) it might be possible for them to return home. When confronted with future shock, however, this option is unlikely to be as available.

Future shock is the product of three related trends; transience, novelty and diversity.

Transience

Impermanence and transience are increasingly becoming important features of modern life because of a major expansion in the scale and scope of change and the accelerating pace of change.

The accelerating pace of change affects people's relationship with things, places, people, organisations and ideas. As acceleration occurs these relationships become foreshortened, telescoped in time. Various factors have affected this:

1. *Things*. Relationships with things have been foreshortened because:

   - Advances in technology and falling manufacturing costs have changed the balance against repairing things in favour of replacement.
   - Technical advances increase the rate of obsolescence.
   - Increased uncertainty about future needs work against investing in things that will last.

2. *Places*. For some, movement means improvement and is welcome, for others relocation produces agonising disruptions. But in spite of the forces mitigating against movement, such as dual-career families, many people do move around and do not have the roots and stability enjoyed by their grandparents.

3. *People*. Relationships are increasingly defined in functional terms and involvement is limited because of:

   - An increase in the number of relationships.
   - A decrease in the duration of relationships.

4. *Organisations*. The nature of peoples' relationships with organisations have changed because:

   - Accelerating change has created the need for continuous organisation development and renewal.
   - Increasing the organisation's adaptability has strained the adaptability of organisational members.
   - Changes in the psychological contract have eroded loyalties to one boss or one organisation.

5. *Ideas*. The entire knowledge system in society is undergoing violent upheaval thus increasing the rate at which people must form and forget their images of reality.

These changes in things, places, people, organisations and ideas have demanded a new level of adaptability in order for individuals and organisations to cope. People respond to an increase in the pace of change in different ways. Those who internalise the principle of acceleration make an unconscious compensation for the compression of time – they modify their durational expectancies. But some find this more difficult than others.

Novelty

This is the second major trend identified by Toffler. He argues that having to live at an accelerating pace is one thing when life situations are more or less familiar, but having to do so when faced by unfamiliar, strange or unprecedented situations is distinctly another. And this is the reality for increasing numbers of people. Today the balance between the familiar and the unfamiliar is changing. In Toffler's words, the novelty ratio is rising.

Diversity

Diversity is the third major trend. The Orwellian view that people will become mindless consumer-creatures, surrounded by standardised goods, educated in standardised schools, fed a diet of standardised mass culture and forced to adopt standardised styles of life could not be further from the truth, according to Toffler. The reality is that most of us are faced with a paralysing surfeit of choice that, especially at work, complicates decision making.

Toffler summarises the consequences of these trends. He argues that when diversity converges with transience and novelty society is rocketed towards an historical crisis of adaptation. The outcome is an environment so ephemeral, unfamiliar and complex that it threatens millions with adaptive breakdown. This breakdown is future shock.

INCREMENTAL AND DISCONTINUOUS CHANGE

How do Toffler's ideas map on to what we know about what is happening in the business world? Tushman and his colleagues at Columbia (1985, 1986) studied hundreds of companies in several industries over time. They found evidence to support existing theories about a consistent pattern of industry evolution.

Early phases of experimentation and low growth give way to more rapid growth as a product gains acceptance and as dominant designs emerge. Later, demand levels off and eventually declines as more advanced or completely different products attract consumers' attention (Figure 1.1).

They also found that within any industrial sector there are consistent patterns in the amount of change that occurs over time. Their evidence, summarised by Nadler and Tushman (1995), suggests that whole industries go through periods of relatively minor change, and these periods are punctuated by intervals of major disturbance, or disequilibrium, when the whole product class and virtually all companies in the industry are affected. Romanelli and Tushman (1994) refer to this process of organisational transformation as 'punctuated equilibrium'.

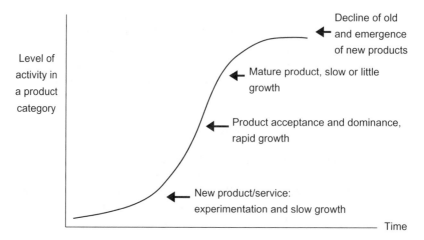

Figure 1.1 Pattern of industry/product category evolution

These periods of major disequalibrium appear to be triggered by a destabilising event or set of events that change the basic dynamics or relationships in a particular industry. These events may come from outside the industry or they may be initiated by one of the industry participants as it strives to gain a competitive advantage. During these periods of disequilibrium the effects are widespread. Almost all companies in the industry experience major change and those that fail to adapt tend to be acquired by others or drop out (Figure 1.2). This evidence points to the existence of two types of change: incremental and discontinuous change.

Incremental change is a type of change associated with those periods when the industry is in equilibrium and the focus for change is 'doing things better' through a process of continuous tinkering, adaptation and modification. Change in these periods builds on what has already been accomplished and has the flavour of continuous improvement.

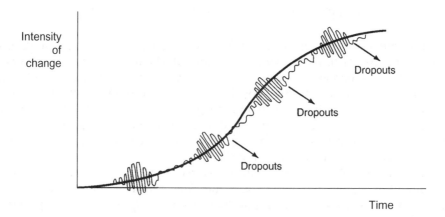

Figure 1.2 Intensity of change over time

Source: Nadler, D., Shaw, R. and Walton, A.E., *Discontinuous Change*, Jossey-Bass, 1995, p. 20.

Discontinuous change is a type of change that occurs during periods of disequilibrium. Many writers, for example Tichy and Devanna (1986), Kotter (1999) and Burke and Litwin (1993), refer to it as transformational change. It involves a break with the past, a step function change rather than an extrapolation of past patterns of change and development. It is based on new relationships and dynamics within the industry that may undermine core competencies, and question the very purpose of the enterprise. This kind of change involves doing things differently rather than doing things better. It might even mean doing different things. An example is the reprographics industry where companies had a core competence in optical reproduction that was undermined by the development of digital scanning.

Tushman and colleagues went on to report that their investigation of company archives revealed that:

- Companies in each product class or industry go through periods of continuous and discontinuous change with some degree of regularity.
- The nature of these patterns can vary across industries (e.g. periods of discontinuous change may follow a 30-year cycle in cement, but a 5-year cycle in mini-computers).
- In almost all industries the rate of change is increasing and the time between periods of discontinuous change is decreasing.

This last point is important because it indicates that managers will be confronted with an ever-greater need to manage discontinuous change (see Brown and Eisenhardt, 1997).

Discontinuous change involves what Toffler refers to as 'novelty'. It challenges the familiar assumptions about how business is done. The increasing rate of change also reflects Toffler's concept of 'transience'.

THE CONSEQUENCES FOR INDIVIDUALS AND ORGANISATIONS

Organisations attempt to make themselves more adaptable by changing their structures, processes and cultures. For example, matrix organisation promotes the more efficient use of scarce resources and facilitates the reconfiguration of resources to match ever changing customer requirements, but these methods of working can lead to role conflicts, role ambiguity and role overload for organisational members.

In many work settings people are being required to unlearn old ways and develop new competencies, or get out. Dated contracts and an increasing reliance on temporary workers are also being used. The effect is to increase organisational flexibility at the expense of individual security and career prospects.

Toffler refers to the possibility of adaptive breakdown – his state of future shock. Many reports document the increasing levels of stress experienced by workers, and much attention has also been focused on those who believe the psychological contract between themselves and their organisation has been violated. All of these developments affect performance, commitment and the physical and psychological well-being of employees. But they also create problems for managers and supervisors. They have to manage people who are upset by change at a time when the same changes are increasing their own workloads. With increasing frequency, especially in times of discontinuous change, managers are having to cope with multiple and concurrent changes. At such times, having to cope with other peoples' emotional response to change is an added burden that is sometimes difficult to manage. This issue will be given more consideration in Chapter 12.

TIME PRESSURE

It is more difficult to manage change, particularly the human aspects of change, when the need for change is urgent.

- Involving people and encouraging participation in the change process can aid diagnosis, reduce resistance and increase commitment, but this kind of approach takes time.
- The less urgent the need for change, the more time there is to experiment. When there is a pressing need for change it is more difficult to search for creative solutions.
- The increasing pace of change often means that there is less time to plan and manage change.

It is possible to differentiate between reactive change and anticipatory change:

- *Reactive change* is an organisation's response to a clear and present requirement for change.
- *Anticipatory change* is initiated without a clear and present external demand. Anticipatory changes might be initiated to gain competitive advantage or to prepare for a destabilising event that might occur sometime in the future.

Combining the degree of continuity or discontinuity with a dimension of time pressure, Nadler and Tushman (1995) produced the typology of change shown in Figure 1.3.

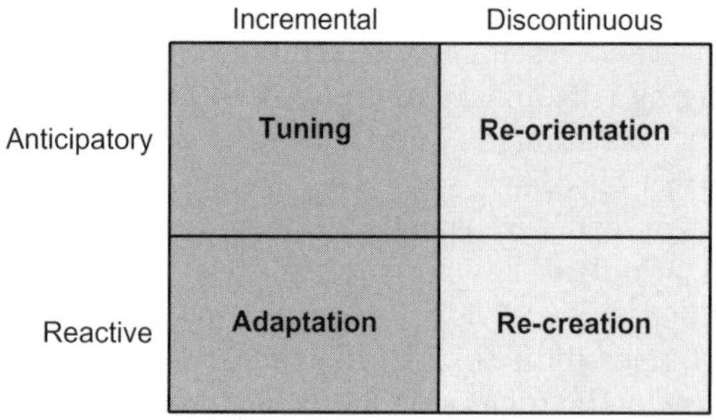

	Incremental	Discontinuous
Anticipatory	Tuning	Re-orientation
Reactive	Adaptation	Re-creation

Figure 1.3 Types of organisational change

Source: Nadler, D., Shaw, R. and Walton, A.E., *Discontinuous Change*, Jossey-Bass, 1995, p. 24

Tuning is change that occurs when there is no immediate requirement to change. It involves seeking better ways of achieving or defending the strategic vision. For example, improving policies, methods, procedures; introducing new technologies; redesigning processes to reduce cost, time to market and so forth, or developing people with required competencies.

This approach to change tends to be initiated internally in order to make minor adjustments to maintain alignment between the internal elements of the organisation and between the organisation's strategy and the external environment.

Adaptation is an incremental and reactive response to a pressing external demand for change. It might involve responding to a successful new marketing strategy adopted by a competitor, or to change in the availability of a key resource. While this kind of change can be minor or major, it tends to be bounded by the existing paradigm. Essentially, it involves, within broad terms, doing more of the same but doing it better in order to remain competitive. This kind of change is not about doing things in fundamentally different ways or about doing fundamentally different things.

Re-orientation and re-creation are types of change that do involve doing things differently or doing different things. They involve transforming the organisation.

Re-orientation involves a fundamental redefinition of the enterprise. It is initiated in *anticipation* of future opportunities or problems. The aim is to ensure that the organisation will be aligned and effective in the future, even if in the short term this involves abandoning existing patterns of alignment. (The concept of alignment and fit will be considered in more detail in Chapter 3.) Because the demand for change may not be obvious to all and may not be seen as pressing, senior management may need to work hard to create a sense of urgency and gain the commitment of others to the need for change. (See Kotter's checklist for leading change, Chapter 9.)

Re-creation is a reactive change that involves transforming the organisation through the fast and simultaneous change of all its basic elements. An often cited example of this kind of change is that introduced by Lee Iacocca when he moved to become the new CEO at Chrysler. He embarked on a process of revolutionary change that involved replacing most of the top team, withdrawing the company from the large-car market and divesting many foreign operations.

Whether the need is for continuous of discontinuous change, the earlier the need is recognised the greater the number of options managers will have when deciding how to mange it. Whenever managers are forced to react to an urgent and pressing need to change they are relatively constrained in what they can do.

SUMMARY

This chapter has considered the nature of change, giving particular attention to issues of continuity and time pressure. The effects of change on individuals and organisations have also been examined and a typology specifying four types of change has been presented.

The nature of the changes that have confronted your organisation over the past few years

You might find it useful to reflect on the nature of the changes that have confronted your organisation (or the part of the organisation that you know best) over the last few years.

- Has the nature of the changes confronting the organisation changed? If so, can you specify what is different?
- Overall would you describe the nature of change as incremental or discontinuous?
- What has been the organisation's typical response to change, reacting or anticipating?

Make a note of your answers on a separate sheet or in the space provided below.

REFERENCES

Brown, S.L. and Eisenhardt, K.M. (1997) 'The Art of Continuous Change: Linking Complexity Theory and Time-Paced Evolution in Relentlessly Shifting Organizations, *Administrative Science Quarterly*, 42, March, pp. 1–34.

Burke, W.W. and Litwin, G.H. (1992) 'A Causal Model of Organizational Performance and Change, *Journal of Management*, 18(3), pp. 523–45.

Kotter, J.P. (1999) *On What Leaders Really Do*, Boston, Mass.: A Harvard Business Review Book

Nadler, D.A. and Tushman, M.L. (1995) 'Types of Organizational Change: From Incremental Improvement to Discontinuous Transformation', in D.A. Nadler, R.B. Shaw and A.E. Walton, *Discontinuous Change: Leading Organizational Transformation*, San Francisco: Jossey-Bass, pp. 15–34.

Romanelli, E. and Tushman, M.L. (1994) 'Organizational Transformation as Punctuated Equilibrium: An Empirical Test', *Academy of Management Journal*, 37(5), pp. 1141–66.

Tichy, N.M. and Devanna, M.A. (1986) *The Transformational Leader*, Chichester: Wiley.

Toffler, A. (1970) *Future Shock*, New York: Random House.

Tushman, M.L., Newman, W. and Romanelli, E. (1986) 'Convergence and Upheaval: Managing the Unsteady Pace of Organization Evolution', *California Management Review*, 29, 1, pp. 29–44.

Tushman, M.L. and Romanelli, E. (1985) 'Organizational Evolution: A Metamorphosis Model of Convergence and Reorientation', in B. Staw and L. Cummings (eds) *Research in Organization Behavior*, vol. 7. Greenwich, Conn: JAI Press.

2

Organisational effectiveness and the role of change management

Change management is about modifying or transforming organisations in order to maintain or improve their effectiveness. Managers are responsible for ensuring that the organisation (or the part of the organisation they manage) performs effectively. To do this they need to know what constitutes effective performance and have some means of assessing whether or not the organisation as a whole or their particular sub-system is performing effectively. They also need to know, if performance is unsatisfactory, what elements of the organisation can be changed in order to improve performance and what steps they can take to secure these changes.

This chapter:

- considers some of the factors that need to be taken into account when assessing organisational effectiveness;
- reviews arguments relating to the manager's ability to affect the way an organisation responds to changed circumstances;
- examines some of the factors, such as the availability of conceptual models, management tools and beliefs about change agency, that can affect the manager's ability to successfully manage change.

ASSESSING ORGANISATIONAL EFFECTIVENESS

Before reading on, make notes, in the space provided overleaf, of the indicators that you believe could be used to assess whether or not your organisation – and your department or unit within the organisation – are effective.

When you have completed this chapter you might like to review these indicators and consider whether any of them need to be revised.

<table>
<tr><td colspan="2" align="center">Indicators of effectiveness</td></tr>
<tr><td align="center">Organisation</td><td align="center">Department/unit</td></tr>
<tr><td></td><td></td></tr>
</table>

DEFINITIONS OF ORGANISATIONAL EFFECTIVENESS

Organisational effectiveness has been defined in many different ways. This section examines a range of criteria that you might need to consider when assessing the effectiveness of an organisation or a unit within an organisation.

Purpose

Many commercial organisations use profit as one of the main indicators of effectiveness, but this indicator might not apply to all organisations. While financial viability may be necessary for the survival of organisations such as religious orders, universities, hospitals or charities, profit might not be viewed as a critical indicator of their effectiveness. The effectiveness of hospitals in the British National Health Service, for example, might be judged on indicators such as bed utilisation, waiting lists and morbidity rates rather than 'profit'. Indicators of effectiveness need to be relevant to the *purpose* of the organisation or unit within an organisation.

Stakeholder perspective

Different stakeholders often use different indicators to assess an organisation's effectiveness. Profit might be more important to shareholders than to workers or customers. Suppliers, customers, employees and people in the wider community affected by the products and services (and pollution) produced by an organisation will all have their own views on what should be taken into account when assessing whether or not it is effective.

Level of assessment

Effectiveness can be assessed at different *levels* (such as the organisation, sub-unit or individual employee), and in terms of the *linkages* between the different elements of the organisation (such as Kotter's processes and cause-and-effect relationships – see Chapter 3).

Alignment

Assessments of effectiveness need to be *aligned* up, down and across the organisation. The indicators used to assess the effectiveness of sub-units need to be aligned 'vertically' to the indicators used to assess the effectiveness of individuals who are members of each unit (via the appraisal process) and to the overall effectiveness of the organisation. The indicators used for different units also need to be aligned 'horizontally' across the organisation. Figure 2.1 depicts a simplified model of the functional structure of an organisation and presents examples of indicators of effectiveness for each function, and objectives that each function might pursue in order to achieve an effective performance.

Managers working in sub-units of the organisation represented in Figure 2.1 might lose sight of the overall goal of the organisation and focus their attention on the achievement of more immediate goals related to functional performance. For example, marketing and sales, in the face of strong price competition, might seek to secure increased sales (related to their goal of maximising revenue from sales) by offering customers fast delivery and customised products. While this strategy might help marketing and sales achieve its own performance targets, it might undermine the effectiveness of the manufacturing and distribution functions (and consequently the effectiveness of the overall organisation). In order to customise products and offer an immediate and flexible response to satisfy customers' 'just-in-

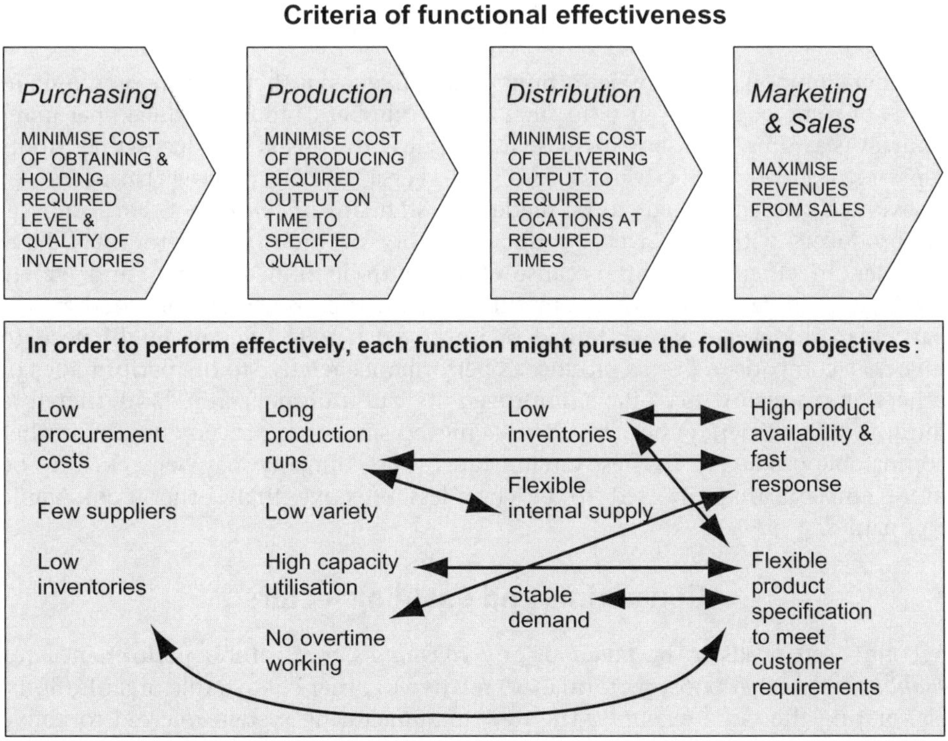

Criteria of functional effectiveness

Purchasing	Production	Distribution	Marketing & Sales
MINIMISE COST OF OBTAINING & HOLDING REQUIRED LEVEL & QUALITY OF INVENTORIES	MINIMISE COST OF PRODUCING REQUIRED OUTPUT ON TIME TO SPECIFIED QUALITY	MINIMISE COST OF DELIVERING OUTPUT TO REQUIRED LOCATIONS AT REQUIRED TIMES	MAXIMISE REVENUES FROM SALES

In order to perform effectively, each function might pursue the following objectives:

Low procurement costs	Long production runs	Low inventories	High product availability & fast response
Few suppliers	Low variety	Flexible internal supply	
Low inventories	High capacity utilisation	Stable demand	Flexible product specification to meet customer requirements
	No overtime working		

Figure 2.1 Examples of functional misalignment

time' delivery requirements, the manufacturing function might have to introduce short product runs, make greater use of overtime working and hold higher stocks of work in progress. The distribution function might have to hold higher inventories of finished goods and, because of unpredictable demand, make more deliveries that involve part loads. The cost of meeting these new manufacturing and distribution requirements might be greater than the net benefits achieved from the increased sales revenue and might threaten the organisation's overall effectiveness. A few examples of sources of possible misalignment are indicated by the double-headed arrows shown in Figure 2.1. As will be seen from this example, it is not uncommon for organisation sub-units (and individual employees) to be rewarded for behaving in ways that have little to do with overall organisational effectiveness.

Time perspective

It has already been noted that in some cases profitability can be a useful indicator of organisational effectiveness. However, just because organisation A is currently more profitable than organisation B does not mean that A is the most effective organisation. Organisation B might be incurring higher costs and lower profits today in order to invest in new plant, product development and staff training in the belief that this will help secure survival and growth over the longer term. The implication of this is that some reference to *time perspective* needs to be included in any definition of effectiveness.

Benchmark

Another common feature of definitions of effectiveness is that they are presented in terms of some output:input ratio such as the number of units produced per man-hour. It is assumed that any increase in output with constant or decreasing inputs represents greater effectiveness and vice versa. When making this kind of assessment reference needs to be made to a standard or *benchmark*. For example, all producers within a given product category or industrial sector may have experienced efficiency gains because of the introduction of a new and widely available manufacturing system. In this context, the assessment of whether one particular producer has maintained or improved its effectiveness might need to involve a comparison of this producer's performance relative to the performance of others. A company may have improved its output:input ratio (and therefore improved its efficiency) but may have achieved smaller improvements than other comparable producers. In these circumstances the company may be deemed to be more efficient than it used to be, but less effective than other comparable companies.

Constraints and enabling factors

Account also needs to be taken of any *constraints* that inhibit performance (or *enabling factors* that boost performance) relative to other comparable organisations. Elaborating the same example, the new manufacturing system referred to above might produce levels of toxic emissions greater than the levels permitted by environmental regulations. These regulations may only apply to a minority of producers located in a particular region or country. In these circumstances, while a producer faced with the strict environmental regulations might not improve output:input ratios as much as some of its competitors, it might achieve considerable success in modifying its production processes in a way that enables it to adopt the new manufacturing technology and improve efficiency enough to produce sufficient profit to survive. A failure to respond in this way may have resulted in the company going out of business. In terms of its ability to minimise the effect of the constraint imposed by the environmental legislation it might be deemed to be an effective organisation.

Summarising the discussion so far, a full definition of organisation effectiveness needs to take account of:

- purpose and desired outcomes;
- the stakeholder perspective from which the assessment is made;
- level of assessment;
- alignment with the various indicators used at different levels and across different functions;
- specified time frame (short, medium or long term);
- benchmark standard; and
- any special constraints or enabling factors that affect performance.

At this point it might be useful to distinguish between effectiveness and efficiency. Carnall (1999) defines efficiency as achieving stated goals within given resource constraints. His definition of effectiveness includes the efficient use of resources to achieve immediate goals but also embraces the need to adapt to changing circumstances in order to remain efficient over the longer term.

Effectiveness and conceptualisations of organisations

This discussion of what constitutes organisational effectiveness can be elaborated further. Goodman and Pennings (1980) argue that our preferred definitions of organisational effectiveness are closely linked to the ways in which we conceptualise organisations.

- *The goals perspective* presents organisations as rationally constructed entities that are formed, and their existence is legitimised, in the quest for certain identifiable goals. The meaning of effectiveness is derived from the accomplishment of these goals.
- *The systems perspective* focuses on the functional complementarity of parts of the organisation and the nature of the organisation's relationship with the environment. The organisation is viewed as an open system that imports inputs from the environment, transforming them into outputs which are then exported. The fundamental task of the organisation is to survive and this is seen to depend on the maintenance of functional complementarity within the organisation and between the organisation and the wider environment. According to Goodman and Pennings, the systems perspective views functional complementarity as being more important than the achievement of some particular goal.

● *The organisation development (OD) perspective* is concerned with the processes of organisational learning that promote organisational renewal and long-term survival. Porras and Robertson (1992) define organisational development as a set of behavioural science-based theories, values, strategies and techniques aimed at the planned change of the organisational work setting for the purpose of enhancing individual development and improving organisational performance through the alteration of organisational members' on-the-job behaviour. Beer (1980) defines organisational development as a system-wide process of data collection, diagnosis, action planning, intervention and evaluation aimed at (a) enhancing congruence between organisational structure, process, strategy, people and culture; (b) developing new and creative organisational solutions; and (c) developing the organisation's self-renewing capacity.

The OD perspective emphasises a set of values that concern the nature of man and the way he or she is employed in an organisational context. Marguilies and Raia (1972) summarise these values as:

1   Providing opportunities for people to function as human beings rather than as resources in the productive process.
2   Providing opportunities for each organisational member, as well as for the organisation itself, to develop its full potential.
3   Seeking to increase the effectiveness of the organisation in terms of all its goals.
4   Attempting to create an environment in which it is possible to find exciting and challenging work.
5   Providing opportunities for people in the organisation to influence the way they relate to work, the organisation and the environment.
6   Treating each human being as a person with a complex set of needs, all of which are important in his or her work and life.

While this perspective has a strong foundation rooted in systems theory and recognises the importance of alignment, it is normative in so far as it emphasises the importance of individual development. This is reflected in (a) indicators of effectiveness that embrace the quality of working life, and (b) determinants of effectiveness that focus on the contribution that organisational members can make to the process of improving organisational effectiveness.

● *The political arena perspective* presents organisations as a collection of internal and external constituencies, each pursuing its own objectives. Organisational effectiveness is defined in terms of the attributes valued by the most powerful constituencies. A constituency's power is determined, at least in part, by the importance of its contribution to the input–transformation–output process. Suppliers or customers are powerful if they are vital to the survival of the organisation. Groups of employees, such as members of a particular trade union, or specific departments are powerful only so long as the organisation needs to rely on them to survive. The more central is the contribution of a constituency to the survival and prosperity of the organisation, the greater its power – so long as there are no rival constituencies that can offer an alternative (substitute) contribution. This political perspective views the organisation as the product of a negotiated order that is managed by the dominant coalition of constituencies, and reflects aspects of both the goals and systems conceptualisations of organisations.

There are common threads in all these different conceptualisations of organisations that point to the essential elements of any definition of effectiveness. Organisations are interdependent open systems that comprise a range of constituencies, each with their own interests and goals. The constituencies (stakeholders) that dominate the political process define the purpose of the organisation and the key indicators of organisational effectiveness. Whether or not an organisation performs effectively (at least over the medium term – see below) will be determined by the extent to which the various elements of the input-transformation-output system are aligned. Over the longer term, organisational effectiveness entails developing and maintaining the processes necessary to adapt as required in order to survive and prosper.

CHANGE AGENCY AND ORGANISATIONAL EFFECTIVENESS

Change agency refers to the ability of a manager or other agent of change to affect the way an organisation responds to change. One approach to the study of change and change management portrays the manager (and other organisational members) as pawns affected by change rather than as agents who can affect change. This approach, which emphasises the forces of economics, environment and context, is referred to by Wilson (1992) as 'determinism'. 'Voluntarism' is an approach to the study of change and change management which emphasises how the actions of managers and other change agents can affect outcomes.

- *The deterministic view* is that the ability of the manager to influence change is limited because the main determining forces lie outside the organisation and the realms of strategic choice for managers. Wilson (1992, p. 42) notes that advocates of this approach view organisations as interdependent elements of a much greater open system, and they regard the characteristics of the wider organisation–environment linkages as the key determinant of strategic change. Thus, for example, no matter how good the CEO of an organisation might be, when faced with a dramatic downturn in the trade cycle or very unfavourable exchange rates, he or she may be able to do little to improve the immediate fortunes of the organisation.
- *The voluntarist view* is that managers can make an important difference. The strategic choice framework provides an example of how the voluntarist approach can work. It challenges the view that there is an ideal type of organisation and a single best way of managing. It recognises functional equivalents and the possibility of equifinality whereby organisational outcomes can be achieved in a variety of different ways. One of the key factors that determines the effectiveness of an organisation is the quality of the strategic choices made by members of the dominant coalition. This approach emphasises the role of human agency and asserts that managers can intervene to affect change in ways that will either promote or undermine organisational effectiveness.

Pettigrew and Whipp (1991) report the outcome of a study of firms in four sectors (automobile manufacture, book publishing, merchant banking and life assurance) and conclude that there are observable differences between the ways in which higher performing firms manage change compared to lesser performing firms. Five factors appear to characterise the way that higher performing firms, in all sectors, managed change; one of these, environmental assessment, will be considered in some detail in Chapter 4.

From the perspective of change agency, the deterministic view offers an over-fatalistic perspective. While, in some situations, there may be external forces that exercise a very powerful effect on organisational performance, there will almost always be scope for managers to intervene in ways that will promote the organisation's interests. Burnes (2000) argues that despite the constraints they face, managers have a far wider scope for shaping decisions than most organisation theories acknowledge. He asserts that 'the scope for choice and the development of political influence is likely to be more pronounced where change, particularly major change, is on the managerial agenda' (2000, p. 180).

Problems can arise, however, when managers and others do not believe in their own ability to act as agents of change; as a consequence they may fail to behave proactively. Their response, and therefore the response of the organisation, may be to react passively in response to external forces for change.

VOLUNTARISM AND CHANGE AGENCY

Two assumptions underpinning the approach to managing change adopted in this book are that (1) managers can make a difference, and (2) they can be trained to manage change more effectively. Effective change managers require (and can be helped to acquire),

- conceptual models and action tools/interventions;
- change management skills; and
- confidence in their own ability to make a difference.

Conceptual models

Change managers require a range of concepts and theories, which essentially fall into two categories: process models of change which are concerned with the *how* of change management, and diagnostic models of change that focus on identifying *what* it is that needs to be changed.

Change managers need concepts and theories that will help them to:

- identify the kinds of change that confront them (for example, incremental or discontinuous);
- understand the *process* of changing;
- help them identify what needs to be attended to (for example, diagnosis, goal-setting etc.) if they are to achieve desired outcomes.

Types of change were discussed in Chapter 1 and process models are considered in Chapter 5.

Managers also need diagnostic models. Many theories exist about the behaviour of individuals and groups in organisations, about organisational processes such as power and influence, leadership, communication, decision-making and conflict, and about the structure and culture of organisations. These individual, group and organisational performance models can be used to help managers identify *what needs to be changed* in order to protect or improve organisational effectiveness. Organisational-level diagnostic models are considered in Chapter 7.

Action tools/interventions

In addition to the conceptual tools that can help change managers understand the change process and diagnose what needs to be changed, they also need to be familiar with a range of different *types of intervention* that they can use to secure a desired change. These will be considered in Chapter 16.

Change managers also need to have some basis for *deciding which interventions to use* in specific circumstances, taking account of contingencies such as the pace of change, the power of stakeholders to resist, and so forth. Models that can be used for this purpose are considered in Chapter 17.

Change agency skills

While conceptual understanding is necessary, it is not sufficient to guarantee that change agents will be able to secure desired changes. When managers are acting as change agents they need to be able to communicate, offer leadership, work with teams, confront, negotiate, motivate and manage relationships with others effectively. Change agency requires these and many other skills that managers use in everyday life. Sometimes change agents are less effective than they might be because they fail to recognise the importance of some of these skills or they fail to apply them when required. Some of these skills are discussed later (Chapter 9 on leadership, Chapter 10 on communicating, Chapter 12 on motivating others to change, and Chapter 13 on helping others to manage their personal transitions). A more detailed discussion of some of the interpersonal skills associated with helping others to change can be found in Hayes (1996) *Developing the Manager as a Helper*.

Reflections on the assessment of effectiveness in your organisation

Review the notes you made at the beginning of this chapter on how you might assess the effectiveness of your organisation and/or your unit in the organisation. In the light of the content of this chapter do you think that you need to revise the criteria/indictors you would use? If so, make a note of the revised indicators.

Indicators of effectiveness	
Organisation	**Department/unit**

BELIEFS ABOUT CHANGE AGENCY

Some managers may have the conceptual knowledge and required skills to equip them to intervene and make a difference, but they may fail to act because they have insufficient faith in their own ability to affect outcomes.

Ineffective change managers are often ineffective because they fail to act in ways that enable them to exercise the control necessary to achieve desired outcomes. Rollo May (1969) argues that in many walks of life people are hypnotised by their own feelings of powerlessness and use this as an excuse for doing nothing. He describes the central core of modern man's neuroses as the undermining of his experience of himself as responsible, and the sapping of his will and ability to make decisions. According to May:

> the lack of will is much more than merely an ethical problem: the modern individual so often has the conviction that even if he did exert his 'will' – or whatever illusion passes for it – his actions wouldn't do any good anyway.

This inner feeling of impotence is a critical problem for some managers and can undermine their ability to act as agents of change.

Two psychologists (Rotter and Phares), after observing that some of their clients seemed to attribute outcomes to luck rather than to factors over which they had some control, embarked on a programme of research which led to the development of the concept of the *locus of control* (Rotter, 1971). The locus of control reflects the degree to which people believe that their own behaviour determines what happens to them. Those who attribute outcomes to their own efforts are referred to as internals, and those who attribute outcomes to external factors such as luck, fate, other people, the state of the economy or other factors over which they have no control, are referred to as externals.

In the context of change management, those who are over-committed to a deterministic view of change may be inclined to believe that the locus of control is external to themselves and to the organisation and, therefore, may develop the view that there is little that they can do to influence events. Those who think this way are less likely to attempt to adopt a proactive approach to the management of change than those who have a more internal view about the locus of control.

Locus of control is related to Seligman's (1975) theory of *learned helplessness*, which argues that a person's expectation about his or her ability to control outcomes is learned. It suggests that managers may begin to question their ability to manage change if, when confronted with a new problem or opportunity, old and well-tried ways of managing fail to deliver desired outcomes. Furthermore, if their early attempts to experiment with alternative ways of managing are equally unsuccessful, this questioning of their own ability may develop into an expectation that they are helpless and the associated belief that there is little that they can do to secure desired outcomes. Seligman argues that this expectation will produce motivational and cognitive deficits.

Motivational deficits involve a *failure to take any voluntary actions designed to control events* following a previous experience with uncontrollable events. If managers believe that they cannot exercise any control over outcomes they will not be motivated to even try. Cognitive deficits involves a *failure to learn* that it is possible to control what happens. If managers believe that they cannot affect outcomes in a particular set of changing circumstances, this belief may stop them recognising opportunities to exercise control, even if there is evidence that their own behaviour has actually had an important impact on outcomes.

The theory suggests that the incentive for managers and others to initiate activity directed towards managing change will depend upon the (learned) expectation that their action can produce some improvement in the problematic situation. If they do not have any confidence in their own ability to manage the change and achieve any improvements they will not try to exercise influence. Both individuals and organisations can develop the expectation that there is little they can do to secure desirable outcomes when confronted by change. However, individuals and organisations can also learn that they can affect their own destiny, and they can learn how to exercise this influence. (The role of learning in change management will be considered in more detail below.)

Reflections on beliefs about change agency in your organisation

Do people in your organisation behave as though they believe that they can make an important difference to the way the organisation will develop in the future? What are the consequences for successful change management?

SUMMARY

This chapter has defined change management as the process of modifying or transforming organisations in order to maintain or improve their effectiveness. We first considered the attributes of organisational effectiveness and the factors that need to be taken into account when assessing the effectiveness of an organisation or unit within it.

We then considered the ability of the manager (and other agents of change) to affect the way an organisation responds to change. After briefly reviewing the deterministic and voluntaristic schools of thought, it was argued that managers can intervene and make an important difference.

Finally we focused attention on the attributes of effective change managers. It was noted that they need to be familiar with relevant conceptual and action tools, possess a range of change agency skills and believe in their own ability to affect the change process.

References

Beer, M (1980) *Organisational Change and Development: A Systems View*, Santa Monica, Cal.: Goodyear.

Burnes, B. (2000) *Managing Change: A Strategic Approach to Organisational Dynamics*, Harlow, England: Pearson.

Carnall, C.A. (1999) *Managing Change in Organisations*, 3rd edn, Harlow, England: Prentice-Hall.

Goodman, P.S. and Penning, J.M. (1980) 'Critical Issues in Assessing Organizational Effectiveness', in E.Lawler, D. Nadler and C. Cammann (eds), *Organizational Assessment*, New York: Wiley, pp. 185–215.

Hayes, J. (1996) *Developing the Manager as a Helper*, London: Routledge.

Marguilies, N and Raia, A.P. (1972) *Organisational Development: Values, Process and Technology*, New York: McGraw-Hill.

May, R. (1969) *Love and Will*, New York: W.W. Norton.

Pettigrew, A. and Whipp, R. (1991) *Managing for Competitive Success*, Oxford: Blackwell.

Porras, J. and Robertson, P.J. (1992) 'Organizational Development Theory, Practice and Research', in M.D. Dunette and L. M. Hough (eds), *Handbook of Organizational Psychology*, 2nd edn, Palo Alto, Cal.: Consulting Psychologists Press, Vol 3, pp. 718–822.

Rotter, J.R. (1971) 'External Control and Internal Control', *Psychology Today*, June, 37.

Seligman, M.E.P. (1975) *Learned Helplessness*, San Francisco: W.H. Freeman.

Tichy, N. and Frombrun, C. (1979) 'Network Analysis in Organisational Settings', *Human Relations*, 32(11), pp 923–65.

Van de Ven, A. and Morgan, M.A. (1980) 'A Revised Framework for Organization Assessment', in E. Lawler, D. Nadler and C. Cammann (eds), *Organizational Assessment*, New York: Wiley, pp. 216–60.

Wilson, D (1992) *A Strategy for Change*, London: Routledge.

3

Systems models, congruency and the concept of 'fit'

This chapter considers the attributes of holistic models of organisational functioning, summarises the main features of open-systems models of organisations and discusses the utility of the concept of alignment or 'fit'.

It was noted in Chapter 2 that there are many theories and models (of motivation, decision-making, group functioning, organisation structure and so forth) that change agents can use to help them understand the functioning of the various components of an organisation. It was also noted that they can use this understanding to help them identify what needs to be changed. Nadler and Tushman (1980) acknowledge the utility of such *'component models'* but caution against combining, in some additive manner, the specific assessments they provide in order to produce an overview of organisational functioning and effectiveness. They argue that there is a need for frameworks and models that provide an understanding of the way in which the *total system* of organisational behaviour functions, and they advocate a more holistic approach.

OPEN-SYSTEMS THEORY

Open-systems theory provides such a framework and views organisations as a system of interrelated components that transact with a larger environment. From the perspective of open systems, some of the main characteristics of organisations are that they are:

- *Embedded within a larger system.* Organisations are dependent on the larger system (environment) for the resources, information and feedback that they require in order to survive.
- *Able to avoid entropy.* Through the exchange of matter, energy and information with the larger environment, organisations can forestall entropy, the

predisposition to decay. They can even increase their vitality over time. People are partially closed systems in that while they can import food, water and air to breath, there are parts of their body that cannot be renewed or replaced. Groups and organisations, on the other hand, have the potential for indefinite life. In their simplest form, as illustrated by Figure 3.1, organisations can be portrayed as open systems in a dynamic relationship with their environment, receiving various inputs that they transform in some way and export as outputs. In order to survive, organisations need to maintain favourable input–output transactions with the environment.

- *Regulated by feedback.* Systems rely on information about their outputs to regulate their inputs and transformation processes. Feedback loops also exist between the various internal components of the system. Consequently changes in any one component can affect changes in other components.
- *Subject to equifinality.* The same outcomes can be produced by configuring the system in different ways.
- *Cyclical in their mode of functioning.* Events are patterned and tend to occur in repetitive cycles of input, throughput and output. For example, the revenue generated from selling outputs is used to fund inputs (purchase more raw materials, pay bank charges, wages and so on) that are used to produce more outputs.
- *Equilibrium-seeking.* Open systems tend to gravitate to a state where all the component parts of the system are in equilibrium and where a steady state exists. Whenever changes occur that upset this balance, different components of the system move to restore the balance (note the links with Lewin's field-theory, discussed in Chapter 5).
- *Bounded.* Open systems are defined by boundaries. External boundaries differentiate the organisation from the larger environment and regulate the flow of information, energy and matter between the system and its environment. Internal boundaries differentiate the various components of the system from each other and regulate the inputs and outputs of sub-systems.

The notion that organisations are systems of interrelated elements embedded in, and strongly influenced by, a larger system is not new. Burns and Stalker (1961) and Lawrence and Lorsch (1967) produced interesting research findings that suggested a link between the internal characteristics of an organisation and the external environment.

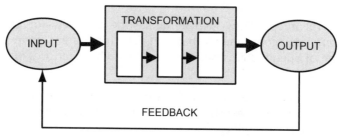

Figure 3.1 The organisation as an open system

CONTINGENCY THEORIES

Burns and Stalker (1961) examined the relationship between the internal structure of 20 British firms and the environments in which they operated. They found that the firms that operated in relatively stable and unchanging environments tended to have more highly structured and formal internal arrangements than firms that operated in unstable environments. They described firms that operated in stable environments as 'mechanistic' because they were characterised by many rules and procedures and were dominated by a hierarchy of authority. The firms that operated in less stable environments were described as 'organic' because they tended to have a free-flowing, de-centralised and adaptive internal organisation. Table 3.1 summarises the main features of mechanistic and organic organisations.

Table 3.1 Mechanistic and organic organisation forms

Mechanistic	Organic
1 Specialised tasks, narrow in scope.	1 Common tasks and interdependencies
2 Tasks rigidly defined	2 Tasks adjusted and redefined as required
3 Strict hierarchy of authority	3 Less adherence to formal authority and rules
4 Centralised knowledge and control	4 Decentralised knowledge and control
5 Hierarchical communication	5 Network communication, diffused channels

The contingency approach advanced by Burns and Stalker received further support from a later study undertaken by Lawrence and Lorsch (1967). They examined three departments (manufacturing, research and sales) in 10 US companies and found that departmental structures varied with environmental uncertainty. The results of their research indicated that production departments tended to have the highest degree of structure, followed by marketing and then research. Their results also indicated that the more complex and uncertain the external environment, the greater the internal differentiation between departments. This happened as departments developed their own attitudes, goals, work orientation and internal structures and processes to accommodate the requirements of their specialised sub-environments. Lawrence and Lorsch's findings also suggested that this internal differentiation tended to lead to problems of internal coordination between departments and, consequently, to a greater need for internal integrating mechanisms.

There are some who question the utility of contingency theory and argue that it fails to provide a convincing explanation for the way in which organisations operate (see Burnes, 2000, pp. 84–5). Congruency theorists, however, interpret the results of these and other studies as offering support for a broader proposition that the alignment or 'fit' between an organisation and the environment and also between the various internal elements of the organisation is a critical determinant of organisational effectiveness.

ALIGNMENT AS A DETERMINANT OF ORGANISATIONAL EFFECTIVENESS

Open-systems theory predicts that changes to any one of the internal or external elements of an organisation's system will cause changes to other elements. Kotter (1980) elaborated this proposition when he developed his integrative model of organisational dynamics, which comprises seven major elements. Figure 3.2 shows these as a set of key organisational processes plus six structural elements. The key organisational processes are classified under two main headings, informational processes such as information gathering, communication and decision-making, and processes that are concerned with the conversion or transportation of matter/energy. Specific processes can be labelled according to their purpose and might include the market-research process, the product development process, the manufacturing process or the leadership process.

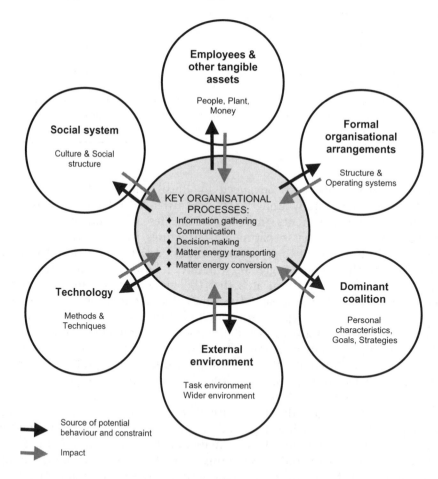

Figure 3.2 Kotter's (1980) integrative model of organisational dynamics

Source: J.P. Kotter, 'An Integrative Model of Organizational Dynamics', in E. Porter, D. Nadler and C. Cammann (eds), *Organizational Assessment*, Wiley, 1980, p. 282.

The six structural elements in Kotter's model are:

- external environment, including the immediate task-related environment and the wider environment (which includes public attitudes, the political system, etc.);
- employees and other tangible assets such as buildings, plant, inventories and cash;
- formal structure, job design and operating systems;
- internal social system including the organisation's culture and social structure;
- technology (or technologies) associated with the organisation's core products;
- dominant coalition – the objectives and strategies of those who control policy-making.

In the *short run*, organisation effectiveness can be defined in terms of the nature of the cause–effect relationships that link all the elements of the system together. For example, if demand for a major product produced by organisations operating in a particular industrial sector begins to slump, the dominant coalition in some organisations will recognise this and take corrective action much faster than the dominant coalition in other organisations. An organisation's response will be influenced by the effectiveness of its information-gathering and decision-making processes and by how quickly these processes can affect other elements in the organisation to adjust matter/energy conversion and transportation processes in ways that will maintain their efficiency. Adjustments might involve cutting production, finding new customers or reducing prices in order to minimise any build-up of stocks of finished goods. Any delays in reacting to changes will result in a wasteful use of resources. In the short run, therefore, effective organisations are those that have key processes that are characterised by levels of decision-making effectiveness and matter–energy efficiency that help to ensure that resources are used effectively.

Kotter argues that over the *medium term* (which he defines as a few months to a few years) the effective organisation is one that is capable of maintaining its short-run effectiveness. He suggests that organisations do this by maintaining the key process elements in an efficient and effective state because it is this that enables them to ensure that the other (six) structural elements are aligned to each other. Sustained misalignment (sometimes referred to as 'poor fit') leads to levels of waste that will eventually threaten the survival of the organisation. He suggests that what constitutes a misaligned relationship between any two or more structural elements is often 'intuitively obvious'. He cites several examples to illustrate the point:

- If the goals and strategies championed by the organisation's dominant coalition are based on inaccurate assumptions about the task environment, the dominant coalition and the task environment are obviously misaligned.
- If the size of the workforce or the organisation's other tangible assets are not sufficient to take advantage of the economies of scale inherent in the organisation's technologies, the two elements are obviously misaligned.
- If the level of specialisation called for in the formal organisational arrangements are inconsistent with skills of the workforce, then again the two elements are misaligned.

The most common sources of non-alignment are changes in the external environment and growth. Kotter argues that organisational systems correct misalignments by taking the path of least resistance; they move towards the solution that requires the minimum use of energy. This usually involves realigning around the element or elements of the organisation that are most difficult and expensive to change (or emerge as the driving force over the longer term, see below). However, if the organisation can afford the waste associated with misalignment, minor examples of poor fit could go uncorrected for a considerable period of time. This argument suggests that, over the medium term, the focus of change management needs to be ensuring that the elements of the organisation are appropriately aligned.

Over the *longer term* (6 to 60 years) Kotter predicts that it is the adaptability of the six structural elements that will be the underlying determinant of effectiveness. He notes that over time one or more of the structural elements (for example, the external environment, technology, the employees or the dominant coalition) typically begins to exert more influence on the key organisational processes than the other elements. This element (or elements) emerges as the driving force that shapes the development of the company. He argues that because of the nature of the interdependence among all of the elements (and the equilibrium-seeking disposition of systems), if one or two elements emerge as the driving force the natural tendency is for the others to follow. They adapt to the driving force in order to maintain alignment. However, this process may not always be as rapid or smooth as required to maintain a sufficient level of alignment, with inevitable consequences for effectiveness. Sustained misalignment will threaten the survival of the company.

Building on the proposition that the organisation's ability to adapt to change over the long term is a function of the state of its structural elements, Kotter provides examples of structural states that do and do not facilitate system adaptation. These are presented in Table 3.2.

Adaptability is important because it determines whether or not the organisation will be able to maintain the required degree of alignment over the long term. Over the longer term, therefore, the focus of change management needs to ensure that the structural elements of the organisation are as adaptable as possible.

A CONGRUENCE MODEL OF ORGANISATIONS

An alternative open-systems model proposed by Nadler and Tushman (1982) also highlights the effect of the congruency of the component parts of the organisation on organisational effectiveness. In addition, it elaborates the relationship between the organisation and its wider environment and focuses more explicit attention on the role of strategy. The model identifies four classes of input:

1　*Environment.* This includes any larger 'suprasystem' (such as a large corporation) that the focal organisation is a part of, markets, financial institutions, supplies, and so forth, and the wider environment that includes the culture(s) within which the organisation operates. It is this environment that provides the opportunities and constraints that the organisation has to contend with.

Table 3.2 Examples of element states that do and do not facilitate system adaptation

	States that are highly constraining and **hard to align** with, thus inhibiting adaptation	States that are not highly constraining and are **easy to align** with
Technology	Organisation possesses a single complex technology that is rapidly becoming outdated and that requires large amounts of capital for equipment	Organisation possesses the most advanced technologies for its products, services, and administrative systems along with a number of alternative technologies it might need in the future
Social system	Key norms are not supportive of organisational flexibility; little trust found in relationships; total power in the system is low; morale is low; little sense of shared purpose	Key norms are supportive of organisational flexibility; high trust found in relationships; total power in the system is high; morale is high; high degree of shared purpose.
Employee and other tangible assets	Plant and equipment is run down; employees, especially middle managers, are unskilled; organisation has some highly specialised human skills and equipment it doesn't need anymore	Plant and equipment in top notch shape; employees, especially middle managers, are highly skilled; organisation possesses equipment and people with skills it doesn't need now but may need in the future
Organisational arrangements	Formal systems are not very sophisticated but are applied in great detail, uniformly across the organisation	Different kinds of formal system exist for structuring, measuring, rewarding, selecting, and developing different types of people working on different tasks; formal systems also exist to monitor change in the organisation and its environment and to change the formal systems accordingly
Dominant coalition	A small, homogeneous, reasonably untalented group with no effective leadership; all about the same age	A large, reasonably heterogeneous yet cohesive group of very talented people who work together well and have plenty of effective leadership; members are of different ages
External environment	The organisation is very dependent on a large number of externalities, with little or no countervailing power	The organisation has only a limited number of strong dependencies, with a moderate amount of countervailing power over all dependencies
	Demand for products and services is shrinking; supplies are hard to get; regulators behave with hostility and inconsistency	Demand for products and services is growing; supplies are plentiful; regulators behave consistently and fairly
	Public angry at the firm; economy in bad shape; political system isn't functioning well; overall, the environment is hostile	Public likes the organisation; economy is in good shape; political system is functioning well; overall, the environment is benevolent

Source: Adapted from J.P. Kotter, 'An Integrative Model of Organizational Dynamics', in E.Porter, D. Nadler and C. Cammann (eds), *Organizational Assessment*,, Wiley, 1980, pp. 292–3.

2   *Resources*, such as liquid capital, physical plant, raw materials, technologies, and labour.

3   *History.* This is important because past strategic decisions and the development of core values and patterns of leadership can affect current patterns of organisational behaviour.

4   *Strategy.* This involves determining how the organisation's resources can be used to best advantage in relation to the opportunities, constraints and demands of the environment. Effective organisations are those that are able to align themselves with the external environment and, as required, reposition themselves to take advantage of any environmental changes such as shifts in markets, technologies and so on. Nadler and Tushman argue that strategy (and associated goals and plans) defines the task (purpose) of the organisation and is the most important input to the organisation's behavioural system. They suggest that effectiveness can be assessed in terms of how well the organisation's performance meets the goals of strategy.

Nadler and Tushman (1980) define the major components of the transformation process as:

1   *Task*, which can be viewed in terms of complexity, predictability, interdependence and skill demands.

2   *Individuals* who are members of the organisation and their response capabilities, intelligence, skills and abilities, experience, training, needs, attitudes, expectations and so forth.

3   *Formal organisational arrangements* that include all the mechanisms used by the organisation to direct, structure or control behaviour.

4   *Informal organisation*, including informal group structures, the quality of intergroup relations, political processes and so on.

Like Kotter, they argue that any useful model of organisations must go beyond merely providing a simple description of the components of the organisation and must consider the dynamic relationships that exist between the various components. They define congruence as the degree to which the needs, demands, goals, objectives and/or structures of any one component of the organisation are consistent with the needs, demands, goals, objectives and/or structures of any other component. Their general hypothesis is that, other things equal, the greater the total degree of congruence between the various components the more effective will be the organisation's behaviour. Figure 3.3 summarises the congruence model and the bold double-headed arrows indicate the six 'fits' between the components of the transformation process (the internal organisation). These are:

- *Individual – formal organisation.* For example, to what extent are individual needs met by the formal organisational arrangements?
- *Individual – task.* For example, to what extent do individuals have the skills necessary to meet task demands and to what extent do the tasks satisfy individual needs?

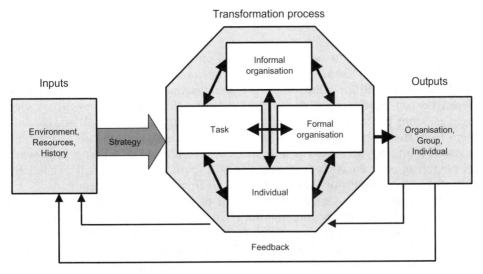

Figure 3.3 Nadler and Tushman's (1980) congruence model

Source: Nadler, D. and Tushman, M., 'A Congruence Model for Organizational Assessment', in E. Porter, D. Nadler and C. Cammann (eds), *Organizational Assessment*, Wiley, 1980, p. 274

- *Individual – informal organisation.* For example, to what extent does the informal organisation satisfy the needs of individuals or make best use of their talents?
- *Task – formal organisation.* For example, to what extent are the formal organisational arrangements adequate to meet the demands of the task?
- *Task – informal organisation.* For example, to what extent does the informal organisation facilitate task performance?
- *Formal – informal organisation.* For example, to what extent are the goals, rewards and structures of the informal organisation consistent with those of the formal organisation?

Many of the components that Nadler and Tushman choose to focus on are different to those that figure in Kotter's model. All models are simplifications of the real world, and the utility of any particular model, in the context of change management, needs to be judged in terms of whether or not it provides a helpful conceptual framework for managing the change process. The four components of the transformation process in Nadler and Tushman's congruence model are derived from Leavitt (1965). The basic hypothesis underpinning congruence would still be valid if these four components were replaced with the five sub-systems (production, supportive, maintenance, adaptive and managerial) identified by Katz and Kahn (1966). It is the congruence or alignment between the organisation and the environment and between the internal components of the organisation that is the key concept that can aid organisational diagnosis and the development of change strategies.

THE UTILITY OF THE CONCEPT OF ALIGNMENT

The concept of alignment has been criticised on the grounds that it is difficult to apply in practice; Wilson (1992), for example, refers to difficulties relating to problems of definition. Some view the organisation and the environment as 'objective' fact, readily open to description and definition, whereas others view them as 'subjective' fact. Problems can arise because managers, and others, perceive them from their own subjective point of view. This makes it difficult to establish any shared understanding of the current or desired level of alignment. Even when people can agree, there is no guarantee that this shared perception will be a reliable indicator of the conditions that will lead to organisational effectiveness.

Another criticism is that alignment might be a more valid concept when the focus is the management of incremental change. When faced with discontinuous change, alignment might be a less helpful concept because the need is to break with the past and introduce radical innovation before seeking to re-establish a new state of alignment around a new task and/or new structural elements.

These criticisms may have some validity, but systems models, alignment and the concept of fit can make an important contribution to effective change management.

SUMMARY

This chapter has considered the attributes of holistic (as opposed to component) models of organisation functioning. It was noted that while component theories are useful for diagnosing specific problems, combining their assessments of different aspects of organisation functioning might not provide an adequate view of organisational effectiveness. Open-systems models of organisations were seen to provide a useful overarching conceptual framework for assessing organisational functioning and effectiveness.

We have summarised the main features of open-systems models of organisations,

- drawing on contingency theory to illustrate the embeddedness of organisations within a larger system and the importance of alignment;
- elaborating Kotter's (1980) integrative model of organisational dynamics to consider the relative importance of alignment and adaptability as determinants of organisational effectiveness over the medium and long term; and
- reviewed Nadler and Tushman's (1982) congruency model of organisations to highlight the importance of strategy in achieving and maintaining alignment.

It concludes with a discussion of the utility of the concept of alignment.

Exercise 3.1   Checking alignment between steps in the transformation process

This exercise draws together some of the issues considered in this and the previous chapter. Think of your department or unit in terms of a process that transforms inputs into outputs.

Step 1   Identify the major inputs and outputs and make a note of them in the space provided below. Depending on the time available, focus on one or more inputs *and* one or more outputs.

Step 2   Select one *input* and identify the department, unit or external supplier that provides it.

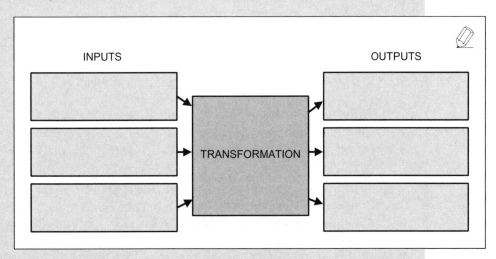

Step 3   Assess how effective you think this supplier is.

- List the indicators that *you* use to assess the effectiveness of the supplier.
- Against each indicator note *your* assessment of how effective the supplier is (use a five-point scale where 1 = very ineffective and 5 = every effective).

Step 4   Think about how members of the supplying department or unit rate their own effectiveness.

- List the indicators that you think *they* use to assess their own effectiveness.
- Against each indicator note how you think *they* rate their own effectiveness.

✎ Indicators I use to assess the effectiveness of the supplier	My assessment	Indicators *they* use to assess their effectiveness	Their assessment

Step 5 Compare the two lists. Do they suggest any actual or potential problems that could undermine organisational effectiveness? If so specify below.

Now repeat steps 2–5 for one of your *outputs*

Step 6 Select one *output* and identify the department, unit or external customer that receives it.

Step 7 Assess how effective you think your department or unit is.

- List the indicators that *you* use to assess the effectiveness of *your* department (with respect to the supply of the focal output).
- Against each indicator note *your* assessment of how effective you think your unit is (use a five-point scale where 1 = very ineffective and 5 = very effective).

Step 8 Think about how members of the receiving unit or department rate the effectiveness of *your* department.

- List the indicators that you think *they* use to assess your department's effectiveness.
- Against each indicator note how you think *they* rate the effectiveness of your department.

✎ Indicators I use to assess the effectiveness of my unit	My assessment	Indicators customers use to assess the effectiveness of my unit	Their assessment

Step 9 Compare the two lists. Do they suggest any actual or potential problems that could undermine organisational effectiveness? If so specify below.

Potential problems with alignment between steps in the transformation process

References

Burnes, B. (2000) *Managing Change: A Strategic Approach to Organisational Dynamics*, Harlow: Pearson.

Burns, T. and Stalker, G.M. (1961) *The Management of Innovation*, London: Tavistock.

Katz, D. and Kahn, R.L. (1966) *The Social Psychology of Organisations*, New York: Wiley.

Kotter, J.P. (1980) 'An Integrative Model of Organisational Dynamics', in E.E. Lawler, D.A Nadler and C. Cammann (eds), *Organizational Assessment*, New York: Wiley, pp. 279–99.

Lawrence, P.R. and Lorsch, J.W. (1967) *Organization and Environment*, Boston, Mass.: Harvard Business School.

Leavitt, H.J. (1965) 'Applied Organizational Change in Industry', in J.G. March (ed.), *Handbook of Organisations*, Chicago: Rand-McNally.

Nadler, D.A. and Tushman, M.L. (1982) 'A Model for Diagnosing Organisational Behavior: Applying a Congruence Perspective', in D.A. Nadler, M.L. Tushman and N.G. Hatvany (eds), *Managing Organisations*, Boston, Mass.: Little, Brown.

Nadler, D.A. and Tushman, M.L. (1980), 'A Congruence Model for Organisational Assessment', in E.E. Lawler, D.A. Nadler and C. Cammann (eds), *Organizational Assessment*. New York: Wiley.

Wilson, D. (1992) *A Strategy for Change*, London: Routledge.

4

Organisational learning and organisational effectiveness

Organisations strive to avoid entropy. The ultimate criterion of effectiveness is survival and the dominant coalition/senior managers seek to achieve this by aligning the organisation with the environment. They do this in order to minimise waste and promote competitiveness.

It was noted in the previous chapter that Nadler and Tushman (1982) highlight the importance of strategy as a vehicle for managing the organisation's alignment with its environment and that Kotter (1980) points to the importance of adaptability as a determinant of long-term effectiveness. The quality of individual and organisational learning has also been identified as another important determinant of an organisation's effectiveness (Lank and Lank, 1995), and de Geus (1988) argues that the ability to learn faster than competitors may be the only sustainable competitive advantage. Miles (1982) argues that organisations have leeway and choice in how they adjust to a changing environment, and that it is this choice that offers the opportunity for learning.

This chapter will provide a brief overview of strategic change management and review the role of individual and organisational learning in the quest for organisational effectiveness.

THE NATURE OF STRATEGY AND STRATEGIC CHANGE MANAGEMENT

Strategy, according to Nadler and Tushman, is a set of key decisions about matching the organisation's resources with the opportunities, constraints and demands in the environment. Strategic change management is concerned with the formulation and implementation of strategy. There are different views about how strategy is formulated. One view (the planning approach) is that strategy formulation *is an intentional and rational process*, whereas a competing view (the emergent approach) is that it is the *outcome* of a complex cultural and political process.

The planning approach.

Those who subscribe to the first school of thought emphasise the logical nature of a process that involves analysis, forecasting and planning. Industrial economists and business planners have developed a range of models and tools that strategic planners can use to determine how the organisation should be developed in order to ensure it remains aligned with its environment, or stretched to take advantage of perceived opportunities.

Quinn (1993) observes that the strategies produced by managers who rely on a rational approach to planning often fail to be implemented successfully. He suggests that in organisations that have developed expensive and elaborate rational planning systems it is not uncommon for senior managers to behave as though they regard strategy formulation and strategy implementation as separate and sequential processes. Problems can arise when strategies are well-developed before implementation starts. This is because those who have developed the strategies may not always have the power to execute them.

Quinn contrasts the rational planning approach with logical incrementalism. This approach falls somewhere between the planning and emergent approaches. It acknowledges that in complex environments it is difficult for any one group to be aware of all the factors that can impact on the organisation's success and that different stakeholders will have different priorities that need to be recognised. Quinn argues that organisations require strategies that will work in practice, even if this involves some sort of political compromise. He also argues that successful senior managers tend to be those who have a view of where they want the organisation to be, but deliberately decide to act incrementally when leading the organisation. They take small steps and build on the experience gained. This incremental approach is more effective, according to Quinn, because it improves the quality of the information used in key decisions; helps overcome the personal and political pressures resisting change; copes with the variety of lead-times and sequencing problems associated with change; and builds the overall awareness, understanding and commitment required to ensure implementation. Based on his observations of senior managers in Xerox, GM and IBM, he concludes that often, in practice, by the time strategies begin to crystallise, elements of them have already been implemented. He reports that through the incremental processes that successful senior managers consciously use to formulate their strategies, they are able to build sufficient organisational momentum and identity with the strategies 'to make them flow towards flexible and successful implementation'.

The emergent approach

The view of those who subscribe to the emergent approach is that the key decisions about matching the organisation's resources with the opportunities, constraints and demands in the environment evolve over time and are the outcome of cultural and political processes in organisations. The nature of the cultural processes will be elaborated below but they manifest themselves in the taken-for-granted assumptions and routines that influence strategic decisions. These processes are bound up with the bargaining and negotiation that occurs between different stakeholders, such as functional or professional groups, that each have their own world views and taken-for-granted assumptions.

While the models and tools associated with the planning approach can be a useful aid to change management (and some of these, such as SWOT and PEST, will be considered in more detail in Chapter 7), the apparent objectivity of the analyses they provide needs to be regarded with some degree of caution. Pettigrew and Whipp (1993) argue that no matter how sophisticated they are they have to be applied by someone. They note that managers rarely collect 'clean' data about the environment; all data has to be perceived and constructed. This process of perception and construction is influenced by the perceiver's values and norms and by the 'shared beliefs' that characterise the cultures that they are a part of.

Johnson (1993) argues that while individuals and groups within organisations may hold varying sets of beliefs, there is likely to exist, at some level, a core set of beliefs and assumptions held relatively in common and taken for granted by all managers. He refers to this as the organisational paradigm (also referred to by others as the shared mental model) and argues that it is this paradigm that influences how managers perceive, interpret and make sense of their environment. He also argues that it is the shared mental model/paradigm that determines whether changes in the environment are perceived as relevant, and if so whether they are perceived to pose threats or offer opportunities. While outsiders may view a change in the environment as a threat to the organisation, members of the organisation, viewing the environment through their shared mental model, may fail to recognise the change or the potential threat it may pose.

Organisational learning and strategy formulation

Exponents of the emergent approach to strategy formulation, such as Pettigrew and Whipp (1993), argue that strategy emerges from the way organisations, at all levels, process information, especially information about the relationship between the organisation and its environment. The quality of this information processing is influenced by the relevance of the shared mental model or taken-for-granted paradigm. If organisations are to develop strategies that will ensure alignment and a strong competitive position, the shared mental model needs to be subject to revision.

This is particularly the case if conditions change in ways that could affect the assumptions and beliefs on which the shared mental model is based. If organisations are to formulate effective strategies they need to have the capacity to learn from their experience and to use this learning to modify the shared mental model that guides the way they manage strategic change.

ORGANISATIONAL LEARNING

Organisational learning involves enhancing the collective ability to act more effectively. The quality of collective/organisational learning is important because it affects both strategy formulation and strategy implementation. The collective nature of learning is especially important in complex and turbulent environments because in such circumstances senior managers may not be the best-placed individuals to identify opportunities and threats. Organisational members, at all levels, who are involved in boundary-spanning activities such as procurement, technical development or sales may have data that could provide a valuable input to strategy formulation. Furthermore, the quality of response to any threats or opportunities that are identified may require individuals and groups located in different functions to collaborate and learn from each other in order to design and produce high-quality products or services in ever-shorter time frames.

Shared mental models, rules and behaviour in organisations

Swieringa and Wierdsma (1992) conceptualise organisations as a set of explicit and implicit rules that prescribe the way members behave (see Figure 4.1). These rules are based on insights which represent what is known and understood. They relate to everything that happens in the organisation. For example, there are rules about the structure of the organisation that prescribe how activities will be grouped and responsibilities allocated, and there are rules about how resources are procured and used and about how people are managed and rewarded. These rules reflect the mental models (subjective theories, shared meanings or beliefs) through which organisational members examine and make sense of their experience. The shared mental model represents the basic assumptions that underpin the organisation's culture. Schein (1990, p. 111) defines culture as (a) the pattern of basic assumptions, (b) invented, discovered or developed by a group, (c) as it learns to cope with its problems of external adaptation and internal integration, (d) that have worked well enough in the past to be considered valid and, therefore, (e) are taught to new members as the (f) correct way to perceive, think, and feel in relation to these problems.

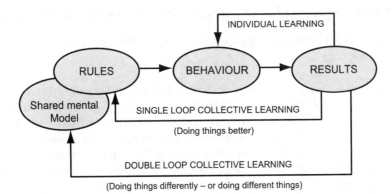

Figure 4.1 Individual and collective learning in organisations

Source: Adapted from Swieringa and Wierdsma (1992).

Learning to behave in accordance with the rules

So long as the rules lead to behaviours that produce desired results there will be no need to change the rules. The only requirement will be for individual learning. Organisational members will have to learn to behave in accordance with the rules. For example, if an individual is promoted into a position that involves being responsible for a budget he or she will not only have to develop an understanding of the rules relating to the management of budgets, but will also have to acquire the knowledge and skills necessary to behave in accordance with these rules.

This kind of learning, however, may not always be sufficient to guarantee organisational success. In today's turbulent and complex environment, old ways of behaving may fail to produce the required results and the organisation may be faced with the need to change, to modify the rules and encourage new behaviours in order to ensure its continued competitiveness and survival.

Collective learning and the modification of rules

Organisational (collective) learning occurs when a group recognises something that offers a more effective way of functioning. It has already been noted that organisations will be more effective when their major components (such as structure, technology, systems and people) are congruent with each other and when there is a good fit between the organisation and the environment. Organisational learning involves achieving and maintaining this fit or, when confronted by discontinuities in the external environment, finding a new and more productive fit. This, in turn, involves organisational members diagnosing the organisation's predicament (including the consequences of their past behaviour), integrating this understanding into their shared mental models and using it as a basis for modifying, as required, the rules that guide decision-making and action. This process is similar to that referred to by Daft and Weick (1984) who describe organisations as open social systems that seek and interpret information about their environment in order to provide a basis for action.

Modifying the rules via single- and double-loop learning

Argyris and Schon (1978) distinguish between two different kinds of organisational (collective) learning.

- *Single-loop learning* entails the detection and correction of errors leading to a modification of the rules within the boundaries of current thinking. It involves organisational members collectively *refining* their mental models about how the world operates in order to do things better. It does not offer any fundamental challenge to current thinking. The effect of single-loop learning is to promote an incremental approach to strategy formulation and change management.
- *Double-loop learning* is a more cognitive process; it occurs when the assumptions and principles that constitute the governing variables or shared mental model are examined and challenged. This kind of learning challenges

accepted ways of thinking and can produce a new understanding of situations and events, which in turn, can lead to the development of new rules that require organisational members to change their behaviour and do things differently or even do different things.

While double-loop learning is often seen as a desirable goal, it can be difficult to attain in practice, a point that will receive further consideration below.

Triggers for double-loop learning

When there is a good fit between the organisation and its environment and when this leads to the achievement of desired levels of performance, there is a high chance that the prevailing shared mental model will be reinforced. The only collective learning in these circumstances will be single-loop learning associated with the detection and correction of errors. This kind of learning is often associated with continuous improvement.

Double loop collective learning is most likely to occur when desired performance levels are not achieved and when feedback signals a need to re-examine the relevance of the shared mental model. Leroy and Ramanantsoa (1997) refer to incongruous events that violate conceptual frameworks as triggers for this kind of learning, and Fiol and Lyles (1983) assert that some type of crisis is necessary to trigger higher level or double-loop learning. Triggers are often associated with discontinuities such as the appointment of a new leader or dramatically altered market conditions.

Can organisations learn or is it only individuals that learn?

The approach to organisational learning presented here focuses on the development of supra-individual or shared mental models that provide a basis for effective action. These shared mental models furnish organisations with a conceptual framework for perceiving and interpreting new information and for determining how stored information can be related to any given situation. They persist over time, despite changes in organisational membership. This implies that organisations have collective memories that are not wholly dependent on the knowledge stored in the minds of current members. It is assumed that knowledge can also be stored in files, procedural manuals, routines, traditions and conventions and that this collective memory enables past experience to be applied to current problems.

Douglas (1986) challenges this view. She concedes that *institutional thinking* can exist in the minds of individuals and she accepts that much of the learning that goes on in an individual's head is influenced by what other organisational members know and by the kinds of information present in the organisational environment. She refers to this process as the 'squeezing' of each other's ideas into a common shape. However, she does not go along with the view that organisations, as collective entities, can learn.

Daft and Weick (1984) are more comfortable with the concept of collective or organisational learning. They base their view of organisations as interpretation systems on the assumption that they have both cognitive systems and memories.

While they recognise that it is individuals who send and receive information and in other ways carry out the interpretation process, they argue that the organisational interpretation process is something more than that which is undertaken by individuals. Individuals come and go, but there is an order and regularity in the way that organisational members continue to respond. The implication is that organisations, as well as individuals, develop mental models.

March (1991) appears to support this view. He presents learning in organisations as a mutual process that leads to a convergence between organisational and individual beliefs. While there may be an external reality that is independent of beliefs about it, both individuals and organisations develop their own mental models and beliefs about reality. The organisation stores the knowledge that it accumulates, over time, from the learning of its members in the form of an organisational code of received truth. This code or mental model (which influences the explicit and implicit rules and procedures that regulate behaviour in the organisation) is modified by the beliefs of individuals, and at the same time individual organisational members are socialised into the beliefs about reality that are associated with the shared mental model or organisational code. Thus, over time, the organisation's mental model affects the beliefs of individuals while it is being affected by those beliefs.

Although March argues that this convergence is generally useful for both the individual and the organisation, he recognises a potential threat to the effectiveness of organisational learning if individuals adjust to the shared mental model or organisational code before the code can learn from them. This threat is most likely to manifest itself and undermine organisational learning when a group develops a strong ideological commitment to the code or shared mental models and dismisses or suppresses deviant thinking as either irrelevant or potentially dangerous.

The revision of shared mental models – the key to collective learning

Shared mental models need to be fluid and open to modification if they are to provide an effective basis for assessing the environment and planning action. Unfortunately, once established, they may be resistant to change. Johnson and Scholes (1999) refer to the *strategic drift* that can occur when the need to modify the paradigm/shared mental model is not recognised, and when managers, blinkered by an outdated set of taken-for-granted beliefs and assumptions, fail to detect changes in the organisation's competitive position. It may not be until this strategic drift manifests itself in an unacceptable poor level of performance that the need to modify the paradigm is eventually recognised.

IMPEDIMENTS TO ORGANISATIONAL LEARNING

The essence of collective learning is the joint construction of meaning, which occurs through sharing and dialogue. However, this process is rarely problem-free. Three sources of difficulty will be considered.

Poor appreciation of the systemic qualities of organisations

Many individuals and groups have a parochial and limited view of their role and this restricts their ability to contribute to organisational learning. Often they focus all their attention on the immediate task and fail to appreciate how this relates to the overall purpose of the organisation. Egan (1988) discusses the need to promote 'business thinking' that relates to the organisation's overall mission and the importance of markets, competitors, customers, and the products and services that satisfy customers' needs and wants. 'Organisation thinking', on the other hand, is essentially inward, about the way the organisation organises its structures and processes to engage in its business. This type of thinking is important but, sometimes, people become too preoccupied with the details of their bit of the organisation and ignore how what they do affects others and how this impacts on the overall effectiveness of the business. Some of the interventions discussed in Chapter 16 are designed to promote systemic thinking.

Lack of accessible channels for dialogue and the sharing of meaning

An important factor that can influence an organisation's ability to learn is the willingness of individual organisational members to share with others the meaning they have constructed for themselves as they encountered new experiences and ideas. Issues of confidentiality may prevent some sharing but there are occasions where knowledge is withheld for what Dixon (1997) describes as political and logistical reasons. These include gaining a personal competitive advantage, or a perceived lack of interest, on the part of others, in what the individual might want to share.

When learning is shared the data on which it is based are open to challenge. Others can reassess the reasoning and logic that led to conclusions. In other words meanings are not just exchanged. Dixon argues that shared meaning is *constructed* in the dialogue between organisational members. She believes that in the process of articulating one's own meanings and comprehending the meanings others have constructed, people alter the meanings they hold. This joint construction of meaning is the essence of organisational learning. Unfortunately, the conditions that facilitate this process are often lacking. This has prompted many organisations to experiment with interventions designed to overcome some of the barriers to understanding between individuals and groups. Some of these interventions are referred to by Dixon, and include; 'whole system in the room' processes such as General Electric's Work Out, Weisbord's Strategic Search Conferences, Beer's Team Syntegrity and Emery's Conference Model; team approaches such as Revans' Action Learning, and others such as Learning Maps. This kind of intervention is considered in Chapter 16.

Ideologies

Reference has already been made to how ideology can distort the free flow of meaning. Walsh (1995) notes how shared mental models can be detrimental to organisational learning. He cites a number of case studies which link 'organisational blunders' to dysfunctional information processing among the organisations' top leadership groups, for example the Facit Corporation's inability to recognise the electronic calculator as a threat to its mechanical calculator business and the Allied commanders' unwillingness to accept the futility of the saturation bombing of Europe in the Second World War. In both these examples the group could be seen as holding a supra-individual schema that distorted its understanding of the information world in a way that made it blind to certain important aspects of its environment. In terms of Swieringa and Wierdsma's model the consequence was that the 'rules' used to guide behaviour were based on an inadequate understanding of the environment and they failed to promote behaviours that would contribute to the organisation's success

Weick (1979, p. 52) points to the phenomenon of groupthink (Janis, 1972) as an example of the dysfunctional consequences when people are dominated by a single self-reinforcing schema:

> Having become true believers of a specific schema, group members direct their attention towards an environment and sample it in such a way that the true belief becomes self-validating and the group becomes even more fervent in its attachment to the schema. What is underestimated is the degree to which the direction and sampling are becoming increasingly narrow under the influence of growing consensus and enthusiasm for the restricted set of beliefs.

Janis describes groupthink as a deterioration of mental efficiency, reality testing and moral judgement that is the result of in-group pressure. He defines eight symptoms of groupthink:

1 The group feels invulnerable. There is excessive optimism and risk-taking.
2 Warnings that things might be going awry are discounted by the group members in the name of rationality.
3 There is an unquestioned belief in the group's morality. The group will ignore questionable stances on moral or ethical issues.
4 Those who dare to oppose the group are called evil, weak or stupid.
5 There is direct pressure on anyone who opposes the prevailing mood of the group.
6 Individuals in the group self-censor if they feel that they are deviating from group norms.
7 There is an illusion of unanimity. Silence is interpreted as consent.
8 There are often self-appointed people in the group who protect it from adverse information. These people are referred to as mind-guards by Janis.

All too often individuals and organisations fail to exploit the full potential for learning because they are unaware of the extent to which their mental models filter out important information. Covey (1989) contends that while people think they are objective and see things as they are, they actually see what they have been conditioned to see. He argues that:

The more aware we are of our basic paradigms, maps or assumptions, and the extent to which we have been influenced by our experience, the more we can take responsibility for those paradigms, examine them, test them against reality, listen to others and be open to their perceptions, thereby getting a larger picture and a far more objective view. (p. 29)

Ideologies, the lack of accessible channels for dialogue and the sharing of meaning, and parochial thinking can all undermine the quality of the collective learning.

Exercise 4.1 Assessing the quality of organisational learning.

Consider the quality of organisational or collective learning in your organisation, or in a part of the organisation you are familiar with. When making your assessment, reflect on the following:

- What is the balance between single- and double-loop collective learning and how does this relate to the kinds of change (continuous or discontinuous) confronting the organisation or unit?
- Do people fully appreciate the systemic nature of the organisation and are they aware of how what they do affects overall organisational effectiveness?
- Are people motivated to share experiences and ideas, and seek a more effective way of operating?
- Is there an ideological commitment to established ways of doing things that discourages innovation and the exploration of new possibilities?

SUMMARY

This chapter opened with a discussion of the nature of strategy and strategic change management. Three different approaches to strategy formulation and implementation were considered and the effect of factors such as culture and organisational politics on the quality of information processing was highlighted.

We then examined the nature of organisational learning and how it contributes to strategic change management, and different kinds of collective learning were discussed. Single-loop learning is concerned with continuous improvement through doing things better; double-loop learning involves challenging current thinking and exploring the possibility of doing things differently or doing different things.

The final section focused on impediments to organisational learning such as a failure to appreciate the systemic nature of organisations, the lack of accessible channels for dialogue and the sharing of meaning and pressures for conformity that constrain creative thinking.

References

Argyris, C. and Schön, D. (1978) *Organizational Learning*, London: Addison-Wesley.

Covey, S.R. (1989) *The Seven Habits of Highly Effective People*, London: Simon & Schuster.

Daft, R.L. and Weick, K.E. (1984) 'Toward a Model of Organisations as Interpreting Systems', *Academy of Management Review*, 9(2), pp. 284–95.

De Geus, A (1988) 'Planning as learning', *Harvard Business Review*, March–April, p. 71.

Dixon, N. (1997) 'The Hallways of Learning', *Organizational Dynamics*, Spring, pp. 23–34.

Douglas, M. (1986) *How Institutions Think*, Syracuse, NY: Syracuse University Press.

Egan, G. (1988) *Change-agent Skills: Assessing and Designing Excellence*, San Diego: University Associates.

Fiol, C.M. and Lyles, M.A. (1983) 'Organizational Learning', *Academy of Management Review*, 10(4), pp. 803–13.

Janis, I.L. (1972) *Victims of Groupthink: A Psychological Study of Foreign Policy Decisions and Fiascos*, Boston: Houghton-Mifflin.

Johnson, G. (1993) 'Processes of Managing Strategic Change', in C. Mabey and B. Mayon-White (eds), *Managing Change*, London: Paul Chapman Publishing in association with the Open University, pp. 58–64.

Johnson, G. and Scholes, K. (1999) *Exploring Corporate Strategy*, 5th edn, London: Prentice-Hall Europe.

Lank, A.G. and Lank, E.A. (1995) 'Legitimising the Gut Feel: The Rise of Intuition in Business, *Journal of Managerial Psychology*, 10(5), pp. 18–23.

Leroy, F. and Ramanantsoa, B. (1997) 'The Cognitive and Behavioural Dimensions of Organizational Learning in a Merger Situation: An Empirical Study', *Journal of Management Studies*, 34(6), pp. 871–94.

March, J.E. (1991) 'Exploration and Exploitation in Organisational Learning', *Organizational Science*, 2(1), pp. 71–87.

Miles, R.H. (1982) *Coffin Nails and Corporate Strategies*, Englewood Cliffs, NJ: Prentice-Hall.

Pettigrew, A. and Whipp, R. (1993) 'Understanding the Environment', in C. Mabey and B. Mayon-White (eds), *Managing Change*, London: Paul Chapman Publishing in association with the Open University, pp. 5–19.

Quinn, J.B. (1993) 'Managing Strategic Change', in C. Mabey and B. Mayon-White (eds), *Managing Change*, London: Paul Chapman Publishing in association with the Open University, pp. 64–84.

Schein, E.H. (1990) 'Organisational Culture', *American Psychologist*, 45(2), pp. 109–19.

Swieringa, J. and Wierdsma, A. (1992) *Becoming A Learning Organisation*, Reading, MA.: Addison-Wesley.

Walsh, J.P. (1995) 'Managerial and Organisational Cognition: Notes from a Trip Down Memory Lane', *Organisational Science*, 6(3), pp. 280–321.

Weick, K.E. (1979) 'Cognitive Processes in Organizations', in B.W. Staw (ed.), *Research in Organizational Behavior*, Vol. 1, Greenwich, Conn.: JA Press, pp. 41–74.

5

Process models of change

In this chapter we open with an activity designed to explore the issues and choices involved in developing an approach to managing organisational change. We then move on to consider the main features of some frequently cited models for conceptualising the change process and present a generic model that will provide the structure for Chapters 6–18 of this book.

Exercise 5.1 Managing a branch-closure programme: an exercise in planning and managing the process of change

The aim of this activity is to explore the issues and choices involved in developing an overall strategy for large-scale change.

The scenario: A long-established bank is facing strong competition from new entrants into the retail banking market. The new entrants specialise in the provision of telephone and internet banking services and have a lower cost base because they do not carry the overheads associated with a large branch network.

A director of the branch network in the traditional bank has proposed a strategy for responding to this competition. It involves closing down 20 per cent of the branch network in order to reduce overheads and increase net revenue per customer. At this stage the details of the strategy have not been finalised. For example, the branches targeted for closure could be city-centre branches occupying expensive properties or small rural branches occupying low-cost premises but with relatively few customers of high net worth to the bank.

Imagine that you are a consultant who has been engaged by the director who initiated the proposal. Your role is to help her:

- explore the feasibility of the proposal to increase profitability by contracting the branch network;
- design a change plan that could be implemented if it is decided to go ahead with the closures.

Step 1 The director, her immediate colleagues and you have brainstormed a list of possible actions that could provide the basis for a strategy for managing this change; these are listed below. You are invited to review the list of actions presented in Table 5.1 and use your experience to:

- Delete any items that, on reflection, you feel are unimportant or irrelevant.
- Add, in the space provided in Table 5.1, any other actions that you feel should be included. You are allowed to add up to four additional actions.
- Think about how the actions might be sequenced from start to finish. For each action, identify whether you think it should occur early or late in the change management process. You can record this view in the space provided on the right hand side of Table 5.1.

Table 5.1 Possible actions

	Action	Early			Late		
1	Identify key stakeholders who might be affected by the change						
2	Provide counselling service and retraining for those who are to be displaced						
3	Inform staff how they, personally, will be affected by the closure plan						
4	Persuade those who are in a position to champion the favoured closure plan to support it in order to help ensure that the Bank maintains its competitive position						
5	Identify a project leader and set up a branch closure team						
6	Announce the scope and scale of the closure plan to all staff						
7	Brief key managers about the closure plan						
8	Identify which branches are to be closed						
9	Review success (or otherwise) of the closure programme and disseminate throughout the organisation any lessons learned about change management						
10	Identify the information that will be required in order to decide the number and location of branches to be closed in order to achieve targeted benefits						
11	Announce closure plan to existing customers						
12	Train members of the branch closure team in change management skills						
13	Identify (and quantify) benefits sought from closures						
14	Develop personnel package for displaced staff						
15	Assess effects of the closures on other aspects of the Bank's functioning						
16	Plan any training that may be required for staff who are to be re-assigned to other work						

	Action	Early			Late	
17	Hold team meetings to brief staff about how the closure plans will affect staff and indicate when they will be informed about how they (personally) will be affected by the change					
18	Identify what steps could be taken to retain high value customers affected by the closures					
19	Provide training for managers and supervisors to assist them help others (and themselves) cope with change					
20	Issue newsletter outlining progress towards full implementation					
21	Decide who should be involved in analysing the information relating to whether a closure plan will deliver sufficient benefits to justify the costs involved					
22	Seek views of customers who might be affected by the closures about what issues should be given attention					
23	Seek views of branch staff about the issues that will have to be given attention if the closure plan is to be successfully accomplished					
24	If it is decided to implement the closure plan, decide who should be involved in identifying which branches are to be closed					
25	Initiate programme to make properties suitable for disposal (eg remove vaults)					
26	Celebrate successes and build on them in order to motivate people to continue working to improve the Bank's competitive position					
27	Decide on date for first closures					
28	Identify any personal gains or losses that might be perceived by those employees who will be affected by the closures					
29	Specify timetable for implementing the closure plan					
30	Consider what might be done to motivate employees to accept the change					
31	Issue a press release about the closure plan					
32	Monitor progress against timetable and anticipated benefits					
33	Explore the best way of disposing of redundant properties					
34	Identify social banking issues raised by the closures (eg what will happen to customers without transport when their local branch closes)					
35	Plan what will happen to displaced staff (redeployment, early retirement, redundancy)					
36						
37						
38						
39						

Step 2 Consider your list of action statements and assemble them into a plan.

- Identify the sequence of actions from start to finish, recognising that some actions may occur in parallel or be repeated.
- Identify relationships between actions in your plan and consider how different actions might be categorised as separate steps or distinctive parts of your plan.
- Summarise your plan (on a separate sheet or in the space provided below) as a flow diagram, including descriptive labels for the main aspects or stages of your plan.

You might find it helpful to print all of the actions listed in Table 5.1 on to separate post-its so that it will be easier to move them about and experiment with different ways of:

- sequencing them, and
- grouping them into categories that reflect the mains steps in your approach to managing the change process.

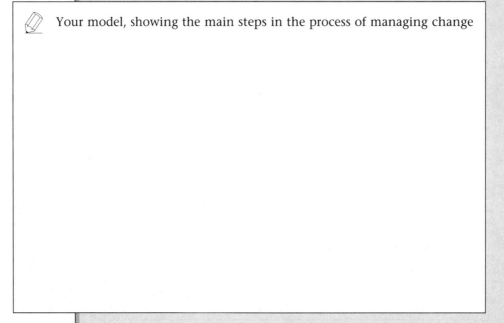

Your model, showing the main steps in the process of managing change

A version of this exercise, *Managing the Merger*, (base on managing a merger between two food retailing organisations) has been developed by John Hayes and Peter Hyde. It has been designed for use with groups and can be purchased from Management Learning Resources, PO Box 28, Carmarthen, SA31 1DT. Email: sales@mlr.co.uk The exercise includes a facilitator's guide and a 'best practice' solution which applies a generic change model to the merger situation.

The next part of this chapter will consider some process issues associated with the management of change and will conclude by presenting a generic model that can be used as a guide when thinking about the best way to manage a particular change. You might find it useful to compare this generic model with the model you developed to manage the branch closures. As you read the remaining chapters of this book you might also find it helpful to reflect on how the content of each chapter might influence your approach to managing this kind of change.

THE NATURE OF CHANGE AS A PROCESS

In Chapter 1, reference was made to the work of Tushman and colleagues and their distinction between incremental and discontinuous change. Weick and Quinn (1999) make a similar distinction and refer to change that is continuous (incremental) and episodic (discontinuous).

- *Continuous change.* They note that a common presumption is that continuous change is emergent. 'The distinctive quality of continuous change is the idea that small continuous adjustments, created simultaneously across units, can cumulate and create substantial change'. Where interdependencies between organisational units are loose these same continuous adjustments can be confined to smaller units, but they can still be 'important as pockets of innovation that may prove appropriate in future environments'.
- *Discontinuous change.* Discontinuous or episodic change, according to Weick and Quinn, occurs during periods of divergence when organisations are moving away from their equilibrium conditions. It is a result of 'a growing misalignment between a inertial deep structure and perceived environmental demands'.

The failure of organisational members to create a continuously adaptive organisation leads to a failure that can be the trigger for planned change (see Dunphy, 1996).

The intentional management of change

Ford and Ford (1995) argue that the intentional management of change occurs when a change agent 'deliberately and consciously sets out to establish conditions and circumstances that are different from what they are now'.

Lewin (1951) provided some useful insights into the nature of change that are very relevant for those who seek to intentionally change the status quo. He argued that the state of no change does not refer to a situation in which everything is stationary. It involves a condition of 'stable quasi-stationary equilibrium' comparable to that of a river which flows with a given velocity in a given direction. A change in the behaviour of an individual, group or organisation can be likened to a change in the river's velocity or direction. In a work situation, for example, certain hostile and friendly actions may occur between two groups in interdepartmental meetings. If the level of hostile behaviour is defined as a problem, a desired change may involve a reduction in hostile behaviour and an increase in friendly behaviour, in other words in a move from one state of stable quasi-stationary equilibrium to another.

Lewin argued that any level of behaviour is maintained in a condition of quasi-stationary equilibrium by a force field comprising a balance of forces pushing for and resisting change. This level of behaviour can be changed by either adding forces for change in the desired direction or by diminishing the opposing or resisting forces.

Both of these approaches can result in change but, according to Lewin, the secondary effects associated with each approach will be different. Where change is brought about by increasing the forces pushing for change this will result in an increase in tension. If this rises beyond a certain level it may be accompanied by high aggressiveness (especially towards the source of the increased pressure for change), high emotionality and low levels of constructive behaviour. On the other hand, where change is brought about by diminishing the forces that oppose or resist change the secondary effect will be a state of relatively low tension.

This argument led Lewin to advocate an approach to managing change that emphasised the importance of reducing the restraining forces in preference to a high-pressured approach that only focused on increasing the forces pushing for change. He argued that approaches which involve the removal of restraining forces within the individual, group or organisation are likely to result in a more permanent change than approaches which involve the application of outside pressure for change.

Achieving a lasting change

Lewin highlighted the concept of permanency. He suggested that successful change requires a three-step procedure that involves the stages of unfreezing, moving and refreezing.

Dawson (1994) and Kantor et al. (1992) argue that the notion of refreezing is not relevant for organisations operating in turbulent environments. They argue that organisations need to be fluid and adaptable and that the last thing they need is to be frozen into some given way of functioning. Lewin's point, however, is that all too often change is short-lived; after a 'shot in the arm', life returns to the way it was before. In his view it is not enough to think of change in terms of simply *reaching* a new state, for example revised management practices that include a new pattern of behaviour towards subordinates. He asserted that permanency, for as long as it is relevant, needs to be an important part of the goal. This state may be very brief and involve little more than taking stock before moving on to yet more change. It is, however, important to think in terms of consolidation in order to minimise the danger of slipping back to the way things were before.

Managing change, therefore, involves helping an individual, group or organisation:

1 unfreeze or unlock from the existing level of behaviour;
2 move to a new level; and
3 refreeze behaviour at this new level.

Hendry (1996) testifies to Lewin's lasting contribution to change management. He notes that 'Scratch any account of creating and managing change and the idea that change is a three stage process which necessarily begins with a process of unfreezing will not be far below the surface'.

STAGES IN THE PROCESS OF MANAGING CHANGE

This section briefly reviews three other process models of change that can be viewed as elaborations of Lewin's basic model.

Lippitt, Watson and Westley (1958) expanded Lewin's three-stage model. After reviewing descriptions of change in persons, groups, organisations and communities they felt that the moving phase divided naturally into three sub-stages:

- The clarification or diagnosis of the client's problem;
- The examination of alternative routes and goals, and establishing goals and intentions for action;
- The transformation of intentions into actual change efforts.

They also argued that change managers can only be effective when they develop and maintain an appropriate relationship with those involved in or affected by the change. This led them to introduce two further stages into the change process; one concerned with the formation and the other with the termination of relationships.

Egan (1988) developed a model that reflects Lewin's three stages of unfreezing, moving and refreezing, but it focuses most attention on diagnosing, visioning and planning for change, that is, on the early stages of Lewin's process model. The first part of Egan's model emphasises three issues:

- The current scenario: assessing problems and opportunities, developing new perspectives, and choosing high impact problems or opportunities for attention.
- The preferred scenario: developing a range of possible futures, evaluating alternative possibilities to establish a viable agenda for change, and gaining commitment to the new agenda.
- Strategies and plans for moving to the preferred scenario: brainstorming strategies for getting there, choosing the best strategy or best-fit package of strategies, and turning these strategies into a viable plan.

The second part of Egan's model relates to the period of transition during which plans have to be implemented. This phase emphasises tactics that can be employed to adapt the plan to the immediate situation and accommodate unforeseen complications, and logistics that involve securing essential resources when required. The final part of the model gives some attention to the consolidation of change.

Beckhard and Harris (1987) present a three-stage model that focuses on defining the present and the future, managing the transition, and maintaining and updating the change. Special consideration is given to some of the issues associated with the moving or transitional stage, including the need for management mechanisms, the development of activity plans and the gaining of commitment from key stakeholders.

These three models highlight the importance of:

- *Diagnosis* – change managers need to give attention to where the organisation is now and to what a more desirable (and attainable) state would look like.
- *Strategies and plans* to move the organisation towards the desired state.
- *Implementation* – translating intentions (strategies and plans) into actual change efforts. Implementation also involves managing the interpersonal and political issues associated with change.

KEY STEPS IN THE CHANGE PROCESS

Change is often managed less effectively than it might be because those responsible for managing it fail to attend to some of the critical aspects of the change process. The model (Hayes and Hyde 1998) presented below provides a conceptual framework for thinking about the management of change, and incorporates many of the features of the process models reviewed above. While the context here is organisational change, the same model can be applied to change at the level of the individual and the group.

At first glance this model suggests that change is a neat, rational and linear process. This is not always the way that it unfolds and is experienced in practice. Sometimes a desired end state is not obvious at the beginning of the process, a point that will be elaborated later. Also the dotted lines in Figure 5.1 represent feedback loops and possible iterations or repetitions in the process. The loop between 'review' and 'external factors' signals that change rarely involves moving from one steady state to another. Typically it is an ongoing process. Often new pressures for change emerge before the current change initiative has been completed.

- *Recognition.* The start of the process is the recognition that external events or internal circumstances require a change to take place. Recognition involves complex processes of perception, interpretation and decision making that, if not managed carefully, can lead to inappropriate outcomes, for example the organisation might fail to change when it needs to or it may change when change is not required.
- *Start of the change process.* The start of the change process involves translating the need for change into a desire for change, deciding who will manage the change and, especially where an external change agent is introduced to help with this process, establishing a workable and effective change relationship.

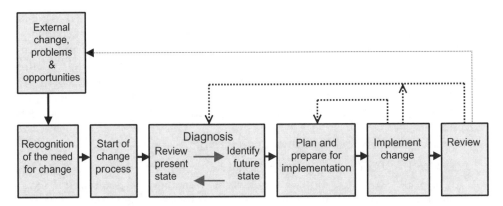

Figure 5.1 Steps in the change process

Source: Hayes and Hyde (1998).

It may be more or less explicit and formal, but at some point it typically involves a review, feasibility study or project. Critical questions that need to be considered at this stage are:

□ Who to involve,
□ What to make public (if anything), and
□ Who should have management responsibility.

It is also important to begin thinking about how to unfreeze others and gain acceptance that change is needed.

● *Diagnosis.* Although reviewing the present and identifying the future state may seem at first sight to be separate and distinct activities, they are often integrated in practice. These two steps frequently go through several iterations, progressing from broad concepts towards something that is sufficiently concrete and detailed to be implemented.

There is also some debate about whether the process should in fact start with looking at the present or the future. The argument for starting with the present is to ensure that the change is not a 'utopian leap' to an unrealistic future which cannot be reached from the current situation. On the other hand, focusing too heavily on the present may limit horizons and lead to the goals of change being too cautious and constrained by current experience. Where radical or transformational change is needed it may be better to consider the direction of change than to concentrate on the start point. For these reasons, Figure 5.1 shows these two elements interacting in the same box.

□ *Reviewing the present state.* The present state of the organisation can often only be understood in terms of the context of its past history and its external environment. The precise objectives for reviewing the present state will depend upon the type of change that is being managed. Common reasons are to:

(1) help identify the required change by diagnosing the cause of a problem, identifying current deficiencies or clarifying opportunities;
(2) establish a baseline so that it is clear what is changing; and
(3) help define the future direction.

Data gained form this kind of review can also be used to help assess how organisational members and other stakeholders will react, and to prepare people for change.

□ *Identifying the future state.* What is required when identifying the future state depends on the kind of change that is being undertaken and on the role of the change managers in the overall process. If the change managers are responsible for initiating the change their task is likely to involve developing a view or 'vision' of what they (and others involved in the diagnostic process) think the organisation ought to look like in the future. If, on the other hand, their role is to implement a change that is being imposed from elsewhere, their task might be more limited to thinking through and visioning the likely impact of the change.

The way the diagnostic stage is managed can affect the way that the need for change is (or is not) translated into a desire for change. Organisational members are more likely to be motivated to let go of the status quo and seek a more desirable state if the diagnostic process:

- ☐ disconfirms their view that all is well with the existing state of affairs
- ☐ if this challenge produces a sufficient level of anxiety to motivate organisational members to search for new possibilities, and
- ☐ the vision of what might be offers sufficient promise to make the effort of changing worthwhile.

● *Prepare and plan for implementation*. Detailed analysis of the future and present state will lead to the identification of a long list of things which will need to be done in order to make the proposed change a reality. There will be different lead times associated with the various tasks, interdependencies between them and resource and other constraints. All of these things need to be taken into account when developing an implementation plan. However, it is important that implementation is not viewed as only a technical activity. Implementation has an important political dimension. It needs to address the extent to which people are ready for and accepting of change and whether the process threatens them in any way. Choices need to be made, such as which method to adopt to implement the change and whether to proceed to full implementation or start with a trial or pilot.

● *Implement change*. Whatever has been planned now needs to be implemented and the focus shifts from planning to action. Attention also needs to be given to monitoring and control to ensure that things happen as intended.

There are two basic approaches to implementing change. Sometimes change involves moving from A to B, where, before implementation, the nature of B is known and clearly defined. This kind of change is sometimes referred to as a 'blueprint' change. Typical examples of a blueprint change include relocation, computerisation of a business process, or the introduction of a new appraisal or grading system. In these circumstances it is easier to view the management of change from the perspective of 'planned change' that involves a pre-determined linear process (following step by step the successive stages in the models of change reviewed above).

Often, however, it is not possible to specify the end point (B) of a change in advance of implementation (see the discussion of logical incrementalism and the emergent approach to the formulation of strategy in Chapter 4). While a need for change might be recognised (because, for example, the organisation is losing market share or is failing to innovate as fast as its competitors), it may be less obvious what needs to be done to improve matters. There may be a broadly defined goal and a direction for change (for example, improving competitiveness), but it may not be possible to provide a very detailed specification of what this end state will look like. In some situations, it may not even be very helpful to think in terms of specific end states because the rate of change in the operating environment may be such that the precise definition of a desirable end state may be subject to constant revision.

In these circumstances, a blueprint approach to change is inappropriate. Change needs to be viewed as a more open-ended and iterative process that emerges or evolves over time. Buchanan and Storey (1997) argue that this is not unusual and that change often unfolds in an iterative fashion and can involve much backtracking.

An emergent or evolutionary approach to change involves taking tentative incremental steps in what it is hoped is the right direction. After each step, the step itself and the direction of the change are reviewed to establish if the step worked and if the direction still holds good. As the process unfolds, it may be possible to define the end state a bit more precisely or to take future steps with more confidence. The dotted lines on Figure 5.1 illustrate the process of feedback and review which is an essential part of this approach to change. Even with blueprint changes, this feedback loop is important because feedback from implementation can lead to the identification of new problems and possibilities. It may have implications for the planning of further activities to bring about change and may even affect the definition of a more desirable end state, thus leading to a revision of the 'blueprint'. Sometimes the feedback may also alert change managers to the possibility that what was originally perceived as a blueprint change might be more appropriately approached and managed as an evolutionary change.

- *Review and consolidate*. The review part of this heading is sometimes taken to imply some form of post-implementation review, but in practice monitoring and reviewing progress are ongoing activities, as progress is measured against key milestones. Consolidation refers to the refreezing aspect of Lewin's model. It involves, among other things, ensuring that there are feedback mechanisms and reward systems in place that will monitor and reinforce desired new behaviours. However, rather than attempting to simply ossify the new state, it also involves building on and updating the change as required.

MANAGING THE PEOPLE ISSUES

As well as the steps described in the model and presented in Figure 5.1, a strategy for managing change must also address a number of people issues that are ongoing throughout the process. Some of these are:

- Power, leadership and stakeholder management
- Communication
- Training and development
- Motivating others to change
- Support for others to help them manage their personal transitions

These issues will be considered later in Chapters 9–13.

Change managers need to address these people issues at all stages of the change process and not just when designing a strategy for implementation. A common mistake is to treat the stages of reviewing the present state and designing the future state as purely technical activities that do not require any strategic thought. They are often viewed as a precursor to the 'real business' of managing change, which is a dangerous attitude to adopt. In Chapter 4 a distinction was made between the planning and emergent approaches to formulating and implementing strategy that is relevant to this discussion. It was noted that the successful implementation of strategies can be threatened when the stages of formulation and implementation are separated, and when there is an overreliance on rational approaches that neglect cultural and political issues. Diagnosing and visioning are not benign activities. Stakeholders may resist any attempt to even consider the possibility that change might be required.

A change strategy is essentially a plan to make things happen. It needs to address all of the things that have to be done to bring about the change. When developing a strategy, change managers need to attend to each step in the change process and to the way the overall process is to be managed. However, all of this needs to be regarded as something that is dynamic and evolving and not a grand plan that can be 'set in stone' from the start. It is also important to recognise that there is no one recipe or prescription about how change 'should' be managed, that can be applied to all situations. Managing change is a complex process. Change managers need to contextualise their approach and develop bespoke strategies that accommodate the cultural and political dynamics that can undermine or facilitate any attempt to manage change. Other actions are associated with issues such as stakeholder management, communication and so forth, which need to be attended to throughout the whole process.

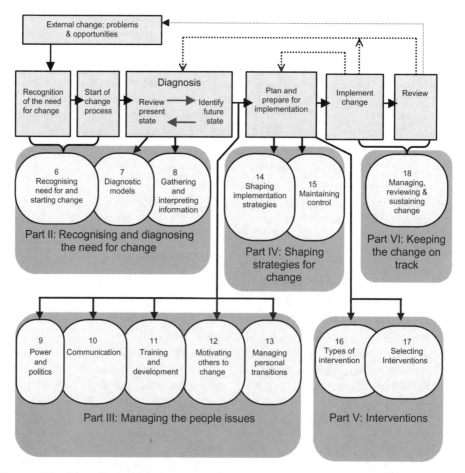

Figure 5.2 The relationship between Chapters 6–18 and the generic process model of change

SUMMARY

This chapter opened with an exercise that invited you to think about how you might go about managing the process of change associated with the branch networks of a large traditional bank. A generic model of the change process was presented, against which to compare, assess and if necessary revise your own approach to change management. This generic model provides the framework for Chapters 6–18. The ways in which Chapters 6–18 relate to the generic model is illustrated in Figure 5.2.

References

Beckhard, R. and Harris, R. (1987) *Organizational Transitions: Managing Complex Change*, 2nd edn, Reading, Mass: Addison-Wesley.

Buchanan, D.A. and Storey, J. (1997) 'Role Taking and Role Switching in Organizational Change: The Four Pluralities', in I. McLoughlin and M. Harris (eds), *Innovation, Organisational Change and Technology*, London: International Thompson.

Dawson, P. (1994) *Organisational Change: A Processual Approach*, London: Chapman.

Dunphy (1996) 'Organisational Change in Corporate Settings, *Human Relations*, 49(5), pp. 541–2.

Egan, G. (1988) *Change Agent Skills B: Managing Innovation and Change*, San Diego, Cal.: University Associates.

Ford, D.J. and Ford, L.W. (1995) 'The Role of Conversation in Producing Intentional Change in Organizations', *Academy of Management Review*, 20(3), pp. 571–600.

Hayes, J and Hyde, P. (1998) *Managing the Merger, a Change Management Simulation*, Novi, Michigan: Organisation Learning Tools (also available from Management Learning Resources, PO Box 28, Carmarthen, SA31 1DT).

Hendry, C. (1996) 'Understanding and Creating Whole Organisational Change through Learning Theory, *Human Relations*, 48(5), pp. 621–41.

Kantor, R.M., Stein, B.A. and Jick, T.D. (1992) *The Challenge of Organizational Change*, New York: Free Press.

Lewin, K. (1951) *Field Theory in Social Science*, New York: Harper & Row. (See also Lewin 1947, 'Frontiers in Group Dynamics', *Human Relations*, 1, pp. 5–41.)

Lippet, R., Watson, J. and Westley, B. (1958) *The Dynamics of Planned Change*, New York: Harcourt Brace, Jovanovich.

Weick, K.E. and Quinn, R.E. (1999) 'Organisational Change and Development', *Annual Review of Psychology*, 50(1), pp. 361–86.

Part II

Recognising and diagnosing the need for change

This part comprises three chapters that review some of the issues that need to be addressed at the early stages of the change process.

Chapter 6   Recognising the need for change and starting the change process

This chapter considers some of the issues associated with starting the change process, including:

- recognising the need for change;
- translating this need into a desire for change;
- deciding who will facilitate the change;
- establishing a working relationship between the change manager(s) and those who might be affected by the change.

After reading this chapter you will be asked to:

- think of an occasion when a need for change in your department was recognised in good time, and an occasion when it was never recognised or only very late in the day; and
- identify some of the factors that might have contributed to these different outcomes.

Chapter 7   Diagnostic models

This chapter is divided into three sections. The first examines the role of models in organisational diagnosis and introduces an exercise designed to help raise your awareness of the implicit models you use when thinking about organisations and assessing the need for change. The second section presents a range of diagnostic models that are commonly used by consultants and managers, and the final section of the chapter will invite you to compare your implicit model with some of the explicit models that are widely used by others. It provides an opportunity for you to reassess the utility of your implicit model and, if shortcomings are identified, to revise it.

Chapter 8   Gathering and interpreting information for diagnosis

This chapter considers some of the issues associated with gathering, analysing and interpreting information about individual, group and organisational functioning. After reading this chapter you will be invited to think about a recent occasion when you (or somebody working close to you) attempted to introduce and manage a change in your part of the organisation, and:

- Reflect on the extent to which this change initiative was based on an accurate diagnosis of the need for change.
- Consider the extent to which this was related to the:

  - ☐ appropriateness of the (implicit or explicit) diagnostic model used,
  - ☐ nature of the information collected, and
  - ☐ way in which it was interpreted.

- Reflect on what steps *you* might take to help improve the quality of the way the need for change is diagnosed in your unit or department.

6

Recognising the need for change and starting the change process

This chapter considers some of the issues associated with starting the change process. These include recognising the need for change, translating this need into a desire for change, deciding who will facilitate the change and establishing a workable and effective change relationship.

RECOGNISING THE NEED FOR CHANGE

It was noted in Chapter 1 that some organisations (or units) are good at anticipating the need for change; these organisations benefit because they have the time to investigate the emerging problem or opportunity and decide how best to respond. Other organisations lack this ability. They may fail to recognise the need for change until they have little choice but to react quickly to an unanticipated set of circumstances. Yet others may never recognise the problem or opportunity. In some circumstances such a failure to recognise and respond can threaten the organisation's long-term survival, but often the change may not be so critical or the organisation may have sufficient 'fat' to survive. Nevertheless the cost may be that it ends up performing at a level that is much below what it might have been.

Where organisations fail to recognise the need for change this may be because members pay insufficient attention to what is happening in the wider environment. Even where organisational members are aware of what is going on outside they may fail to recognise its implications for the organisation. In Chapter 4, reference was made to how ideologies and inappropriate shared mental models can undermine an organisation's ability to interpret and understand what is going on in the environment. At the level of the organisation this can lead to strategic drift, and at the level of the unit or sub-system it can lead to a similar lack of alignment and consequent inefficiencies.

Nadler and Shaw (1995) illustrate this with their argument that one of the paradoxes of organisational life is that success often sets the stage for failure. This is because, when organisations are successful, managers become locked into the patterns of behaviour that produced the original success. These patterns become codified or institutionalised and are rarely questioned. Nadler and Shaw elaborate their argument with the proposition that success often leads to growth and growth leads to complexity and greater differentiation. As this happens, attention shifts away from how the organisation relates with the environment (it is taken for granted that this relationship will be successful), and is switched to managing the new and more complex relationships within the organisation. Customers and supplies receive less attention and competitive gains of rival organisations (for example in terms of reduced costs or shorter time to market) are ignored. Where this complacency and internal focus leads to declining performance the organisation may behave as if the solution is to do more of what led to success in the past. Nadler and Shaw refer to the organisation becoming 'learning disabled'. It becomes incapable of looking outside, reflecting on success and failure, accepting new ideas and developing new insights. If unchecked the ultimate outcome of this trap of success can be what they refer to as the 'death spiral' (see Figure 6.1).

Another problem, referred to in Chapter 10, is that the organisational members who recognise the need for change may not be in a position to do anything about it. They may be located low down in the organisational hierarchy or, in communication network terms, they may be isolated and unable to communicate with those who have the power to make things happen.

Recognising the need for change is an essential step in starting the change process. You might want to reflect on your own experience and consider how good your unit or organisation has been at recognising the need for change.

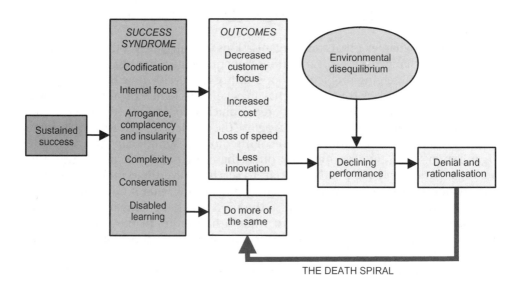

Figure 6.1 The trap of success

Source: Nadler, D. and Shaw, R. 'Change Leadership', in D. Nadler, R. Shaw and A.E. Walton, *Discontinuous Change*, Jossey-Bass, 1995, p. 11.

TRANSLATING RECOGNITION OF NEED FOR CHANGE
INTO DESIRE FOR CHANGE

Organisational members may recognise a problem or opportunity but this may not be translated into a desire for change because the individuals or groups who recognise the need for change may fear that, while it will benefit the organisation, it may disadvantage them.

Another problem may be that those who recognise the need for change may have little confidence in their own ability or the ability of others to implement the change and achieve a more desirable state (see the section on beliefs about change agency in Chapter 2 and the discussion on how leadership can affect these beliefs in Chapter 9). This lack of confidence may be related to a history of failures to bring about change or to a feeling that the competencies, commitment and other resources required for change will not be available in the current situation. Pugh (1993) argues that those who are most likely to want to change are those who are basically successful but who are experiencing tension or failure in some particular part of their work. This group will have both the confidence and the motivation to change. The next most likely to change are the successful because they will have the required confidence. However, because of their success they may be satisfied with the status quo and lack the motivation to change. The least likely to understand and accept the need for change are the unsuccessful. While they may be the ones who need to change most, they are also the ones who are likely to lack confidence in their own ability to improve their predicament. Consequently, they may prefer the status quo (the devil they know) to the possible outcome of a failed effort to change (the devil they don't know).

This has implications for deciding where to initiate the change effort. When faced with the possibility of alternative start points, the change agent might decide to start working with those who have the confidence and motivation to engage in the change process because early successes can inspire others to get involved.

Exercise 6.1 Recognising the need for change

Think of an occasion within the last three years when your unit (or your organisation) recognised the need for change in good time, and think of another occasion when it failed to do this. In the space overleaf, list those factors that you suspect may have contributed to these different outcomes.

Factors that contributed to the recognition of the need for change	Factors that contributed to the failure to recognise the need for change

Reflect on your unit or organisation's past record of recognising the need for change, and note, in the space below, anything that you or others could do to help ensure that in the future your unit or organisation will be more alert to the need for change.

DOING SOMETHING ABOUT IT – STARTING THE CHANGE PROCESS

After persuading others of the need for change it is necessary to decide *who* will, at least in the first instance, manage/facilitate the change. The change agent could be an insider, a member of the system or sub-system that is the target for change, or an outsider. An insider might be chosen in situations where:

- the person responsible for managing the unit or sub-system that is to be the (initial) target for change is committed to acting as change agent;
- it is agreed that some other insider has the time, knowledge and commitment to manage the change more effectively than an outsider;
- the system does not have the resources to employ an outsider;
- issues of confidentiality and trust prohibit the use of an outsider; or
- it proved impossible to identify a suitable outside consultant.

An outsider might be chosen where:

- there is nobody on the inside who has the time or competence to act as facilitator/change agent; or
- it is felt that all of the competent insiders have a vested interest in the outcome and therefore might be less acceptable to all parties than a neutral outsider.

ESTABLISHING A CHANGE RELATIONSHIP

Where the change agent is a member of the target system, entering the change relationship may simply involve agreeing with members of the target system that:

- there is a problem or opportunity that requires attention; and
- there is a need to engage in some form of preliminary data gathering in order to determine what further action is required.

A brand manager who is unhappy with the time it takes to introduce a change in the way a product is packaged may enlist the support of others to benchmark their performance against that of leading competitors. Similarly, a manager of a sports centre might set up a meeting with staff to consider possible reasons why an increasing proportion of existing members are failing to renew their membership.

Because the change agent is an insider and known to others, many of the issues that can be problematical and require careful attention when introducing an external consultant/change agent can often be managed informally and without too much difficulty. Where the change agent is an outsider (coming from another part of the organisation or from outside), the establishment of a change relationship can be a more complex, and sometimes a more formal, process.

ISSUES THAT CAN AFFECT THE QUALITY OF THE RELATIONSHIP

One of the key issues is building trust and confidence. Some individuals and groups are less comfortable than others when it comes to being open and discussing their affairs with outsiders. This might be because they fear that it might be difficult to communicate the nature of their problem (or opportunity) to others and that others may view them as incompetent or foolish. Alternatively, it may be because they fear that seeking help will threaten their autonomy and make them too dependent on others.

The early stages of the relationship-building process can be critical because clients quickly form impressions about the change-agent's competence, ability to help, friendliness and inferred motives. In terms of competence and ability, some clients want a consultant/change agent who has sufficient expertise to be able to 'see a way through' and tell them what to do. They might expect the change agent to undertake a diagnostic study and prepare a written report. In these circumstances the competence they are seeking from the consultant is related to the 'content' of the problem or opportunity. Others might want a more collaborative relationship and expect the change agent to work with them to help them solve their own problems. The competence that is valued in this type of relationship is related more to the *process* of problem-solving and managing change rather than to the *content* of a problem. The important point to make at this stage is that both parties need to reach some agreement about the role of the external consultant/change agent.

In terms of friendliness and approachability, what many clients want is a helper who is, on the one hand, sympathetic to their needs and values, but, on the other hand, is sufficiently neutral to offer objective comment, feedback and other assistance. In terms of inferred motives, where clients feel that they can trust the consultant/change agent and believe that they are 'on their side' and are 'working for them' they will be more likely to share sensitive information and be receptive to feedback or suggestions about helpful processes and so on. However, where the change agent is seen as untrustworthy, incompetent or 'not for them' the clients will be much more likely to react defensively and resist any attempt to influence their thinking.

Developing a relationship with an external change agent can take time, and sometimes clients test the helper's competence, attitudes, perceived role and trustworthiness by presenting them with what they regard as a safe or peripheral problem. If they are satisfied with the change agent's performance the client may move on to present what they believe to be the real problem.

Identifying the client

From the perspective of the change agent, an issue that must be managed carefully is the identification of the client. The person who invites an outsider into a situation may not be the person or group that ends up as the focal client. The change agent needs to be ready to amend the definition of the client if a preliminary diagnosis suggests that the problem is not confined to one group or unit, but involves multiple units, several levels of the hierarchy or people outside the organisation such as customers, suppliers, trade associations, unions or others.

Problems can arise when external change agents define the client as the person/ group who invited them into the situation. If they are blind to the need to redefine who the client is they may end up, inadvertently, working to promote or protect a sectional interest rather that the effectiveness of the organisation.

One way of defining the client is in terms of the person or persons who 'own' the problem and are responsible for doing something about it. Thus, for example, the client might be either the manager who seeks help to improve the effectiveness of his or her department, or the department as a whole. Cummings and Worley (2001) define the client as those organisational members who can directly impact the change issue, whether it is solving a particular problem or improving an already successful situation. This definition is more likely to identify the client as a group or the members of a sub-system rather than as an individual. Cummings and Worley specify the client in terms of all those who can directly impact on the change because they argue that if key members of the client group are excluded from the entering and contracting process they may be reluctant to work with the change agent.

The author learned about this from direct experience. He was invited by the personnel director of an international oil company to help with a problem in a distant oil refinery. He was flown to the nearest major airport, put up in a hotel and, next morning, flown by a small plane to the refinery's own airstrip. Eventually he found himself in a meeting room in the refinery with all the senior managers. After some brief introductions the refinery manager started the meeting by asking the consultant why he was there. It was clear that the personnel director had not involved the refinery manager in the decision to engage an external consultant. This was strongly resented and by the time the consultant had arrived at the refinery there was little he could do to build an effective working relationship with the management team. However, some months later, the same refinery manager approached the consultant and invited him back to the refinery to work on a different problem. On this occasion it was his problem and his decision to involve an outsider. The rejection first time round had nothing to do with the consultant's competence. The refinery manager had been very unhappy that somebody else had decided that he had a problem and that, without any consultation, had decided that he needed external help to resolve it.

Clarifying the issue

Reference has already been made to the possibility that the presented symptoms or problem may not be related to the issue that the client is most concerned about. There are other problems associated with deciding what the real issue is. Those who seek help from consultants to resolve a problem often present the difficulty as somebody else's problem. The head of HR of a manufacturing company invited the author to meet the finance director over lunch. The problem that the finance director (who was also the deputy chairman of the board) wanted to talk about was to do with the poor state of communications between the board and senior management. He defined the problem in terms of the quality of the senior managers. Eventually, after the board had considered the problem in more detail, it was redefined as something to do with the board itself, about conflicting views regarding the role of the board and political issues that affected how the board functioned.

Another issue is that problems are often presented to others in terms of implied solutions. For example, 'We need help to:

- improve the appraisal system,
- build a more cohesive team,
- improve communications'.

The communications problem might be further defined in terms of improving the communicating skills of certain individuals. However, a preliminary investigation may suggest that while communications are a problem, an important factor contributing to the problem is the structure of the organisation and the effect this has on the communication networks. In such a situation, improving the communication skills of selected individuals or replacing existing members with others might do little to resolve the underlying structural problem.

Change agents need to keep an open mind about the nature of the problem until there has been some kind of preliminary investigation. However, it is important that the change agent pays careful attention to the felt needs of the client.

Exercise 6.2 Starting the change process

Think of an occasion when you acted as a change agent. It might have been at work or elsewhere (home, club, etc.), and it might have involved an individual, group or larger system. Did it go smoothly from the start or did you hit problems initiating the change process?

If you did hit problems, did they relate to any of the issues considered in this chapter? Reflect on this experience and, in the space below, make a note of any learning points that might help you to avoid similar problems in the future.

SUMMARY

This chapter has considered some of the issues associated with starting the change process. These include recognising the need for change, translating this into a desire for change, deciding who will manage the change and, especially where an external consultant is introduced to help with this process, establishing a workable and effective change relationship. Associated issues for the change agent include being clear who the client is, and keeping an open mind about the precise nature of the problem while seeking to clarify the issues that are of concern to the client.

References

Cummings, T.G. and Worley, C.G. (2001) *Organization Development and Change*, 7th edn, Cincinnati, Ohio: West.

Nadler, D.A. and Shaw, R.B. (1995) 'Change Leadership: Core Competency for the Twenty-first Century', in D.A. Nadler, R.B. Shaw and A.E. Walton (eds), *Discontinuous Change: Leading Organisational Transformation*, San Francisco: Jossey-Bass, pp. 3–14.

Pugh, D. (1993) 'Understanding and Managing Organizational Change', in C. Mabey and B. Mayon-White (eds), *Managing Change*, London: Paul Chapman in association with the Open University, pp. 108–12.

7

Diagnostic models

Chapters 7 and 8 are concerned with *what* it is that needs to be changed to move towards a more desirable state and improve organisational effectiveness. In this chapter we first examine the role of models in organisational diagnosis, and introduce an exercise designed to help raise awareness of the implicit models we use when thinking about organisations and assessing the need for change. We then present a range of diagnostic models that are commonly used by consultants and managers. In the final section we invite you to compare your implicit model with some of the explicit models that are widely used by others. It provides an opportunity to reassess the utility of your implicit model and, if shortcomings are identified, to revise it.

THE ROLE OF MODELS IN ORGANISATIONAL DIAGNOSIS

Organisational behaviour, at all its different levels, is a very complex phenomenon. It is impossible for anyone to pay attention to, or understand the interactions between, all the many elements or variables that can have an effect on how an organisation functions. Consequently we simplify the real world by developing models that typically focus attention on:

- a limited number of *key elements* that are seen to offer a good representation of the real world;
- the ways these elements interact with each other, sometimes referred to as *causal relationships* or laws of effect; and
- the *outputs* produced by these interactions.

Models that include explicit reference to outputs offer the possibility of evaluating performance and assessing effectiveness.

We all develop our own implicit theories or conceptual models about how organisations function, and we use these models to:

- guide the kind of information that we attend to;
- interpret what we see; and
- decide how to act.

We develop these models on the basis of our personal experience, either as organisational members or external observers of organisational behaviour. Sometimes these models provide a good basis for understanding what is going on and predicting what kind of actions or interventions would produce desired change. Often, however, they are very subjective and biased, they overemphasise some aspects of organisational functioning and completely neglect others. Consequently they do not always provide a useful guide for management practice and the management of change.

The aim of the exercise presented below is to help you develop a greater level of awareness of your own model of organisational functioning. This will help you assess whether your own personal model is consistent with or relevant to the problems or opportunities that you need to address. It will also help you compare you model with alternatives and modify it to improve its utility.

Making personal models more explicit can be of benefit to all of the people involved in managing a change. It can provide an opportunity for them to share their models, debate their relative merits, and move towards the development of a collective model that can be used to provide a basis for joint diagnosis and concerted action.

Exercise 7.1   Raising awareness of your implicit model of organisational functioning

This exercise is based on a procedure for collaborative model building devised by Tichy and Hornstein (1980) and involves five steps. The first requires you to prepare a short assessment of the current state of your organisation. The next four steps involve reflecting on how you arrived at this assessment to tease out the main features of your implicit model of organisational functioning.

Step 1   Assess the current state of your organisation. Prepare a short note that describes your organisation (either the total organisation or an important unit that you are familiar with) and assesses or diagnoses its current state. Make reference to the issues that you feel require attention. These issues might be problems and/or opportunities. If you feel that these issues are already being managed effectively justify this view and indicate what it is that gives you this impression. If, on the other hand, you feel that there is a need for some kind of change to ensure that these issues will be managed more effectively, again justify this view.

Do *not* explain the kind of interventions that you think are necessary to bring about any required changes. The aim of this exercise is to diagnose the current state of the organisation (and assess whether it is and will continue to perform effectively), not to provide a prescription of actions required to improve matters.

Step 2 Identify the information you used to make this assessment. Think about the things that you considered when making your assessment in the first step of this exercise. Identify and list the 'bits of information' that you attended to. Focus on the information that you actually attended to. Try not to let the kind of information that you think you 'should' have considered influence your list.

Identify, if possible, at least 25 different bits of information and record them in the space provided. Table 7.1 provides some examples of the bits of information that people might attend to when assessing the state of their organisation. These are only offered as examples to stimulate your thinking; your own list may not contain any of these.

Table 7.1 Examples of the kind of information that might be attended to

Leader's ability to influence internal politics	The allocation of roles and responsibilities	Selection and placement of staff
Mission or purpose of the organisation/unit	Quality of supervision	Management information systems
Levels in the hierarchy	System used to evaluate performance	Informal groups and coalitions
State of physical plant/equipment	Culture (norms, traditions etc.)	Future sources of income/revenue
Co-ordinating mechanisms	Technological change	Morale and motivation
Customer satisfaction	Costs	Quality of communications
Cash flow	Inventory levels	Margins
Staff turnover	Reward systems	Competitive threats

Step 3 Developing categories for organising your diagnostic information. Some of the bits of information that you used to make your assessment might be related and it might be possible to group them together into a number of more inclusive categories.

- Do this by grouping related bits of information into the category boxes provided below. (Typically people identify between 4 and 12 categories, but there are no restrictions on the number of categories you might identify.)
- When you have categorised your bits of information, describe the rationale you used for including information in each category.

These categories reflect the main elements or variables of your diagnostic model.

Category Name	*Category Name*
Items included in category: Briefly state rationale for including items:	Items included in category: Briefly state rationale for including items:

Category Name	*Category Name*
Items included in category: Briefly state rationale for including items:	Items included in category: Briefly state rationale for including items:

Category Name	*Category Name*
Items included in category: Briefly state rationale for including items:	Items included in category: Briefly state rationale for including items:

Category Name	*Category Name*
Items included in category: Briefly state rationale for including items:	Items included in category: Briefly state rationale for including items:

Step 4   Specifying relationships between categories/elements. The categories identified above reflect the elements of your implicit diagnostic model. Step 4 of the model-building process focuses on interdependencies and causal relationships between the elements. These can be identified by considering whether a change in any one element will have an effect on any other element.

- Using the format of Table 7.2, list the elements (categories) identified in Step 3 down the left-hand column and across the top of the table.
- Take each element down the left-hand column in turn and assess the impact a change in this element might have on every other element, using a three-point scale where 0 = no or slight impact; 1 = moderate impact; and 2 = high impact.

Table 7.2   Interdependencies between elements

Elements / Effect of change on:	1	2	3	4	5	6	7	8	9	10
1	–									
2		–								
3			–							
4				–						
5					–					
6						–				
7							–			
8								–		
9									–	
10										–

Note: Even though elements might be interrelated and affect each other, one element (e.g. A) can have a greater effect on another (e.g. B) than vice versa. This is illustrated in Table 7.3.

Table 7.3   An example of a matrix of interdependencies

Categories	A	B	C	D	E
A	–	2	1	0	2
B	1	–	1	0	0
C	0	1	–	0	1
D	0	0	1	–	2
E	2	0	1	2	–

Step 5   Your implicit model can be represented diagrammatically:

- Draw a circle for each of the elements that you identified in Table 7.2.
- Label each circle with the name of the element it represents.
- Draw lines between those elements that have any impact on each other. Use a solid line to show a strong relationship between categories (with the arrow-head indicating the direction of a cause and effect relationship), and a dotted line to show a moderate link (do not join elements that have only a slight or no impact on each other).

The model represented by Table 7.3 is presented diagrammatically in Figure 7.1

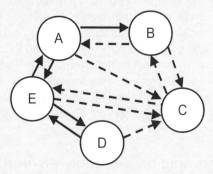

Figure 7.1   A causal map of a diagnostic model

Now draw your own diagnostic model

* As noted above, this exercise is based on a procedure for collaborative model-building devised by Tichy and Hornstein (1980).

In the next section we present a range of widely used models of organisational functioning; you might wish to compare your own model with these alternatives.

A REVIEW OF DIFFERENT MODELS FOR ORGANISATIONAL DIAGNOSIS

In Chapter 2 reference was made to how organisations can be conceptualised from a number of different perspectives. Each of these emphasises different elements, different causal relationships and different definitions of effectiveness. In Chapter 3 a distinction was made between component models that provide insights into the functioning of specific components of an organisation, and models that provide an overview of the total system. In this section, all the models that are considered are, to a greater or lesser extent, overall rather than component models.

The first set of models to be considered is primarily concerned with diagnosing the fit between the organisation and its environment. Examples include PEST, SWOT and Strebel's cycle of competitive behaviour. The second set is mainly concerned with diagnosing the organisation's internal alignment. Examples include Weisbord's six-box organisational model, and Pascale and Athos' 7S model. The third set is concerned with open-systems models that give greater attention to both internal and external alignment. Examples include Kotter's integrative model of organisational dynamics and Nadler and Tushman's congruence model of organisations (both considered in Chapter 3) and the Burke–Litwin causal model of organisational performance and change.

Diagnosing organisation–environment fit

There are a number of models that focus on assessing the environment and how environmental changes might affect organisational performance.

PEST analysis

This approach can be used by managers to examine the organisation's environment and search for evidence of change that might signal a problem or opportunity. The mnemonic refers to Political, Economic, Socio-cultural and Technological factors.

Political factors include new legislation in areas such as environmental management, consumer protection and employment; regulation of markets in areas such as telecommunications and broadcasting; fiscal policies, and so forth. Organisations that operate in international markets need to be aware how legislative changes or changes in the level of political stability in different parts of the world might influence their operations.

Economic factors include issues such as exchange rates, cost of borrowing, change in levels of disposable income, cost of raw materials, and the trade cycle.

Socio-cultural factors include demographic trends such a fall in the birth rate or an ageing population. They also include shifting attitudes towards education, training, work and leisure which can have knock-on effects on the availability of trained labour, consumption patterns and so on. Cultural factors can also affect business ethics and the way business is done in different parts of the world.

Technological factors include issues such as the levels of investment competitors are making in research and development and the outcome of this investment; the availability of new materials, products, production processes, means of distribution, and so forth; the rate of obsolescence and the need to reinvest in plant and people.

SWOT analysis

This approach focuses on Strengths, Weaknesses, Opportunities and Threats. In addition to assessing the opportunities and threats that a PEST analysis might reveal, it also includes an assessment of the organisation's strengths and weaknesses and its capability of responding to the threats and opportunities that confront it.

Strebel's (1996) evolutionary cycle of competitive behaviour

Strebel's model can be used to anticipate technological and economic changes in the environment and initiate planned organisational changes that will enable a company to remain one step ahead of the competition. Strebel posits that there is an evolutionary cycle of competitive behaviour and that different phases of the cycle are marked by break points. He also suggests that, given proper attention to competitive trends, these break points can be predicted in advance. The two phases of the cycle are innovation and efficiency.

The start of the innovative phase of the cycle (bottom left of Figure 7.2) is characterised by a sharp increase in divergence and begins when an innovation by one competitor is seen to create a new business opportunity. This triggers others to innovate and gives rise to a greater variety in the offerings (products and services) available to customers. This process continues until there is little scope for further innovation that offers suppliers or customers much in the way of added value. At this point divergence of offerings begins to decline as the best features of past innovations are imitated by competitors.

The next phase of the cycle begins when one or more providers begin to turn their attention to efficiency rather than innovation. Cost reduction is seen as the route to maintaining market share and increasing profit. They achieve this by improving systems and processes to reduce delivered cost. While each phase of the cycle can present opportunities for some, it can also pose threats for others. In the efficiency phase of the cycle only the fittest survive and inefficient competitors are driven out of business.

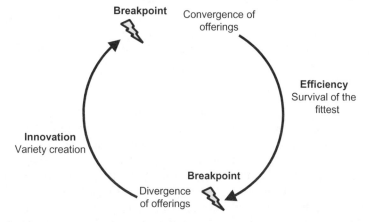

Figure 7.2   Strebel's (1996) cycle of competitive behaviour

Source: Strebel, P., 'Breakpoint: How to Stay in the Game', *Mastering Management*, 1996, Part 17, *Financial Times*.

When most of the opportunities for gaining competitive advantage from improving efficiency have been exploited, attention might switch once again to innovation, and the cycle will repeat itself. Strebel (1996) suggests indicators that can be used to anticipate breakpoints. He also notes that convergence is usually easier to anticipate than divergence because it involves a move towards greater similarity in existing products and services whereas divergence is based on potential new offerings and their existence might not be known until a competitor offers them to customers.

Diagnosing internal alignment

Two examples of models that are widely used to diagnose internal alignment are Pascale and Athos' 7S model and Weisbord's six-box organisational model.

Pascale and Athos' (1981) 7S model

This model highlights seven elements of organisations that are seen to make an important contribution to organisational effectiveness. However, it does not make explicit reference to outcomes or to the external environment. The 7S framework points to a range of useful diagnostic questions such as:

1 *Strategy*. Purpose of the business; nature of the competition; relationship between espoused and actual strategy.
2 *Structure*. Division of activities; integration and coordination mechanisms; nature of informal organisation.
3 *Systems*. Formal procedures for measurement, reward and resource allocation; informal routines for communicating, resolving conflicts and so forth.
4 *Staff*. Demographic, educational and attitudinal characteristics of organisational members.
5 *Style*. Typical behaviour patterns of key groups such as managers and other professionals and of the organisation as a whole.
6 *Shared values*. Core beliefs and values and how these influence the organisation's orientation to customers, employees, shareholders and society at large.
7 *Skills*. The organisation's core competencies and distinctive capabilities.

Weisbord's (1978) six-box model

Weisbord presents his systemic model as a 'practice theory' that synthesises knowledge and experience for change agents. It provides a conceptual map of six elements or boxes that can be used to apply any specific (component) theories to the assessment of these elements in a way that can reveal new connections and relationships between elements. It is an open systems model that recognises the importance of organisation–environment relationships but focuses most attention on what needs to be done internally to ensure that the organisation becomes/ remains a high-performance organisation able to adapt to external changes.

The six boxes are presented in Figure 7.3. Weisbord argues that the effectiveness of an organisation's functioning depends on what goes on in and between the six boxes. There are two aspects of each box that deserve attention: the formal and the

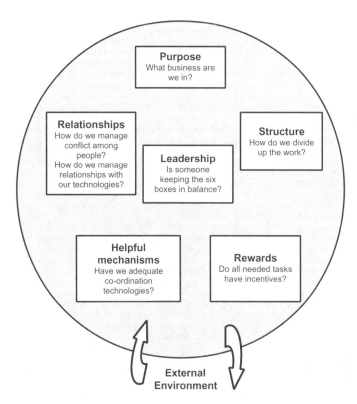

Figure 7.3 Weisbord's (1978) six-box model

Source: Weisbord, M.R., *Organizational Diagnosis*, Addison-Wesley, 1978, p. 9.

informal. He argues that the formal aspects of an organisation (for example, stated goals or the structure as represented by an organisation chart) might bear little relation to what happens in practice. Attention needs to be given to the frequency with which people take certain actions in relation to how important these actions are for organisational performance. This leads to a consideration of why people do what they do, and what needs to be changed to promote more effective behaviour. Leadership is seen to have a special role to play in coordinating what goes on in the other five boxes.

Weisbord suggests that a useful starting point for any diagnostic exercise is to:

- focus on one major output (of a unit or the total organisation);
- explore the extent to which the producers and the consumers of the output are satisfied with it; and
- trace the reasons for any dissatisfaction to what is happening in or between the six boxes that represent the unit or organisation under consideration.

Models that attend to both internal and external alignment

Kotter's (1980) integrative model of organisational dynamics and Nadler and Tushman's (1981) congruence model of organisations have been the focus of attention in Chapter 3. Both will be summarised here, but most attention will be reserved for the Burke–Litwin causal model of organisational performance and change.

Kotter's (1980) integrative model of organisational dynamics

This model comprises seven elements as summarised in Figure 7.4. A distinctive feature of this model, as noted in Chapter 3, is the important role played by the key organisational processes such as information gathering, communication, decision-

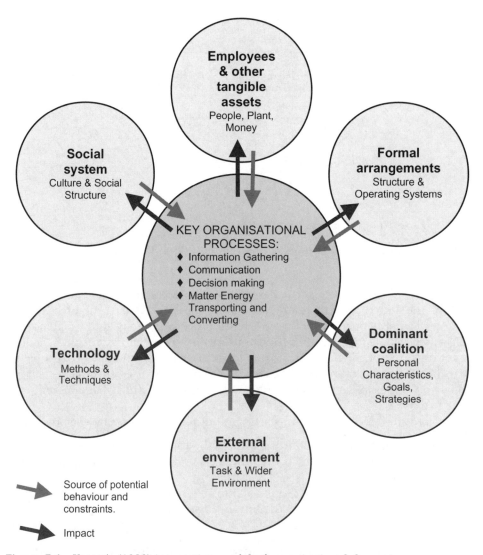

Figure 7.4 Kotter's (1980) integrative model of organisational dynamics

Source: Kotter, J.P., 'An Integrative Model of Organizational Dynamics', in E. Porter, D. Nadler and C. Cammann (eds), *Organizational Assessment*, Wiley, 1980, p. 282.

making and matter–energy transformation. Another is that it offers three perspectives on effectiveness. Short-run effectiveness is determined by the quality of the processes and cause and effect relationships that link all the elements of the system together. In the medium term, effectiveness is influenced by the organisation's ability to sustain its short-term effectiveness. This is determined by the degree of alignment of its main elements. Over the longer term, effectiveness is determined by the organisation's ability to adapt to internal and external changes.

Nadler and Tushman's (1980) congruence model

Nadler and Tushman's model conceptualises the organisation as a transformation process that takes inputs from the environment and transforms them into individual, group and organisational outputs. The transformation process includes four major elements: task, individuals, formal organisational arrangements and the informal organisation (see Chapter 3 for a more detailed description). Effectiveness is determined by the degree of congruence (alignment) that exists between the organisation and its environment and between the four internal elements of the organisation. Strategy is presented as an input that manages the organisation's alignment with the wider world (see Figure 7.5). Congruence (alignment) is defined as the degree to which the needs, demands, goals, objectives and structures of any one element are consistent with the needs, demands, goals, objectives and structures of any other element.

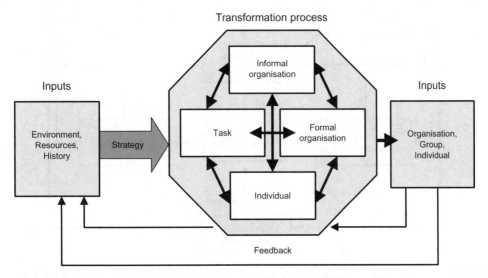

Figure 7.5 Nadler and Tushman's (1980) congruence model

Source: Nadler, D. and Tushman, M., 'A Congruence Model for Organizational Assessment', in E. Porter, D. Nadler and C. Cammann (eds), *Organizational Assessment*, Wiley, 1980, p. 261.

The Burke–Litwin (1992) causal model of organisational performance and change

This model points to causal linkages that determine the level of performance and affect the process of change. It also differentiates between two types of change: transformational change that occurs as a response to important shifts in the external environment, and transactional change that occurs in response to the need for more short-term incremental improvement. These features distinguish this model from the others considered in this section.

The model, illustrated in Figure 7.6, comprises 12 interrelated elements. It is an open systems model in which the inputs are represented by the external environment element at the top of the figure, and the outputs by the individual

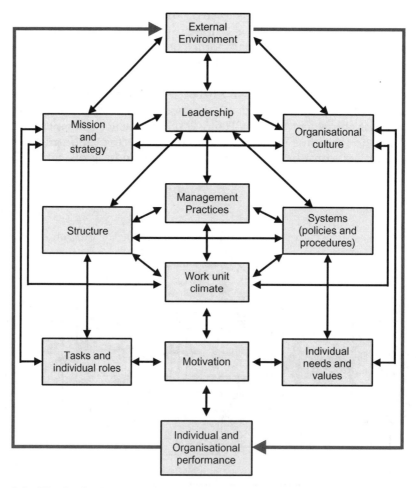

Figure 7.6 The Burke–Litwin (1992) causal model of organisational performance and change

Source: Burke, W.W. and Litwin, G.H., 'A Causal Model of Organizational Performance and Change', *Journal of Management*, 1992, 18(3), p. 528.

and organisational performance element at the bottom of the diagram. Feedback loops go in both directions: the organisation's performance affects its external environment and the external environment affects performance. The remaining 10 elements represent the process of transforming inputs into outputs, and reflect different levels of this process. Strategy and culture, for example, reflect aspects of the whole organisational or total system. Climate is an element associated with the local unit level, and motivation, individual needs and values, and job–person fit are individual-level elements.

The model is presented vertically (rather than across the page from left to right, like the Nadler and Tushman model) to reflect causal relationships and the relative impact of elements on each other. Burke and Litwin posit that those elements located higher in the model, such as strategy, leadership and culture, exert greater impact on other elements than vice versa. In other words, even though elements located lower down in the model can have some impact on those above them, position in the model reflects 'weight' or net causal impact.

This said, the model does not prescribe that change *should* always start with elements at the top of the model. It is a predictive rather than a prescriptive model. It specifies the nature of causal relationships and predicts the likely effect of changing certain elements rather than others. The decision about where to intervene first might be influenced by whether the aim is to secure transformational or transactional change. The model elaborates these two distinct sets of organisational dynamics. One is associated with organisational transformation and the need for a fundamental shift in values and behaviour, and the other is associated with behaviour at the more everyday level.

Transformational change is required when an organisation has to respond to the kind of environmental discontinuities that were considered in Chapter 1. This kind of change involves a paradigm shift and completely new behaviours. Instead of changes designed to help the organisation do things better (incremental change) the organisation needs to do things differently or do different things. As noted in Chapter 4 this calls for the principles, assumptions and values that underpin the implicit and explicit rules that guide behaviour to be revised. It involves a change in the organisation's culture. It also calls for a change in the organisation's mission and strategy, and for managers especially, but not only senior managers, to provide a lead and to behave in ways that clarify the new strategy and encourage others to act in ways that will support it. Where the need is for this kind of change attention needs to be focused on the transformational elements highlighted in Figure 7.7.

Transactional change is associated with 'fine tuning', with how the organisation functions within the existing paradigm. It emphasises single rather than double-loop learning, as specified in the model of organisational learning discussed in Chapter 4 (see Figure 4.1). The focus of attention needs to be the structures, management practices and systems that affect the work climate, which in turn impacts on motivation and performance (at both the unit and individual level).

Interventions designed to bring about organisational transformation that target 'higher-level' elements in the model will eventually and inevitably have an impact on all other elements in the system because of their weight and relative impact. If, however, the target of interventions is primarily the elements in the lower part of the model, aimed at achieving what Burke and Litwin refer to as transactional change, the impact is more likely to remain at local unit level. Interventions

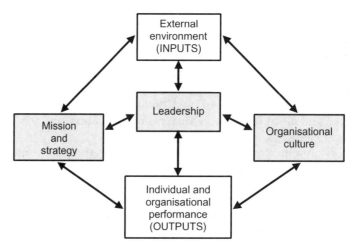

Figure 7.7 The transformational factors

targeted at this type of element might have relatively little, if any, impact on overall organisational culture and strategy. Burke and Litwin (1992) also present an impressive (if selective) summary of studies that provide empirical support for the causal linkages hypothesised by their model.

REVISING YOUR PERSONAL MODEL OF ORGANISATIONAL FUNCTIONING

The previous section has presented a brief summary of some widely used models of organisational functioning and has identified some of the main differences between them. You are advised to develop a 'healthy scepticism' towards the utility of different models and to constantly reassess which is most appropriate for the purpose at hand.

Characteristics of a good model

All the models considered above are simplifications of the real world. None are guaranteed to accommodate all circumstances and provide a reliable basis for understanding why things are the way they are, or identify actions that can be taken to produce a desired outcome. Depending on circumstances and purpose, some theories or models might have greater utility than others.

Three characteristics of 'good' diagnostic models are that they:

- are relevant to the particular issues under consideration;
- help change agents recognise cause and effect relationships;
- focus on elements that they can influence.

Points to consider when refining your own model

When identifying a model that you might use to guide your diagnosis and planning you might usefully reflect on two points:

- How do the available models relate to your personal experience? For example, to what extent do the models considered above (or other models that you are aware of) accommodate or ignore elements and causal relationships that your experience has led you to believe are important? It might be unwise to slavishly apply a model that ignores aspects of organisational functioning that your own experience tells you are significant.
- Do any of the available models include elements and/or relationships that you have never previously considered but which, on reflection, might help you make better sense of your own experience? You need to be alert to the danger of rejecting alternative models too hastily. You might find that a model that is quite different from your own personal model can provide useful new insights. Even if you decide not to adopt an alternative model in its entirety, you might decide to incorporate some aspects of it into your own model.

Giving proper consideration to these issues can prompt you to refine and improve your own personal model of organisational functioning. Before moving on to the next chapter, you might find it useful to reflect on the model you articulated in Exercise 7.1 above.

SUMMARY

This chapter has:

- Examined the role of models in organisational diagnosis.
- Presented an exercise designed to help you raise awareness of your implicit model of organisational functioning.
- Provided an overview of some widely used diagnostic models that you can use as a benchmark when assessing the validity and utility of the model you currently use.
- Suggested some guidelines for revising your current model or selecting an alternative that might improve the quality of your diagnosis.

The next chapter examines some of the issues that you need to consider when deciding how to collect information for diagnosis.

References

Burke, W.W. and Litwin, G.H. (1992) 'A Causal Model of Organizational Performance and Change', *Journal of Management*,18(3), pp. 523–45.

Kotter, J.P. (1980) 'An Integrative Model of Organizational Dynamics', in E.E. Lawler, D.A Nadler and C. Cammann (eds), *Organizational Assessment*, New York: Wiley. pp. 279–99.

Nadler, D.A. and Tushman, M.L. (1980) 'A Congruence Model for Organisational Assessment', in E.E. Lawler, D.A. Nadler and C. Cammann, *Organizational Assessment*. New York: Wiley, pp. 261–78.

Pascale, R. and Athos, A. (1981) *The Art of Japanese Management*, New York: Warner Books.

Strebel, P. (1996) 'Breakpoint: How to Stay in the Game', *Mastering Management*, Part 17, London: *Financial Times*.

Tichy, N.M and Hornstein, H.A. (1980) 'Collaborative Organisation Model Building', in E.E. Lawler, D.A. Nadler and C. Cammann, *Organizational Assessment*, Chichester: Wiley, pp. 300–16.

Weisbord, M.R. (1978) 'Organisation Diagnosis: Six Places to Look for Trouble With or Without a Theory, *Group and Organization Studies*, December, pp. 430–47.

8

Gathering and interpreting information for diagnosis

Diagnosing the need for change involves a process of gathering, analysing and interpreting information about individual, group and organisational functioning. The main steps in this process are:

1. Selecting a conceptual model for diagnosis;
2. Clarifying information requirements;
3. Information gathering;
4. Analysis;
5. Interpretation.

In those circumstances where the information is collected by an internal or external change agent working on behalf of a client group, the information will need to be fed back to the other organisational members who will be involved in the diagnosis. This often occurs after those who have collected the data have completed a preliminary analysis but before the information has been interpreted.

SELECTING A DIAGNOSTIC MODEL

It was noted in Chapter 7 that organisational behaviour, at all its different levels, is a very complex phenomenon and that it is impossible for managers to pay attention to every aspect of organisational functioning. We cope with this complexity, sometimes unconsciously, by developing or adopting conceptual models that simplify the real world and focus attention on a limited number of elements and relationships. Some of the explicit models of organisational functioning that are available to change agents relate to how the organisation functions as a total system. Others (component models) focus on selected elements of the overall system, such as leadership, structure, job design, competencies and so on. A range of total-system models was considered in the previous chapter and most good texts on organisational behaviour critically review a wide range of component models.

Conceptual models play a key role in the diagnostic process because they help us decide which aspects of organisational behaviour require attention and they provide a focus for information-gathering. They also provide a basis for interpreting the information that has been collected. When selecting a model for diagnosis the obvious first point that has to be considered is the extent to which the model is relevant to the issue(s) under consideration, for example, loss of market share, dysfunctional intergroup conflict, high labour turnover, and so forth.

An effective model is one that identifies specific elements and/or cause and effect relationships that contribute to the problem or opportunity, and indicates which of these have most weight (or effect) on other aspects of organisational functioning and performance. Evidence, from personal experience or published research, about the ability of a conceptual model to explain and predict cause and effect relationships can help the change manager select an appropriate model for diagnosis. However, the ultimate aim of organisational diagnosis is more than improving our understanding of why something is the way that it is. It also involves using this understanding to plan action to improve organisation effectiveness.

Consequently, if a diagnostic model is to have any practical utility, it needs to highlight aspects of organisational functioning that, either directly or indirectly, the change manager can do something about.

CLARIFYING INFORMATION REQUIREMENTS

Exercise 7.1 invited you to think about the information you would use in order to diagnose the current state of your organisation. This information was then categorised and used to help you make explicit your personal model of organisational functioning. However, this process can be reversed. When a diagnostic model has been selected the change manager can identify the items of information that will be required to assess how an organisation (unit or group) is performing and to distinguish what is going well and what is going not so well.

In Chapter 7 the Burke–Litwin causal model of organisational performance was presented. The 12 elements of the model are defined in Table 8.1, together with examples of the kind of questions that might be used to elicit information about each element. The examples are taken from an instrument used in a diagnostic exercise in the BBC. The survey instrument included a minimum of four questions relating to each element of the model; respondents were invited to respond to the questions on a five-point scale.

INFORMATION GATHERING

This stage of the process begins with a series of planning decisions relating to which methods of data collection to employ and whether data can/should be collected from every possible source or from a representative sample of the total population of sources.

Table 8.1 Examples of questions asked in the 1993 BBC staff survey

ELEMENTS	INDICATIVE QUESTIONS
External environment Any outside condition or situation that influences the performance of the organisation. These conditions include such things as marketplaces, world financial conditions, political/governmental circumstances, etc.	Regarding the pace of change, what would you say the organisation as a whole is experiencing (from static to very rapid change)?
Mission/strategy What organisational members believe is the central purpose of the organisation and how the organisation intends to achieve that purpose over an extended time	How widely accepted are the organisation's goals among employees?
Leadership Executive behaviour that encourages others to take needed actions	To what extent do senior managers make an effort to keep in touch with employees at your level in the organisation?
Culture 'The way things are done about here.' The collection of overt and covert rules, values and principles that guide behaviour and that have been strongly influenced by history, custom and practice	To what extent are the standard ways of operating in the organisation difficult to change?
Structure The arrangements of functions and people into specific areas and levels of responsibility, decision-making authority, and relationships	To what extent is the organisation's structure clear to everyone?
Management practices/action What managers do in the normal course of events to use human and material resources to carry out the organisation's strategy	To what extent does your manager communicate in an open and direct manner?
Systems Standardised policies and mechanisms that facilitate work. They typically manifest themselves in the organisation's reward systems and in control systems such as goal and budget development and human resource development	To what extent are the following communication mechanisms in the organisation effective? (e.g. grapevine)
Climate The collective current impressions, expectations, and feelings of the members of local work units. These affect members' relations with supervisors, with one another and with other units	Where you work in the organisation, to what extent is there trust and mutual respect among employees?
Task requirements and individual skills The behaviour required for task effectiveness, including specific skills and knowledge required for people to accomplish the work assigned and for which they feel directly responsible (often referred to as the job-person match)	How challenged do you feel in your present job?
Motivation Aroused behavioural tendencies to move towards goals, take needed action, and persist until satisfaction is attained	To what extent do you feel encouraged to reach higher levels and standards of performance in your work?
Individual needs and values The specific psychological factors that provide desire and worth for individual actions and thoughts	(From disagree strongly to agree strongly) I have a job that matters
Performance The outcomes or results, with indicators of effort and achievement. Examples include productivity, customer or staff satisfaction, profit, and service quality	To what extent is the organisation currently achieving the highest level of employee performance of which they are capable?

METHODS FOR COLLECTING INFORMATION

There are a number of different techniques or methods that can be used to collect information. They include individual and group interviews, questionnaires, projective methods such as drawings and collages, observation and the use of secondary data, sometimes referred to as unobtrusive measures. Cummings and Worley (2001) provide a useful discussion of most of these methods; only their main features are summarised in this chapter.

Interviews

Individual and group interviews are a rich source of information about what is going on in an organisation. People can be asked to *describe* aspects of the organisation and how it functions, and they can also be asked to make *judgements* about how effectively the organisation, or an aspect of it, functions and how they feel about this (their *affective reaction*). For example, after describing how the appraisal system operates in an organisation, some employees might judge it to be ineffective but indicate that they are quite happy about this because the ineffective system works to their personal advantage.

Individual interviews have some added advantages. Respondents might be persuaded to share private views that they may be reluctant to express in a more open forum. The interaction between interviewer and respondent can offer the possibility that respondents might be stimulated to articulate and make explicit vague feelings and views that they had not previously formulated at a conscious level. Interviews are also adaptive. If respondents raise issues that the interviewer had not anticipated, the interview schedule can be modified to allow these emerging issues to be explored in more detail. The interview also offers the opportunity for the interviewer/change agent to build rapport and develop trust with respondents and motivate them to develop a constructive attitude towards the change programme.

Interaction between respondents in a group interview can generate information that might not be forthcoming in an individual interview. For example, if individuals from different units or levels in the organisation express different views, these differences might promote a useful discussion of why the conflicting perceptions exist and what problems or opportunities they might point to. There are, however, a number of potential problems associated with using the interview to collect information.

Interviews can be very time consuming and costly, although group interviews are less so than individual interviews. In addition, coding and interpreting responses can be a problem, especially when interviews are unstructured. Coding and interpretation can be simplified by adopting a more structured approach, asking all respondents the same set of predetermined questions and limiting the use of open-ended questions. However, the gains from adopting a more structured approach need to be balanced against the potential loss of rich data that can be gleaned from a more unstructured conversation, for example where the interviewer leads off with some general open-ended questions and then follows the respondent's chain of thought.

Bias is another problem that can arise from the way interviewers organise the order of topics to be covered and from the way they formulate questions. Especial care needs to be taken to avoid the use of leading questions that signal to the respondent that there is a desired response.

Questionnaires

Questionnaires are sometimes referred to as self-administered interviews. They are designed to obtain information by asking organisational members (and others) a predetermined set of questions about their perceptions, judgements and feelings. Using questionnaires to collect diagnostic information can be more cost-effective than using interviews because they can be administered simultaneously to large numbers of people without the need to employ expensive interviewers. Also, they can be designed around fixed response type questions that ease the burden of analysis.

However, they do have a number of disadvantages. They are non-empathic; when using questionnaires to collect information it can be difficult for change managers to build rapport and communicate empathy with respondents. This can have an adverse effect on respondents' motivation to give full and honest answers to the questions asked.

Questionnaires are also much less adaptive than interviews. Interviewers can modify their approach in response to the interviewee's reaction to questions and can explore unanticipated issues. The format of the questionnaire, on the other hand, has to be decided in advance. Problems can arise because respondents fail to understand or misinterpret the meaning of questions. Important questions may also be omitted; a problem that is difficult to resolve once the questionnaire has been administered.

Another problem is self-report bias. Questionnaires (like interviews) collect information from people who may, either deliberately or otherwise, bias their response. Responses to questions are based on the respondents' perceptions of what is going on. These perceptions may be based on incomplete or false information. Also, there is a tendency for respondents to present their own behaviour in the most positive light and to protect their own interests. The design of the questionnaire can also bias responses. For example, people may fall into a pattern of answering co-located questions in a similar manner or their attention may wander and they may take less care when answering questions towards the end of the questionnaire.

Projective methods

These might include, for example, drawings and collages as a useful way of collecting information about issues that people may find difficult to express in other ways. Fordyce and Weil (1983) suggest that by asking sub-groups to (a) prepare a collage around themes such as 'how do you feel about this team?' or 'what is happening to the organisation?' and (b) to present and explain it to the total group in a plenary session, organisational members can be helped to express and explore issues at a fairly deep and personal level. A similar procedure is to invite individuals to prepare and share drawings that show certain aspects of organisational life. For example, individuals might be asked to draw a circle for each member of their group, making the circles larger or smaller depending on the influence they have over the way the group works. They may also be asked to elaborate their drawing by locating the circles for different members of the group in terms of how closely they need to work together to get the job done. A further elaboration might be to ask them to join the circles with blue lines where the people they represent have a personally close relationship and with red lines if they are far apart in terms of communication, rapport and empathy.

These kinds of approaches to surfacing information can be good icebreakers and can provide an easy route to the discussion of sensitive issues that are rarely discussed openly. However, while they may be well-received by some groups, others may reject them as childish games.

Observations

Observing behaviour as it occurs is one approach to collecting information that avoids self-report bias. One of the key issues associated with this approach is deciding how the observation can be organised to focus attention on required behaviour and avoid being distracted or swamped by irrelevant information. When collecting information about behaviour in a group setting, for example, the degree of structure for observing and recording can vary from using broad categories such as leadership or communication to the use of detailed category sets such as the Interaction Process Analysis framework developed by Bales (1950).

An advantage of this approach to information collection is that the observer may recognise patterns of behaviour that those being observed may be unaware of and, therefore, are unable to report in interviews or in their responses to questionnaires. Another advantage is that observations relate to current behaviour and are less likely than self-reports to be contaminated by historical factors.

Observation is also an adaptive approach to collecting information. What is observed might cue the observer to explore connected aspects of current practice. Some of the disadvantages of this approach include problems associated with coding and interpretation, cost and possible observer bias.

Unobtrusive measures

In many organisational settings there are large amounts of information that are collected as a normal part of day-to-day operations. It can relate to various aspects of organisational functioning such as costs, down-time, wastage rates, absenteeism, labour turnover, delivery times, margins, complaints, number and type of meetings, and so on. This kind of information is referred to as unobtrusive because the fact that it is being collected for diagnosis is unlikely to prompt any specific response bias. It is also likely to be readily accepted by organisational members and, because of the nature of many of the records that contain this kind of information, it may be easy to quantify.

However, even when records are maintained, it may be difficult to access information in the required form. For example, information about individuals such as the outcome of performance appraisals, increments awarded, absenteeism and sickness rates may all be contained in each individual's personal record but may not be available in any aggregate form for all members of a particular department.

Sampling

Sometimes, for example when collecting information from members of a relatively small work group, it may be possible to include every member of the group in the survey. However, when a diagnostic exercise involves collecting information about a whole department, or the total organisation, it may be necessary to consider ways of sampling people, activities and records in a way that will provide sufficient information to provide a representative picture of what is going on.

Important issues that need to be considered when drawing a sample relate to sample size, relative to the total population, and composition. For example, how many people should be interviewed, events observed or records inspected, and which individuals, events or records should be included in the sample? The answer to the size or 'how many' question depends on the degree of confidence in the findings that is required and, if the information is to be subjected to statistical analysis, the type of analysis that is to be used. The answer to the composition or 'which' question depends on the complexity of the total population. If the total population is relatively homogeneous the selection of members to be included in the sample might be done on a random basis, using random number tables, or by selecting every nth member of the total population. If, however, the total population contains different sub-groups it might be important to ensure all of them are represented in the sample. This involves segregating the total population into a number of mutually exclusive sub-populations and drawing a sample from each. The composite sample that results from this process is referred to as a stratified sample.

ANALYSIS

Once information has been collected it needs to be analysed. For example, in response to a question such as 'How challenged do you feel in your present job?' only some of those surveyed might have offered a positive response. The change agent may want to know what proportion of the sample responded in this way compared to those who responded in the same way in other organisations in order to be able to assess whether lack of challenging work is a problem. It might also be useful to consider whether there is any relationship between those who do not feel challenged and the unit they work in or their level in the hierarchy.

Analytical procedures organise information in ways that can provide answers to diagnostic questions, and analytical techniques can be classified as qualitative or quantitative.

Qualitative techniques

These tend to be more concerned with meaning and underlying patterns than with scientific tests. Cummings and Worley (2001) refer to content analysis and force-field analysis as two qualitative analytical techniques that are frequently used in organisational diagnostic exercises.

Content analysis

This method attempts to summarise respondents' comments into meaningful categories. This involves identifying comments or answers that tend to recur most frequently and grouping them in ways that provide a set of mutually exclusive and exhaustive categories or themes. For example, in response to a question such as 'What do you like best about your work?' a number of responses might refer to working with friendly colleagues, considerate supervisors and having the opportunity to communicate with co-workers while doing the job. All of these comments might be regarded as referring to a common theme, the social aspects of the job. A different set of comments might refer to the degree of challenge offered by the work, the opportunity to be creative and the freedom to experiment with new methods. All of these comments might be regarded as referring to different aspects of the nature of the work itself. These two categories might then be used as a basis for analysing the content of all the information collected from respondents. When a category set is exhaustive it is possible to allocate every response to a category, and when it is mutually exclusive each item of information will fall into one particular category. After all responses have been classified, one way of determining the importance of the different categories is to identify those that have been referred to most often.

NUDist is a software tool that can be used for coding and analysing qualitative data, and provides a relatively easy method of comparing the responses from different respondents to particular questions.

Force-field analysis

Based on Lewin's (1951) three-step model of change discussed in Chapter 5, this method also involves categorising information. The distinctive feature of force-field analysis, however, is that it involves organising the categories into two broad types; those relating to forces or pressures for change, and those relating to forces or pressures supporting the (problematic) status quo and resisting change.

It was noted in Chapter 5 that Lewin viewed the level of behaviour in any situation as the result of a force-field comprising a balance of the forces pushing for change (for some different level of behaviour) and the forces resisting that change. Diagnosing situations in terms of driving and restraining forces can provide a useful basis for developing action plans to secure desired change. When the forces pushing in one direction exceed the forces pushing in the opposite direction the dynamic equilibrium changes (Figure 8.1). The level of behaviour can be changed towards a

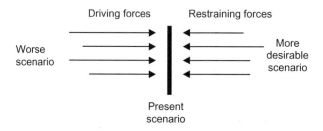

Figure 8.1 A force field

more desirable state by increasing the strength of forces for change in the desired direction (increasing the driving forces), or by diminishing the strength of restraining forces.

Quantitative techniques

Some of the very basic techniques most frequently used by change agents when analysing quantitative information are means, standard deviations, correlation coefficients and difference tests. The mean is a measure that indicates the average response or behaviour. For example, over the last year, the eight employees in department X might have averaged five days' sick leave. The standard deviation indicates the extent to which there is high or low variation around this mean; for example six members of the department may have had no sick leave whereas the other two may have had 20 days each. Correlation coefficients measure the strength of the relationship between variables; for example sick leave might be inversely related to job satisfaction. Difference tests indicate whether the scores achieved by one group (for example an average of five days' sick leave for members of department X) are significantly different from those achieved by members of other groups (different departments in the same organisation or some benchmark score or industry norm). More details on these and other techniques can be found in any standard text on statistics.

INTERPRETATION

Conceptual models provide a basis for interpreting diagnostic information and identifying what needs to be changed to achieve a more desirable state of affairs. The results of the 1993 staff survey in the BBC, which was designed around the Burke–Litwin causal model of organisational performance, indicated some priorities for change. The elements most in need of change were structure, leadership and factors affecting motivation, but there was also evidence that there was scope for improvement in many other areas. A very brief summary of the results of this survey is presented in Figure 8.2.

Political considerations

Collecting information is not an innocuous or benign activity. Nadler (1977) argues that the collection and distribution of information can change the nature of power relationships. Data collection can generate energy around the activities or behaviours that are being measured for a number of reasons. For example:

- It may result in information that an individual or group has previously withheld in order to secure some political advantage being widely distributed, thereby undermining their power and influence.
- It opens up the possibility of comparing the current performance of an individual or group with their own past performance, with the performance of others or with some benchmark. These possibilities might be perceived as threatening, especially where there is a link between performance and rewards.

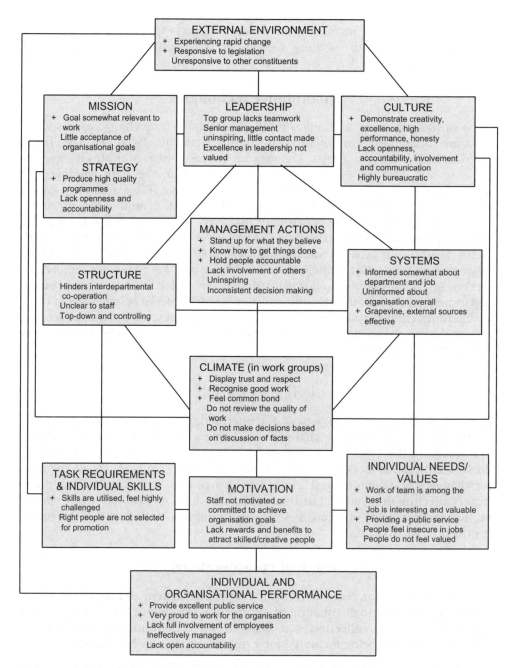

Figure 8.2   Results of the 1993 BBC staff survey

The energy generated by data collection can be directed towards assisting or undermining the change agent's attempt to diagnose the need for change. How the energy will be directed will be influenced by the perceptions people have about the possible future uses that may be made of the data. If, for example, employees expect the information collected in a diagnostic survey to be used in an open, non-threatening and helpful manner they may be motivated to provide accurate information. If, on the other hand, they expect it to be used in a punitive manner they may attempt to withhold or distort data. This point is illustrated in a case reported by Porter, Lawler and Hackman (1975). They refer to a group of employees who worked together to assemble complicated large steel frameworks. Their method of working varied depending on whether or not they were being observed by anyone who might influence the rate they were paid for the job. The group had discovered that by tightening certain bolts first, the frame would be slightly sprung and all the other bolts would bind and be very difficult to tighten. When they used this method they gave the impression that they were working hard all of the time. When they were not being observed they followed a different sequence of tightening bolts and the work was much easier and the job could be completed in less time.

Change managers need to be alert to the possibility that they will encounter resistance even at this very early stage in the change process.

Exercise 8.1   Evaluating your use of diagnostic information

Think about a recent occasion when you (or somebody working close to you) attempted to introduce and manage a change in your part of the organisation.

1. Reflect on the extent to which this change initiative was based on an accurate diagnosis of the need for change.
2. Consider to what extent this was related to:

   - The appropriateness of the (implicit or explicit) diagnostic model used
   - The nature of the information collected
   - The way in which it was interpreted.

3. Reflect on what steps *you* might take to help improve the quality of the way the need for change is diagnosed in your unit or department.

SUMMARY

This chapter has examined the process of gathering and interpreting information for the purpose of diagnosis. Attention has been focused on five main steps:

1. Selection of an appropriate conceptual model for diagnosis;
2. Clarification of information requirements;
3. Information-gathering;
4. Analysis;
5. Interpretation.

Attention has also been drawn to the political issues associated with data collection that can frustrate attempts to gain an accurate impression of organisational functioning.

References

Bales, R.F. (1950) *Interaction Process Analysis: A Method for the Study of Small Groups*, Cambridge, Mass.: Addison-Wesley.

Cummings, T.G. and Worley, C.G. (2001) *Organisational Development and Change*, 7th edn, Cincinnati, Ohio: South Western.

Fordyce, J.K. and Weil, R. (1983) 'Methods for finding out what is going on', in W. French, C.H. Bell and R. Zawacki (eds), *Organisation Development: Theory, Practice and Research*, Plano, Texas: Business publication, pp.124–32

Lewin, K. (1951) *Field Theory in Social Science*, New York: Harper & Row.

Nadler, D. (1977) *Feedback and Organization Development: Using Data-based Methods*, Reading, Mass.: Addison-Wesley.

Porter, L.W., Lawler, E. E. and Hackman, J. R. (1975) *Behavior in Organizations*, New York: McGraw-Hill.

Part III

Managing the people issues

It was noted in Chapter 5 that there are a number of issues that have to be attended to throughout the change process. These are considered in the next five chapters.

Chapter 9   Power, leadership and stakeholder management

This chapter explores the politics of organisational change and the need to enlist the support of key stakeholders. While reading the chapter you will be invited to think about a recent change in your organisation and with the advantage of hindsight:

- identify the stakeholders involved in the change;
- classify them according to the power they had to influence the change and their stake in the outcome;
- assess the extent to which the change manager was aware of these stakeholders and took proper account of them when managing the change.

This chapter also examines the role of leadership in the management of change. You will be invited to:

- identify examples of managers in your organisation who have or have not been successful in their attempts to manage change;
- use Kotter's model of transformational leadership to identify strengths and weaknesses in their leadership style.

Chapter 10   Communicating

This chapter considers the role of communication in the management of change. Often the focus is exclusively on the 'what, when, who and how' of communicating from the perspective of the change manager communicating to others. In this unit attention is also given to issues associated with change managers perceiving, interpreting and using information communicated to them by others. After studying this unit you will be invited to consider how the quality of communication has helped or hindered change in your organisation.

Chapter 11   Training and development

Organisational change is typically associated with some degree of individual change, which is often the outcome of an informal and natural process of learning and development. However, there may be occasions when those responsible for managing an organisational change decide that some form of deliberate training intervention is required in order to help individuals develop new knowledge, skills, attitudes and behaviours. Such interventions can be highly structured and very focused on the achievement of closely specified outcomes, or they can be designed to help organisational members learn how to learn and encourage them to actively involve themselves in a self directed process of professional development.

This chapter considers the main elements of an effective training strategy and how training can contribute to the successful implementation of a change plan. After reading this chapter you will be invited to critically assess the way training has been used in your organisation to help achieve organisational change.

Chapter 12   Motivating others to change

This chapter considers how the general level of commitment in an organisation can affect the level of support for change and identifies some of the most common sources of resistance to change. The utility of expectancy theory for assessing and managing resistance to change is explored. The second half of the chapter involves an exercise designed to help you use expectancy theory to motivate others to change.

Chapter 13   Managing personal transitions

This chapter addresses the way organisational members experience change. It examines the response to change (irrespective of whether the change is viewed as an opportunity or a threat) as a progression through a number of stages of psychological reaction. It also considers how an understanding of the way individuals react to change can help managers plan and implement organisational change in ways that will maximise benefit and minimise cost for both the organisation and those affected by the change.

Before reading this chapter you will be invited to reflect on how you reacted to a change that was lasting in its effects, took place over a relatively short period of time and affected a number of key assumptions you made about how you related with the world around you. The information generated by this exercise will be used to validate a generic stage model of transition.

These five 'people issues' are considered at this point for convenience. While they must be attended to when developing, implementing and managing a change programme (the focus of parts IV, V and VI) they are also relevant at the very early stages of the change process. For example, at the start of the process, only some of the constituencies that have a stake in the future of the organisation may have been involved in (a) recognising the need for change, and (b) undertaking a preliminary diagnosis.

At some point, decisions will have to be made about whether and when to involve others in the diagnostic and visioning process. Related decisions will include which others to involve and how to involve them. Associated with this issue of stakeholder management is the development of a communications strategy. It may not be possible to keep the likelihood of change secret. Consequently, even in the early stages of the process (well before the details of an implementation strategy have been planned), it may be necessary to decide who is to be told what and when they should be told.

Those involved in managing the early stages of the change process may also require some training in diagnostic methods or they may need to participate in a team-building exercise to ensure that they can work effectively as a change management group. It is also possible that some of those who become involved in the early stages of the process may be hostile to the prospect of change and attention may need to be given to how they can be motivated to make a constructive contribution. Even when people support the change they may experience problems letting go of the status quo and they might need some help to cope with the process of transition.

9

Power, leadership and stakeholder management

When thinking about managing change, some people assume that organisations are well-integrated entities within which everybody works harmoniously together in order to achieve a set of shared goals. They appear to believe that decisions are made logically and rationally, that people share similar views of the world around them and that they act to promote the interests of the organisation as a whole. The reality is often very different.

ORGANISATIONS AS POLITICAL ARENAS

In Chapter 2, organisations were conceptualised as a collection of internal (and external) constituencies, each pursuing their own objectives. This view presents organisations as political arenas within which individuals and groups attempt to influence each other in the pursuit of self-interest. Those who adopt this political perspective argue that when there is a conflict of interests it is the power and influence of the individuals and groups involved that determines the outcome of the decision process, not logic and rational argument. This perspective submits that those responsible for managing change cannot afford to ignore issues of power and influence.

McCall (1979) asserts that the constituencies that are most powerful are those that:

- are in a position to deal with important problems facing the organisation;
- have control over significant resources valued by others;
- are lucky or skilled enough to bring problems and resources together at the same time;
- are centrally connected in the work flow of the organisation;
- are not easily replaced; and
- have successfully used power in the past.

Those with power may perceive a proposed change as a threat to their power base. They may view it, for example, as moving others into better positions to deal with the most pressing problems facing the organisation, or they may fear that it will reduce their ability to control significant resources. On the other hand, those who lack power, or who would welcome more power, may perceive the change as an opportunity and work to support it.

These different perspectives encourage political behaviour, actions on behalf of different constituents or stakeholders designed to maximise their power and their ability to secure preferred outcomes. Freeman (1984) defines a stakeholder as any group or individual who can affect or is affected by the achievement of the organisation's objectives. Change managers need to be alert to possible ways in which stakeholders may respond to a proposed change and be aware of who is likely to be predisposed to either support or sabotage the initiative. In order to ensure the successful introduction of change it is essential to secure the assistance of key stakeholders and to build a critical mass of support.

STAKEHOLDER MANAGEMENT: IDENTIFYING AND INFLUENCING INDIVIDUALS AND GROUPS WHO MIGHT SUPPORT OR RESIST THE CHANGE

The first step in stakeholder management involves identifying key stakeholders and assessing their ability to influence the outcome of the change initiative. Change managers need to be aware of the individuals or groups who may be affected by (have a stake in) the change; their commitment to the change; and their ability to influence the outcome.

Who is affected by (has a stake in) the change?

Because organisations are open systems, changes to any one part of an organisation can affect many individuals and groups. Some of those affected may not be employees of the organisation. Clarkson (1995) elaborates Freeman's earlier definition and, in addition to employees, includes shareholders, investors, customers and suppliers, plus the Government and communities that provide infrastructure and markets, whose laws must be obeyed, and to whom taxes and other obligations may be due. Members of the wider community who may be affected by such issues as pollution, job opportunities and house prices may also need to be considered.

Jawahar and McLaughlin (2001) also note that, over time, organisations change and as a result the identity of critical stakeholders may change because of their potential to satisfy critical organisational needs.

What is their commitment to and ability to influence the outcome of the change?

Stakeholders can have a positive, neutral or negative interest in the change. In addition, as noted earlier, stakeholders differ in terms of their power. While change managers may pay careful attention to some powerful stakeholders, they may completely overlook others. Recent examples illustrate this point. Local residents were offended (to the point of rioting) by a proposal to rename bingo halls located in their largely Islamic neighbourhoods 'Mecca Bingo'. Customers of the Bank of Scotland (including the West Lothian Council with a £250 million account) threatened to close their accounts in protest at the Bank's proposed joint business venture with US evangelist Pat Robertson after he proclaimed that Scotland was a 'dark land' and a stronghold of homosexuality.

Shaw and Maletz (1995) classify stakeholders according to both their power to influence outcomes and their commitment to the change. They differentiate between 'blockers' (stakeholders who proactively intervene to prevent the change from succeeding) and 'sponsors' (stakeholders who proactively work to ensure that the change effort succeeds).

An alternative way of classifying stakeholders combines how much the stakeholder is affected by the change (their stake in the outcome) and their power to influence the outcome. A simple 2×2 matrix, based on ideas developed by Piercy (1989) and Grundy (1998), provides a useful typology that is presented in Figure 9.1. Stakeholders who are directly affected by the change (have a high stake in the outcome) can be differentiated in terms of their power to influence the outcome. Sponsors and blockers are more powerful than the helpless victims or beneficiaries. However, those who may be helpless today may be in a much more powerful position sometime in the future, and this possibility may influence how the change managers decide to respond to their concerns.

Stakeholders who are not *directly* affected by the change can also be differentiated in terms of their power to influence the outcome. Meddlers, for example, could include journalists who are motivated to achieve their own outcome of selling more newspapers. They may seek to do this by leaking the news of redundancies or by presenting a story about a change in a way that will be controversial. Bystanders are those who are aware of the change but are not affected by it and do not have the power to influence the outcome.

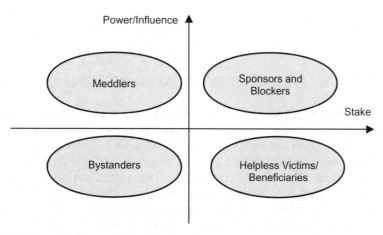

Figure 9.1 Classification of key stakeholders

Once stakeholders have been identified, change managers need to determine how they should relate to them (Chapter 14 considers some of the issues that might need to be considered). Where there is a need to win the support of powerful stakeholders the change managers might focus on providing additional information, building relationships and addressing stakeholder concerns. However, there may be circumstances where 'blockers' or meddlers cannot be influenced and where it might be necessary to look for ways of reducing their power, isolating them or even removing them from the situation.

Exercise 9.1   Stakeholder analysis

Think about a recent change in your organisation. With the advantage of hindsight:

- Identify the stakeholders involved in the change.
- Classify them (according to the power they had to influence the change and their stake in the outcome) as 'Sponsors and Blockers', 'Helpless Victims or Beneficiaries', 'Bystanders' or 'Meddlers'.
- Assess the extent to which the change managers were aware of these stakeholders and took proper account of them when managing the change.

THE ROLE OF LEADERSHIP IN THE MANAGEMENT OF CHANGE

Nadler and Shaw (1995) and Tichy and Devanna (1986) argue that what has worked in the past can become the cause of failure in the present (see Chapter 6 and the discussion of the trap of success). Leaders need to be able to recognise when change is required and need to be aware how they can act to facilitate the change process. Tichy and Devanna also draw attention to a theme that was developed, later, by Kotter (1990) – the struggle between leadership and management. They argue that management is concerned with the maintenance of the existing organisation. Leadership, on the other hand, is more concerned with change. This creates a tension between 'doing things right' and 'doing the right things'.

DIFFERENCES BETWEEN LEADERSHIP AND MANAGEMENT

Kotter (1990) argues that both managers and leaders have to attend to three functions: deciding what needs to be done, developing the capacity to do it, and ensuring that it is done. However, there is a marked difference in the way that managers and leaders attend to these functions.

Deciding what needs to be done

- *Managers* decide what needs to be done through a process of goal setting, establishing detailed steps for achieving these goals and identifying and allocating the resources necessary for their achievement (through planning and budgeting).
- *Leaders*, on the other hand, focus on setting a direction and developing the strategies necessary to move in that direction (creating a vision).

In terms of the ideas discussed in Chapter 4, management is more focused on developing plans to do things better, whereas leadership involves more double-loop thinking about what is the right thing to do. It involves attending to a wide range of cues that might signal emerging opportunities or problems, and setting a direction that will maximise future benefit. However, visions need to serve the interests of key stakeholders. Kotter argues that visions that ignore the legitimate needs and rights of some stakeholders, favouring certain stakeholders over others, may never be achieved.

Developing the capacity to do it

- *Managers* develop the capacity to accomplish their agenda by organising and staffing.
- *Leaders* focus on aligning people, communicating the new direction and creating coalitions committed to getting there. Successful leaders empower others to make the vision happen.

Kotter argues that a central feature of modern organisations is interdependence, where no one has complete autonomy, and where most members of the organisation are tied to many others by their work, technology, management systems and hierarchy. He argues that these linkages present a special challenge when organisations attempt to change. 'Unless many individuals line up and move together in the same direction, people will tend to fall all over one another'.

Transformational leaders have the ability to identify those who might be able to support or sabotage an initiative, network with them and communicate in a credible way what needs to be done. Aligning people in this way empowers them, even people at lower levels of the organisation. When there is a clear (and shared) sense of direction, committed stakeholders, including subordinates, are more likely to feel able to take action without encountering undue conflict with others or being reprimanded by superiors.

Ensuring that it is done

- *Managers* ensure people accomplish plans by controlling and problem-solving.
- *Leaders* are more concerned with motivating and inspiring. Kotter believes that inspiring others and generating highly energised behaviour can help them overcome the inevitable barriers to change that they will encounter as the initiative unfolds. He identifies four ways in which leaders can do this.

  - ☐ Articulating the vision in ways that are in accord with the values of the people they are addressing.
  - ☐ Involving people in deciding how to achieve the vision, thereby giving them some sense of control.
  - ☐ Supporting others' efforts to realise the vision by providing coaching, feedback and role modelling.
  - ☐ Recognising and rewarding success.

Managerial work, in times of change, is increasingly a leadership task. Managers are the people who, typically, are in the best position to provide the leadership required to ensure that a change will be successful. However, if they are to provide this leadership they need to recognise that their role involves a dual responsibility, for management (to keep the system operating effectively) and for leadership (to revitalise and renew the system to ensure that it will remain effective over the longer term).

The thrust of the argument developed in Chapter 1 is that not only is the pace of change increasing, but that there is also a shift in emphasis away from incremental towards discontinuous or transformational change. The implication of this is that leadership and the provision of a sense of direction is becoming a more important part of managerial work.

In the first instance the initiator of change might be an individual or a small group of individuals. These people might be viewed as the ones who are leading the change, but Kotter (1999) argues that this leadership has to be multiplied and shared if the change is to be successful. Managers, throughout the system, have to accept that they have a leadership role to play. They have to contribute to creating a vision, aligning relationships and inspiring others.

A CHECKLIST FOR LEADING CHANGE

In a much cited paper, Kotter (1995) articulates eight steps in the change process and highlights, in terms of leadership, what needs to be done to ensure success at each stage.

1 *Establishing a sense of urgency.* Change managers often underestimate how hard it can be to drive people out of their comfort zones. Unfreezing involves alerting organisational members to the need for change and motivating them to let go of the status quo. Many factors can make this difficult to attain. These include a history of past success and the lack of an immediate crisis. After British Gas was privatised many senior managers refused to recognise that there was any real

threat to the organisation's monopoly position. Those attempting to lead change in the business had to work very hard to convince colleagues that they should begin to prepare for major discontinuities. Chapter 6 considers a range of issues that require the leader's attention at the beginning of a change.

2 *Forming a powerful coalition.* Kotter argues that unless those who recognise the need for change can put together a strong enough team to direct the process, the change initiative is unlikely to get off the ground. He suggests that while this 'guiding coalition' might not include all the senior managers it is much more likely to succeed if, in terms of titles, information, experience, reputations and contacts, it is seen to signal a real commitment to change.

3 *Creating a vision.* The guiding coalition needs to develop a shared vision that can be easily communicated to others affected by the change. In his book *Leading Change*, Kotter (1996) summarises six criteria for an effective vision:

- *Imaginable*: conveys a picture of what the future will look like.
- *Desirable*: appeals to the long-term interests of employees, customers, stockholders, and others who have a stake in the enterprise.
- *Feasible*: comprises realistic, attainable goals.
- *Focused*: is clear enough to provide guidance in decision-making.
- *Flexible*: is general enough to allow individual initiatives and alternative responses in the light of changing conditions.
- *Communicable*: is easy to communicate; can be successfully explained within five minutes.

Sometimes interventions such as visioning workshops (see Chapter 16) can be helpful in developing a vision that satisfies these criteria.

4 *Communicating the vision.* Communication is considered in more detail in Chapter 10. However, in terms of communicating the vision, people – all those affected by the change – need to hear the message repeatedly. Kotter asserts that in many change programmes the vision is under-communicated by a factor of ten! He also emphasises that communicating a vision involves more than the spoken and written word. Organisational members (and other stakeholders) watch those responsible for managing the change for indications of their commitment. It is important that they 'walk the talk' and communicate the vision by example.

5 *Empowering others to act on the vision.* Transformational leadership involves identifying and removing obstacles that can stop people acting to implement the vision. Some of these obstacles might include tangible aspects of the organisation such as reward systems that penalise valued behaviour, restrictive rules and regulations or inflexible organisational structures. Others may be less tangible and involve beliefs and assumptions that stifle initiative. Empowering others to act includes creating a climate in which people believe in themselves and are confident that they have the support of others to make things happen. The importance of beliefs about change agency are considered in Chapter 2.

6 *Planning for and creating short-term wins.* Kotter argues that achieving major change can take time. The danger with this is that the change effort can slow down as people lose the initial sense of urgency and their attention drifts elsewhere, possibly to pressing operational matters. One way of minimising this

risk is for those leading the change to seek out short term wins and plan for visible (interim) performance improvements that can be celebrated along the way.

7   *Consolidating improvements and producing still more change.* Building on the previous point, while Kotter advocates celebrating early wins, he cautions against declaring victory too soon because this can kill momentum. Leaders should capitalise on early wins to motivate others to introduce further changes to systems and structures that are consistent (aligned) with the transformation vision.

8   *Institutionalising new approaches.* Leaders need to ensure that changes are consolidated. They can help achieve this by showing others how the changes have produced new approaches, behaviours and attitudes that have improved performance. Kotter argues that leaders should take every opportunity to demonstrate benefit and reinforce these changes until they become an accepted part of the culture and the 'way things are done around here'.

Many of these points will be referred to again in other chapters of this book.

Exercise 9.2

Identify two change managers who have been key figures in attempting to introduce and manage change in your organisation. One should be a person who you judge to have been very successful at managing change. The other should be one who you judge to have been much less successful.

Assess their approach to managing change using Kotter's checklist for leading change. Consider whether there is any evidence to suggest that the most successful change managers are those who ensure that Kotter's eight points are attended to.

SUMMARY

This chapter has explored the politics of organisational change and pointed to the importance of enlisting support from key stakeholders. The role of leadership in change management has been summarised as creating a vision, aligning relationships around the vision and inspiring others to achieve the vision. We closed with an eight-point checklist of what leaders can do to promote change.

References

Clarkson, M.B.E. (1995) 'A Stakeholder Framework for Analysing and Evaluating Corporate Social Performance', *Academy of Management Review*, 20, pp. 92–117.

Freeman, R.E. (1984) *Strategic Management: A Stakeholders Approach*, Boston: HarperCollins.

Grundy, T. (1998) 'Strategy Implementation and Project Management, *International Journal of Project Management*, 16, 1, pp. 48–50.

Jawahar, I.M. and McLaughlin, G.L. (2001) 'Towards a Descriptive Theory: An Organizational Life Cycle Approach', *Academy of Management Review*, 26(3), pp. 397–414.

Kotter, J.P. (1990) 'What Leaders Really Do', *Harvard Business Review*, May-June, reproduced in J.P. Kotter (1999) *On What Leaders Really Do, op. cit.*

Kotter, J.P. (1995) 'Leading Change: Why Transformation Efforts Fail', *Harvard Business Review*, March-April.

Kotter, J.P. (1996) *Leading Change*, Boston, Mass.: Harvard Business School Press.

Kotter, J.P. (1999) *On What Leaders Really Do*, Boston, Mass.: A Harvard Business Review Book.

McCall, M.W. (1979) 'Power, Influence and Authority', in S. Kerr (ed.), *Organizational Behaviour*, Columbus, Ohio: Grid Publishing, pp. 185–206.

Nadler, D.A. and Shaw, R.B. (1995) 'Change Leadership: A Core Competency for the Twenty-First Century', in D.A. Nadler, R.B. Shaw and A.E. Walton (eds), *Discontinuous Change: Leading Organizational Transformation*, San Francisco: Jossey-Bass, pp. 3–14.

Piercy, N. (1989) 'Diagnosing and Solving Implementation Problems in Strategic Planning, *Journal of General Management*, 15(1).

Shaw, B.R. and Maletz, M.C. (1995) 'Business Processes: Embracing the Logic and Limits of Reengineering', in D.A. Nadler, R.B. Shaw and A.E. Walton (eds), *Discontinuous Change: Leading Organizational Transformation*, San Francisco: Jossey-Bass, pp. 169–89.

Tichy, N.M. and Devanna, M.A. (1986) *The Transformational Leader*, Chichester: Wiley.

10

Communicating

The quality of communications can have an important impact on the success or otherwise of a change programme. It was noted in Chapter 3 that communication is a key process that can influence how effectively an organisation adjusts to a change. It was also noted in Chapter 4 how the nature of collective learning is affected by the structures and processes that facilitate or inhibit individuals and groups sharing the meanings they construct for themselves as they encounter new experiences and ideas. And in the previous chapter it was noted that communicating the vision has a vital role to play in leading change. This chapter briefly considers the features of communication networks that relate to the management of change, the effect of interpersonal relations on the quality of communication and the questions relating to communications that need to be considered when deciding *how* to manage the change process.

FEATURES OF COMMUNICATION NETWORKS

Four features of communication networks will be considered: directionality, role, content and channel.

- *Directionality*. The management of change is often a top-down process. It involves those responsible for managing change informing others lower down the organisation about the need for change, what is going to happen and what is required of them. It also involves a stream of upward communication that provides them with much of the information they require in order to clarify the need for change, and develop and implement a change programme.

O'Reilly and Pondy (1979) list some of the consequences of directionality on the content of messages. Senders transmitting messages up the organisation hierarchy send information that they perceive to be relevant *and* which reflects favourably on their (or their unit's) performance. Where possible, they screen out information that reflects unfavourably on them. Consequently people further up the organisation may not receive all the information that may be relevant to the issues they have to manage.

Senders transmitting messages downwards have a tendency to screen out any information that they perceive to be not directly relevant to the subordinates' task. There is also a tendency for them to elaborate this task-related information to ensure that it is properly understood. This 'need to know' attitude can lead to problems when change managers fail to pass on information that might have helped others understand the need for change or helped them feel more involved in the change process.

● *Role.* The nature of what is communicated can be affected by the roles that organisational members occupy. The nature of an *inter-role relationship* is important; a person might communicate certain things to a colleague that s/he would not communicate to an external consultant, an auditor, a member of another department, their boss, a subordinate or a customer. This issue will be discussed in more detail when the effect of trust and power on the quality of interpersonal relationships is considered.

The nature of a role can be an important determinant of whether the role occupant will be an *isolate* or a *participant* in the organisation's affairs. Some roles are potentially more isolated than others: a finance officer may be better networked within the organisation than a salesperson who is responsible for a remote territory; an employee on an assembly line may have relatively few opportunities to communicate with others and therefore may be deprived of opportunities to contribute to collective learning. This may be much less of a problem for somebody located in an open-plan office who is constantly interacting with colleagues. Some of the interventions that will be considered in Chapter 16 are designed to create opportunities for dialogue, sharing and the provision of feedback that are so important in situations characterised by uncertainty and change. When planning to communicate with people about a proposed change it is important to take account of those who occupy isolated roles. People who feel that they have been neglected or excluded are more likely to be alienated than those who feel that they are in a position to participate in the change.

Some members of the organisation occupy *boundary-spanning roles* that enable them to transfer information from one constituency to another. For example, people in sales, customer support and product development occupy roles that link the organisation with the wider environment. Within the organisation there are also roles that straddle the boundaries between internal constituencies; the occupants of these kinds of roles may have access to important information that could be used to identify emerging problems or opportunities. MacDonald (1995) argues that critical information is often imported into organisations through informal and individual contacts and that the persons who are the boundary-spanners who acquire this information may not be the people who can use it as a basis for managing change. They may have to pass their information on to others who are in a better position to respond. However, these 'others' may not recognise the importance of the information or may receive a message that is different to that which the originator of the message intended to convey.

Distortion can occur because information is passed on to others by *gatekeepers*. Gatekeepers are those who are in a position to interpret and screen information before transmitting it to others. Almost everybody in the organisation is to some extent a gatekeeper, but some roles offer their occupants considerable power to control the content and timing of the information that is passed on to decision-makers. Change managers need to be aware of who controls the flows of information that are important to them. One way of reducing dependence on some gatekeepers is to build an element of redundancy into the communication network in order to provide the possibility of obtaining information from more than one source.

- *Content.* MacDonald (1995) draws attention to the importance of attending to external information and integrating this with the information that is routinely available to organisational members if the organisation is to learn and change. A common problem, however, is that this external information is often unfamiliar and responding to it frequently leads to disruption and uncertainty. Consequently, organisational members tend to prefer the more familiar internal information that is easier to integrate into the prevailing mental models and paradigms that are used for making sense of the situation that confronts them.

  Other important aspects of content are whether it is perceived as good news or bad news, how senders expect it to be received and the implications this may have for their well-being. Change managers need to be alert to these content issues and especially to the need to give careful consideration to the potential relevance of information that at first sight may appear to be of little consequence.

- *Channel.* Information and meaning can be communicated in many different ways: written communication via hard copy, electronic communication via email, video-conferencing, telephone, face-to-face communication on a one-to-one, one-to-group or group-to-group basis, and so on. O'Reilly and Pondy (1979) suggest that written communication may be effective when the sender and receiver have different vocabularies or problem orientations, and that oral communication may be most effective when there is a need to exchange views, seek feedback and provide an immediate opportunity for clarification. They note, however, that while organisation members may prefer certain media and while certain forms of communication may have clear advantages in specific circumstances, external factors may limit the freedom to select a particular mode of communication. For example, distance may prohibit face-to-face interaction, budget constraints may demand the use of written communication rather than video conferencing, and time constraints may rule out the use of lengthy meetings.

INTERPERSONAL EFFECTS ON THE QUALITY OF COMMUNICATION

In the process of managing change, change managers/agents will often seek information from others and others will attempt to seek information from them.

Factors such as *trust* and *influence* can have an important effect on the quality of the information that is exchanged. O'Reilly and Pondy refer to studies that show that lack of trust is associated with a tendency for senders to withhold unfavourable but relevant information while passing on favourable but irrelevant information. There is also evidence that senders are guarded in what they are prepared to share with those others who are able to influence what happens to them.

Obtaining full and frank answers from others is not an easy task. Interpersonal interactions are complex social encounters in which the behaviour of each party is influenced by the other. An often-used model of information gathering presents the process solely in terms of an information seeker (change manager) getting information from respondents (organisational members). This model is an oversimplification because it fails to take full account of the interactive nature of the encounter (see Figure 10.1).

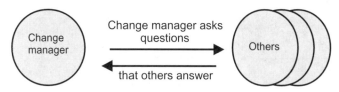

Figure 10.1 An oversimplified model of the interview

Organisational members are aware that the change managers/agents are observing what they say and do and that they may be making judgements about them and their future role. Consequently they may not openly and honestly answer all the questions they are asked. They may attempt to manage the way they respond so as to maximise their personal benefit from the interaction rather than help the change managers achieve their purpose. (Note, this example could just as easily be presented in terms of organisational members 'interviewing' a change manager.)

Goffman (1959), Mangham (1978) and others have used drama as a metaphor for describing and explaining a wide range of interactions, and this metaphor can usefully be applied to this kind of social encounter. Goffman talks about putting on a performance for an audience and argues that people's portrayal of action will be determined by their assessment of the audience. He also notes that actors use mirrors so that they can practise and become an object to themselves, backstage, before going 'on-stage' and becoming an object to others. Similarly, organisational members may anticipate the nature of their audience, the change managers, and rehearse the way they want to present themselves.

A better representation of the interaction between change managers and organisational members is illustrated in Figure 10.2. The change managers are likely to structure the situation and behave in ways that they feel will best project their definition of the purpose of the encounter and the role they want to assume in the interaction. This behaviour not only says a lot about how the change managers wish to be seen, but also about who they take the other organisational members to be and the role they are expected to play. The change managers (A) attempt to influence the others' interpretation of the situation and to focus their attention on those issues which they (the change managers) regard as important, and much of what takes place at this stage involves cognitive scene-setting.

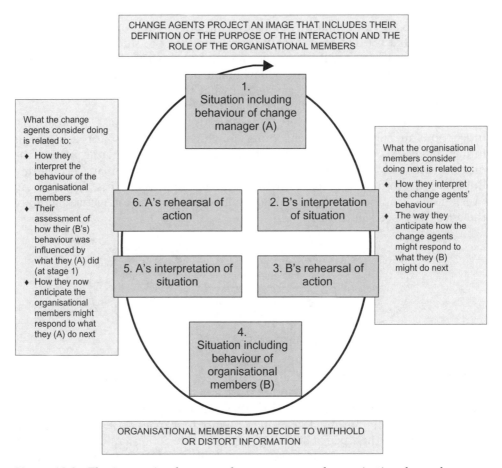

Figure 10.2 The interaction between change agents and organisational members

At stage 2, in Figure 10.2, the organisational members (B) seek to understand what it is that the change managers (A) are projecting and what implications this has for them. Do the change managers, for example, appear to see the encounter as an information-gathering exercise designed to provide them with the information they need to determine what has to be changed? Alternatively, do they see it as the first step towards involving organisational members in the management of the change process?

Organisational members might detect a difference between the performance the change managers (A) consciously and deliberately give, and what Mangham (1978) refers to as the information they 'give off'. The change managers (A) may attempt to perform in a way that gives the impression to others (B) that they are committed to a shared approach to the management of change; however, they may actually 'give off' signals, verbal and non-verbal, that contradict this intended impression. Thus, as the interaction progresses through stages 3 and 4 the organisational members (B) may decide to cooperate and give the change managers (A) the information they are seeking. Alternatively, they may decide not to be completely open and to distort or withhold information until they are more confident about the change managers' intentions.

Reference has already been made to rehearsal of action. At stage 3, organisational members have to decide, on the basis of their interpretation of the situation, how to respond to the change managers. Farr (1984) discussing the work of Mead, notes that Man not only acts but re-acts to his own actions. He reacts to his own behaviour on the basis of the actual or *anticipated* reaction of others. He can anticipate their reactions through simulation or rehearsal. He can try out, in his own mind, a few pieces of behaviour and test them for fit. Mangham even suggests that he can simulate several stages into alternative futures for an interaction, a form of mental chess in which various moves and their consequences are tested.

Once the organisational members (B) have decided what to do and have responded to the change managers' (A) initial behaviour, the situation changes. Both A and B, at stage 4 on the circle, are faced with a situation that includes the most recent behaviour of B. If the change managers failed to make their purpose explicit (at stage 1), organisational members may misinterpret their behaviour and act in ways that the change managers either did not anticipate or feel is inappropriate to the situation.

The change managers have to assess this situation (stage 5) and attempt to understand the meaning of the organisational members' behaviour. Their interpretation of the organisational members' response offers a basis for assessing the relevance and validity of any information communicated by them. Good interviewers/information gatherers have the ability to empathise with the other party; they can assume the other's role in the interaction, putting themselves in the other's shoes and replaying in their mind the situation the respondents/ organisational members' face. And they can interpret the other's behaviour, including their answers to questions, from this perspective.

On the basis of their interpretation of the situation, including the organisational members' (B) behaviour, the change managers (A) can rehearse the next move (stage 6) before deciding what to do and/or say. This then forms part of the unfolding scene to which B will have to respond, and so the process continues.

The point of this example is that the nature of the encounter will influence how both parties will interpret what they see and hear. It will also influence the quantity and quality of the information that each is prepared to offer. Change managers/ agents need to give careful thought to how others will interpret their actions. Their interpretation will be an important determinant of what others are prepared to communicate to change managers and how they will behave in response to information passed to them by the change managers.

QUESTIONS TO BE CONSIDERED REGARDING COMMUNICATION ISSUES

Often the discussion of communication issues associated with the management of change tends to focus exclusively on the 'what, when, who and how' of communication from the perspective of the change agent/manager communicating to others. The discussion in this section has also emphasised issues associated with change managers/agents perceiving, interpreting and using information provided by others.

There are no magic formulae about the 'what, when, who and how' of communication that can provide ready answers for all situations. In some circumstances change agents may advocate a policy of complete openness about all issues to everybody as soon as possible. In other circumstances information might be highly restricted because it is deemed to be commercially sensitive, or it might be decided that information should not be widely shared until after certain high-level decisions have been made. Counter arguments might focus on the difficulty of keeping the need for change secret and the importance of not losing control of communications to the informal grapevine.

What is important is that adequate attention is given to ensuring that all relevant information is sought and is attended to by change managers, and that they pay careful attention to the information that they need to communicate to others.

Exercise 10.1   Assessing the quality of communications

Think about a recent attempt to introduce and manage change in your organisation or a particular part of the organisation that you are familiar with, and reflect on how the quality of communication helped or hindered the change process.

● Did the change manager(s) communicate effectively to all those involved in or affected by the change?
● If not, to what extent was this related to 'network factors' such as directionality, role, familiarity of content, or channel, or to interpersonal factors that interfered with the quality of communication?

What could the change manager(s) have done differently that might have improved the quality of communications?

References

Farr, R. (1984) 'Interviewing: The Social Psychology of the Inter-View', in Cary L. Cooper and Peter Makin (eds), *Psychology for Managers*, London: British Psychological Society.

Goffman, E. (1959) *The Presentation of Self in Everyday Life*, New York: Doubleday.

Mangham, I.L. (1978) *Interactions and Interventions in Organizations*, Chichester: Wiley.

MacDonald, S. (1995) 'Learning to Change: An Information Perspective on Learning in the Organisation', *Organizational Science*, 6(5), pp. 557–68.

O'Reilly, C.A. and Pondy, L.R. (1979) 'Organisational Communication', in S. Kerr (ed.) *Organisational Behavior*, Columbus, Ohio: Grid publications, pp.119–49.

11

Training and development

Organisational change is typically associated with some degree of individual change, and this individual change is often the outcome of an informal and natural process of learning and development. However, there may be occasions when those responsible for managing an organisational change decide that some form of deliberate training intervention is required in order to help individuals develop new knowledge, skills, attitudes and behaviours. Such interventions can be highly structured and very focused on the achievement of closely specified outcomes, or they can be designed to help organisational members learn how to learn and encourage them to actively involve themselves in a self-directed process of professional development.

Training and development is considered here rather than in Part V because it is one of the people issues identified in Chapter 5 that require constant attention at every stage of the change process.

Training interventions tend to be targeted at two main types of organisational member. On the one hand there are those who are required to perform new roles associated with managing the change. They may require training, for example, in order to lead a task force charged with diagnosing organisational problems and identifying what needs to be changed. On the other hand there are those who, as a result of the change, will be required to behave differently and may require training in order to be able to achieve new standards of performance. This chapter will consider, briefly, how training can help to reestablish alignment between the competencies of organisational members and other elements of the system such as task and structure. Attention will also be given to the main aspects of a systematic approach to the development of effective training interventions.

ACHIEVING A MATCH BETWEEN ORGANISATIONAL MEMBERS AND CHANGING TASK DEMANDS

When change calls for new behaviours on the part of organisational members, a number of factors will determine whether or not these new behaviours will be forthcoming. These include the quality of the match between competencies and task demands, the effect of reward systems on the motivation to deliver revised performance outcomes, and the availability of feedback to enable individuals and their managers to assess whether the new performance standards are being achieved. This chapter is concerned with the first of these.

Sometimes organisational members will already possess all the competencies they require in order to achieve the new performance standards. All that such people will need (in terms of their ability to perform in new ways) is information about the revised performance outcomes that they will have to achieve.

At other times the people affected by the change may not possess the competencies they will need, and in these circumstances a number of options may be available to those managing the change. They may explore ways of redesigning the task to match the existing competencies of organisational members; they may replace existing staff with others who already have the required competencies; or they may help existing staff to acquire the required new competencies.

A SYSTEMATIC APPROACH TO TRAINING

Goldstein (1993) and others argue that effective training involves three main steps: the analysis of training needs, the design and delivery of training and the evaluation of training effectiveness.

Training-needs analysis

A training-needs analysis starts with a system-level review to determine how the proposed change will affect organisational goals, objectives and task demands. This overview provides the information necessary to identify where more specific task and person analyses are required. For example, the move from an optical to a digital scanning technology in the reprographics equipment sector changed the nature of the tasks performed by many organisational units. In this case, a system-level review might have pointed to a need for a more detailed analysis in departments such as product design, assembly, technical support, sales and so forth. However, in other departments, such as finance, the system-level review might have identified few implications for the nature of the task performed and the competencies required.

The next step, a task analysis, focuses on specific jobs or roles and examines how modifications to the task of a unit will affect the nature of the performance that will be demanded from members of that unit. It also points to the competencies (knowledge, skill, attitude or behaviour) that people performing these new or modified roles will require in order to perform to the new standard. Elaborating the example of the reprographics equipment manufacturer, a task analysis of, for example, the selling function might have revealed how the introduction of digital scanning technology changed the nature of the performance required by sales persons to sell digital as opposed to optical reprographics equipment.

The person analysis seeks to identify discrepancies between the required competencies, as determined by the task analysis, and the existing competencies of the organisational members available to perform these revised tasks. This analysis provides the information necessary to (a) identify which individuals or groups will require training, and (b) specify training objectives in terms of what trainees need to know and how they will be required to behave.

The most useful way of expressing training objectives is in terms of *behavioural objectives* that specify what trainees will be able to do after training. For example, one of the training objectives for the reprographics equipment sales representatives might be 'to be able to accurately describe how the new technology affects the performance of the new range of copiers produced by the company'. Another might be 'to be able to demonstrate to customers how to maintain the equipment to keep it operating at peak efficiency'.

The design and delivery of training

Smith (1991) suggests that the choice of training method should, at least in part, be determined by the kind of competencies that the training is designed to impart. For example, training methods that are good at imparting knowledge and information include lectures, and reading books and manuals. Where the focus is attitudes, role play or informal discussion groups might be selected. Where the aim is to develop cognitive strategies, case studies, simulations, projects or mentoring might be used; and where the focus is perceptual and involves motor skills a variety of methods might be considered – these could include the discrimination method that is designed to help trainees detect differences between items that are very similar, and the progressive parts method which is a schedule for organising the practice of complex motor skills.

Reid and Barrington (1999) classify training strategies under five main headings: training on-the-job; planned organisation experience; in-house courses; planned experience outside the organisation; and external courses. They also recommend four criteria that can be used to determine which of these strategies will be most appropriate:

- Compatibility with training objectives.
- Estimated likelihood of transfer of learning to the work situation.
- Availability of resources (such as time, money and skilled staff).
- Trainee-related factors.

They illustrate how these factors can influence choice of training method with an example that can easily be adapted here to apply to preparing managers to participate in an organisation-wide change programme. The change agent might be required to set up and manage a project team to develop a strategy to implement a series of changes agreed by the company's management committee. It might be decided that the team should include managers representing a range of departments that will be affected by the changes. The objectives of the training for team members might include:

1   imparting knowledge (so that trainees will understand, be able to describe to others and recognise actions that will help achieve the aims of the change programme);

2 developing positive attitudes (so that trainees will be committed to the aims of the programme and to working constructively with other members of the team to achieve these aims); and

3 developing group process skills (so that trainees will be able to diagnose what is going on in the group and act in ways that will contribute to group effectiveness).

In terms of compatibility with training needs, the change agent might quickly reject some strategies, such as on-the-job training, because there may be no project teams currently operating in the company that could provide the required work experience. External courses, such as outward-bound forms of team training, might offer a good way of developing positive attitudes towards colleagues and developing group process skills. However, in order to satisfy some of the other training needs, the change agent or somebody else from the company would have to be involved and the course would have to be adapted to provide some sessions that deal with the aims of the change programme. This would also require the external course to be restricted to managers from the same company who are to work together in the new project team. A specially designed in-company course might be an attractive option. It could include a mix of formal inputs on the aims of the change programme, informal discussion sessions to explore trainees' reactions to these aims, and group activities that could be used as a vehicle for developing group process skills.

In terms of the transfer of learning, both the external course, if it were restricted to prospective members of the project team, and the in-house course could facilitate the transfer of group process skills and positive attitudes towards other trainees to the work situation. The in-house course could also score high on the transfer of learning if the group activities involved working on real issues that the team would have to deal with once it 'went live'.

In terms of availability of resources, time might be a factor that would preclude the use of internal or external planned work experience. Also cost, in terms of money in the budget rather than the opportunity cost of the change agent's time, might be a factor that would work against the external course. The in-house course might cost less but the change agent would have to find the time to develop the training materials and the work-related group activities. The change agent may be confident that s/he has the necessary skills to design and deliver the in-house programme; s/he might also be aware of an external consultant who could be employed to help at a cost that would be considerably less than the cost of the external course.

In terms of trainee-related factors, from a business perspective it may be impossible to release all the managers at the same time to participate in a week-long external course. Also, for domestic reasons, some members of the proposed project team may find it very difficult to be away from home for a whole week. Taking into account all these factors the change agent may opt for the in-house course.

The evaluation of training effectiveness

The role of evaluation in the context of change management will be discussed in some detail in Chapter 18, together with some of the issues that can affect the validity of evaluation exercises. The focus of attention here is the kind of criteria that can be used when evaluating the effectiveness of training interventions. Kirkpatrick (1983) argues that training can be evaluated at four levels:

- At level 1 the criterion is how trainees *reacted* to the training. Did they feel it was relevant, interesting, demanding, etc.?
- At level 2 the criterion is *what they learned*. It is not unknown for trainees to react favourably to the training but to learn relatively little, or only achieve acceptable standards of learning in respect of some, but not all, of the learning goals. This kind of feedback has obvious implications for those responsible for selecting the training strategy and designing the details of the learning activity.
- At level 3 the criterion is *behaviour*. Trainees may have reacted positively to the training and learned what it was intended they should learn. However, back on the job their behaviour may have changed little, if at all. In other words, what was learned on the course may not have been transferred to the work situation. It is relatively easy to apply the relevant principles of learning to design a training activity that will encourage learning; it is much more difficult to design a training activity that will ensure that the learning is transferred and used in the work situation. A common problem that inhibits transfer is the social pressure that trainees are subjected to after they return from training. While they may have learned best practice when on the course, back on the job colleagues often pressure them to revert back to the traditional ways of working.
- At level 4 the criterion is *results*. It is possible for the training to produce the intended changes in behaviour, but this behaviour change may not produce the intended results. Sales representatives may have started to call more regularly on customers but this may not produce the increase in sales that had been anticipated. This kind of feedback indicates a need for a fundamental rethink of the training strategy.

SUMMARY

This chapter has considered how training can contribute to the change process, with attention directed towards the main elements of an effective approach to training. These are:

1 A training-needs analysis, which involves three steps:

- a system-level review to determine which parts of the organisation will be affected by the change;
- a more focused task analysis to determine how the pattern of task demands and required competencies will change; and
- a person analysis to identify the extent to which existing organisational members possess the required competencies.

2 The design and delivery of training.
3 The evaluation of the training.

Exercise 11.1   Assessing the way training is used in the change process

Reflect on either an organisation-wide change or a change targeted at a particular department or unit in your organisation. Consider the following points and then make a brief assessment of the way training was used to help achieve change.

● Was there any evidence indicating that the organisation and/or particular change managers were prepared to invest in training to support change?
● Was the attention given to training inadequate, about right, 'over the top'?
● Was the training targeted at the individuals and groups most in need of training?
● Was the training provided compatible with training requirements and delivered in a way that maximised the transfer of learning to the work situation?

Assessment of the way training was used to help achieve change:

References

Goldstein, I.L. (1993) *Training in Organisations*, 3rd edn, Monterey, Cal.: Brooks/Cole.

Kirkpatrick, D.L. (1983) 'Four Steps in Measuring Training Effectiveness', *Personnel Administrator*, 28(11), pp. 19–25.

Reid, M. and Barrington, H. (1999) *Training Interventions*, London: Institute of Personnel and Development.

Smith, M. (1991) 'Training in Organisations', in M. Smith (ed.), *Analysing Organizational Behaviour*, London: Macmillan – now Palgrave, pp. 49–76.

12

Motivating others to change

It was noted in Chapter 3 that organisations, like all open systems, seek to maintain a state of equilibrium, they tend to gravitate to a condition where all the component parts of the system are aligned with each other. Intentionally intervening to change the organisation by modifying one component of the system can disturb this state of equilibrium and can create pressure to restore it. Restoration can be achieved by realigning other components with those that have been changed, or by resisting the change and seeking to re-establish the status quo.

In all organisational systems, there is a natural tendency to resist change. This chapter will:

1 consider how the general level of commitment in an organisation can affect the extent to which organisational members will support new initiatives;
2 review and synthesise some of the views on resistance to change presented by Kotter and Schlesinger (1979), Zaltman and Duncan (1977), Nadler (1993) and Pugh (1993);
3 examine the utility of expectancy theory as a basis for assessing the motivation of an individual or group to support or resist change; and
4 consider how change strategies can be designed to motivate individuals and groups to change.

ORGANISATIONAL COMMITMENT AND THE LEVEL OF SUPPORT FOR CHANGE

People's past experience of change can affect their level of commitment to the organisation and their willingness to support further change.

Over forty years ago, Argyris first defined the *psychological contract* as the perceptions of both parties to the employment relationship of their obligations implied in the relationship. More recently, Guest *et al.* (1996) referred to it in terms of perceptions of fairness, trust and the extent to which the 'deal' is perceived to have been delivered. It is an unwritten set of expectations between every member of an organisation and those who represent the organisation to them, and it incorporates concepts such as fairness, reciprocity and a sense of mutual obligation. For example, organisations may expect employees to be loyal, keep trade secrets, work hard and do their best for the organisation. In return, employees may expect that they will receive an equitable level of remuneration, will be treated fairly and with dignity, will have some level of security of employment and, possibly, some level of autonomy and an opportunity to learn and develop. If employees feel that their employer/managers have kept their side of the psychological contract they are likely to respond by displaying a high level of commitment to the organisation. If, on the other hand, they feel that the organisation has failed to keep its side of the bargain they may respond by redefining their side of the psychological contract. They may invest less effort in their work, be less inclined to innovate and less inclined to respond to the innovations or changes proposed by others.

Exercise 12.1   Violations of the psychological contract

Think of an incident at work when the organisation/management fell short of what might have been reasonably expected of them in their treatment of an individual or group of employees. In the space below, list any effects this incident had on the level of commitment of the individual or group and on their willingness to support change?

You might also consider what was the effect on others. People observe how others are treated and this affects their views about how they may be treated in the future if they are involved in some kind of change. Note, in the space below, any 'ripple effect' that this incident had on the commitment of others and their willingness to support change.

Managers often expect that those who have been retained after a programme of redundancies will be relieved and grateful and will respond with higher levels of commitment and performance. Research on the 'survivor syndrome' (see Doherty and Horsted, 1995) suggests that this may not be the case. Survivors may respond in a number of ways, ranging from shock, anger, animosity towards management, guilt, concern for those gone, and anxiety, to relief that they still have a job or fear of losing their job in the future. The evidence suggests that survivors often display less confidence and a lack of commitment, trust and loyalty to the organisation.

As Bob Worcester, chair of MORI, once said: ' Don't worry about those staff who turn off and go: worry about those who turn off – and stay!'

REASONS FOR RESISTING SPECIFIC CHANGES

Kotter and Schlesinger identify four main reasons why people resist change:

1 *Parochial self-interest.*   People resist change when they think that it will cause them to lose something of value. It is not uncommon for stakeholders to focus on their own best interests rather than those of the organisation. Pugh (1993) suggests that all too often managers fail to anticipate resistance because they only consider change from a rational resource allocation perspective and fail to appreciate that many organisational members are much more concerned about the impact it will have on them personally. They will assess its impact in terms of how it might affect ways of working, job opportunities, career prospects, job satisfaction and so on, and in terms of how it might undermine or enhance their power and status and the prestige of the groups to which they belong.

   Zaltman and Duncan (1977) view threats to power and influence as one of the most important sources of resistance to change. They observe that the prospect of a merger often gives rise to fears on the part of individuals, groups and even entire organisations that they will lose control over decision-making. They also note that managers, even very senior managers, may resist the use of certain approaches to the management of change if they feel that they may undermine their power and authority. They illustrate this with an example of head teachers who were resistant to the use of a survey feedback approach to organisation development because it enabled teachers and district-level personnel to have access to data and to use it, along with the heads, to propose solutions to problems. Some of the head teachers were concerned that this approach would increase the power of the teachers and undermine their own power to influence how the schools are managed.

2 *Misunderstanding and lack of trust.*   Misunderstandings can be a frequent source of resistance. Stakeholders often resist change because they do not understand the implications it may have for them. Such misunderstandings may lead them to perceive that the change will cost them more than they will gain.

   Misunderstandings are most likely to arise when trust is lacking between the person(s) initiating the change and the stakeholders who feel that they will be affected by it. Managers/change agents often fail to anticipate this kind of resistance, especially when they are introducing a change that they perceive will be of benefit to those involved, because they assume that people only resist changes that undermine their best interests. The author was asked by the CEO of a chemical company to investigate why the workforce had rejected a productivity agreement that senior management believed offered considerable advantage to both the organisation and process workers. It turned out that the message that had been communicated to the workforce was, in some important respects, different from the proposal that the senior management team had agreed to make (see Chapter 10). These differences had arisen as the proposal had been passed down the management chain. However, this communication problem had been compounded by the fact that the process workers felt that the offer was too good to be true and that management was intent on manipulating them in some way.

3   *Different assessments.*   Kotter and Schlesinger (1979) suggest that another common reason why some stakeholders resist change is that they assess the situation differently from those initiating the change and see more costs than benefits resulting from it, not only for themselves but also for the organisation or other constituencies that are important to them. They argue that managers who initiate change sometimes assume that (a) they have all the relevant information required to conduct an adequate organisation analysis, and that (b) those that will be affected by the change have the same facts. Often neither assumption is correct. Also those initiating change often fail to take account of how the change might affect stakeholders who are not organisational members. External stakeholders can be an important source of resistance. This problem was discussed in Chapter 9.

Zaltman and Duncan (1977) point to how selective attention and retention can prevent individuals or groups appreciating that the current state of affairs is unsatisfactory. The mental models that influence how they perceive, interpret and make sense of their environment (referred to in Chapter 4) can have a strong effect on how organisational members assess their circumstances and whether or not they perceive any problems that require remedial action. Their mental models can also affect the kind of solution that will be favoured if a problem is perceived to exist. It is not unusual for resistance to occur, even when organisational members and their managers have a shared view of the nature of a problem, because both parties have conflicting views about what should be done to resolve it.

4   *Low tolerance for change.*   Stakeholders also resist change when they are concerned that they will not be able to develop the new skills and behaviours that will be required of them. All people are limited in their ability to change, but some are much more limited than others. In Chapter 1 reference was made to Toffler's view that people respond to the increasing rate of change in different ways and that some are more able than others to internalise the principle of acceleration, modify their durational expectancies and make an unconscious compensation for the compression of time. Toffler also considers the phenomenon of adaptive breakdown, which he refers to as future shock.

Even when stakeholders intellectually understand the need for change they, sometimes, are emotionally unable to make the transition (see Chapter 12). The change may involve a grieving process similar to that which occurs when a person loses a loved one. Perceived loss can affect people in different ways but often this involves some element of denial and a reluctance to 'let go'.

EXPECTANCY THEORY AND THE MOTIVATION TO SUPPORT OR RESIST CHANGE

Expectancy theory considers how expectations influence motivation. It offers a useful conceptual framework for assessing whether a stakeholder is likely to support or resist an impending change. Expectancy theorists (for example Vroom, 1964) argue that behaviour is a function of two factors – expectancies about the future and the attractiveness of outcomes.

- *Outcomes* can be evaluated in terms of their value or attractiveness; Vroom refers to this as 'valence'. If stakeholders expect the change to reduce the availability of valued outcomes they are likely to offer resistance. If, on the other hand, they expect it to increase the availability of valued outcomes they are more likely to offer support.
- *Expectancies*. It is not only the potential availability of valued outcomes that will determine whether a stakeholder will support or resist a change. Stakeholder motivation will also be influenced by expectancies about the likelihood that they will actually receive valued outcomes in practice. The theory focuses attention on two expectancies about the future:
  (a) *Effort to performance expectancy*. This refers to the person's expectation (subjective probability about the likelihood) that s/he can perform at a given level (in other words, that effort will lead to successful performance).
  (b) *Performance to outcome expectancy*. This refers to a person's expectation that some level of performance will lead to desired outcomes (or the avoidance of negative outcomes).

From a motivational perspective it is the expectation or belief about the relationship between effort, performance and valued outcome that will determine whether a stakeholder will be motivated to support or resist a change. The basic elements of this theory are illustrated in Figure 12.1.

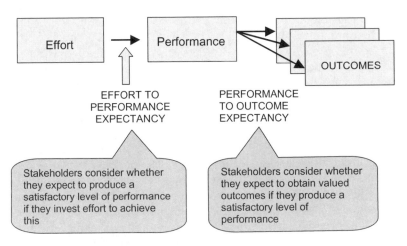

Figure 12.1 The expectancy model of motivation

Equity of treatment

The model can be extended to include the stakeholder's expectations about equity of outcome in the changed situation. If stakeholders believe that comparable others will receive more favourable treatment (in terms of valued outcomes) as a result of the change this will affect their assessment of the attractiveness of the outcomes they expect to receive. Some stakeholders who expect, in absolute terms, to receive a net increase in valued outcomes may resist the change because they feel that they are being treated unfairly relative to comparable others.

Understanding and competence

The model can also be extended to include key factors that may affect effort–performance expectancies. These include the stakeholder's understanding of the nature of the required performance (and the rules that govern how a performance should be produced), and the competencies required to deliver a satisfactory level of performance. These will be discussed below (and see Figure 12.2).

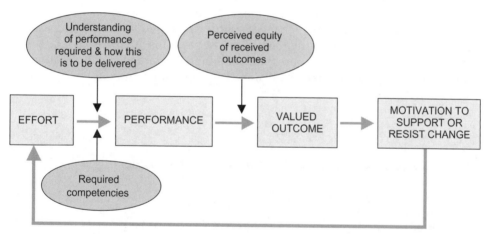

Figure 12.2 An expectancy model of the motivation to support or resist change

ASSESSING THE AVAILABILITY OF VALUED OUTCOMES

The first step in assessing how stakeholders will respond to change is to identify how the change will affect the availability of valued outcomes in the changed situation. In order to do this the change manager needs to:

- be aware of the kinds of outcome that are valued by the stakeholders who will be affected by the change;
- have some understanding of the extent to which the current situation provides these outcomes; and
- have some understanding of the extent to which valued outcomes will be (at least potentially) available in the changed situation.

This assessment will provide a useful first indication of the extent to which stakeholders will support or resist the change. It will also indicate the extent to which they are likely to be motivated to perform in ways that will contribute to organisational effectiveness in the changed situation.

When people are confronted by an impending change they often fear that they will lose some of the outcomes that they value in the existing situation. However, they may also anticipate some gains. These gains might be more of the outcomes that they already enjoy, or some completely new benefits. In order to anticipate how stakeholders will feel about a change it is necessary to empathise with them in order to construct a balance sheet of (what we think) they will perceive as gains or losses. Different people value different outcomes, and even the same person may value different outcomes at different points in time. The more that we know about stakeholders the better placed we will be to construct a balance sheet of their gains and losses. Listed in the box are some broad headings that might suggest the kinds of outcomes that could be important to stakeholders.

Each of these headings can be elaborated to include a more detailed list of associated outcomes. For example, under the heading of pay, employees might feel that the impending change is likely to reduce the availability of valued outcomes because they will be required to work longer hours or at a faster rate for the same pay. On the other hand, the change might be viewed as enhancing valued outcomes if it leads to a regrading that will boost pay. This might also be the case if it offers a shift to annualised hours that will eliminate unpredictable variations in weekly pay and provide a guaranteed annual income can be used to secure a bank loan or a mortgage.

Types of outcomes that could be important to stakeholders

Pay

Working conditions

Interesting/meaningful work

Autonomy

Opportunity for competition or
collaboration

Opportunities to be creative

Power and influence

Belonging/involvement

Location

Security

Working with considerate
supervisors

Satisfaction

Challenge

Achievement

Recognition

Status

Openness/sharing

Use knowledge and skills

The broad headings listed are intended as prompts; they do not provide an exhaustive list. Different kinds of stakeholder may value different kinds of outcome.

Exercise 12.2   Assessing the availability of valued outcomes

1 Think about a recent or impending change at work or elsewhere, and identify a key stakeholder affected by the change.
2 List all the *valued outcomes* that you believe the stakeholder receives in the *current situation*. Review the list and indicate whether you feel that the change will produce a gain (✓), no change (?) or a loss (✗) for each outcome.

Valued outcome in existing situation	✓	?	✗	Rank

3 Next, extend the list by adding any *new outcomes* that you anticipate will be available to the stakeholder in the *changed situation* and indicate your assessment of whether the stakeholder will view them as a gain (✓), neutrally (?) or as a loss (✗).

Valued outcome in changed situation	✓	?	✗	Rank

4 Finally, review the content of the full table and *rank* how you think the stakeholder will value the outcomes. In the column headed 'Rank', enter 1 next to the most valued outcome, 2 next to the second most valued, and so on.

5 *Assess net gain or loss.* In order to make an overall assessment of the potential net gain or loss for the stakeholder it is necessary to take account of both the number of gains and losses identified in the above table, and also the relative importance of the different valued outcomes to the stake holder. The ranking is intended to provide a basis for weighting the significance of each gain and loss. Is the stakeholder likely to view the net effect of the change as a:

GAIN	
LOSS	

6 Consider whether those responsible for managing the change were/are aware of how the change was/is likely to affect the availability of outcomes that are valued by the selected stakeholders.
7 Consider whether this information might have improved the way the change was/is being managed.

EXPECTANCIES ABOUT EFFORT-PERFORMANCE AND PERFORMANCE-OUTCOME RELATIONSHIPS AND EQUITY OF NET BENEFITS

Although the change manager may see potential net gains for the people affected by the change, the individuals concerned may not share this assessment.

Whether stakeholders will be motivated to support or resist the change will depend on *their* expectations about:

- their ability to deliver a satisfactory level of performance in the changed situation;
- whether a satisfactory (or even exceptional) level of performance will lead to the achievement of valued outcomes in the changed situation; and
- whether the net benefits accruing to them will be equitable when compared to the net benefits accruing to comparable others in the changed situation.

In order to better understand the extent to which stakeholders will resist or support change, the change manager needs to consider the following three issues.

Anticipate stakeholder expectations regarding whether they will be able to produce a satisfactory level of performance in the changed situation

There will be less resistance (more support) in those situations where stakeholders expect to be able to deliver a satisfactory level of performance in the changed situation. Individuals or groups are more likely to resist a change when they expect that, irrespective of how hard they work, the change will undermine their ability to produce a satisfactory level of performance.

Diagnosis

In order to anticipate how the change might affect stakeholder expectations about their ability to produce a satisfactory level of performance in the changed situation, the change manager needs to:

■ Consider whether any misunderstandings might arise about the processes and procedures that will apply in the changed situation. Stakeholders may assume that any new rules that define the nature of a satisfactory level of performance, or new rules that regulate working practices may undermine their ability to produce a satisfactory level of performance.

For example, individuals may assume that in the changed situation they will have less autonomy and that they will be required to work in a group setting. They may also fear that in this group setting their performance will be dependent on inputs from others who are poor or unreliable performers. Their fears may be well-founded, but they may also be based on misunderstandings about the nature of the change or the other people they may have to work with.

Possible action

The change manager may be able to reduce resistance from this source by:

☐ helping people develop a clear understanding of how the change will affect the way they will be required to work (*education*);
☐ helping them understand the consequences that these new processes and procedures may have for their ability to deliver a performance (*education and persuasion*);
☐ providing them with an opportunity to be involved in the planning of the change. This might reassure them that the change will be managed in a way that will minimise those factors that could undermine their ability to deliver a satisfactory level of performance (*participation and involvement*).

- Consider the relevance of existing core competencies in the changed situation.

  For example, in those situations where a stakeholder's core competencies become more highly valued the individual is more likely to support the change. However, where core competencies are perceived to be less relevant (or even redundant) the change is more likely to be resisted because the stakeholder may fear that s/he will not be able to produce a satisfactory level of performance.

Possible action

The change agent may be able to reduce the resistance from this source by:

- □ considering possibilities for redeploying people to roles that will better utilise existing competencies (*planning*);
- □ involving people in identifying possibilities for redeployment (*participation*);
- □ providing training to develop more relevant competencies (*training and development*).

Anticipate stakeholder expectations about the relationship between performance and the achievement of valued outcomes in the changed situation

There will be less resistance (and more support) for a change in those situations where stakeholders expect that the delivery of a satisfactory level of performance will be linked to the achievement of valued outcomes. In those situations where they expect the change to undermine the achievement of valued outcomes they are more likely to resist the change and to be less motivated to perform in the changed situation.

Diagnosis

In order to anticipate how the change might affect stakeholder expectations about the relationship between performance and the achievement of valued outcomes, the change agent needs to:

- Empathise with the stakeholders affected by the change in order to develop a better understanding of how they might expect the change to affect the link between performance and the achievement of valued outcomes.

  For example, if an individual values promotion and expects that in the changed situation there will be a closer link between advancement and level of performance, s/he may support the change and be motivated to perform well in the changed situation. If, however, the individual expects the change to weaken this link, then it will increase the possibility that the change will be resisted.

Possible action

The change agent may be able to reduce resistance from this source by:

☐ considering ways of modifying the change to strengthen the links between performance and the achievement of valued outcomes (*planning*);

☐ persuading individuals that the change will actually strengthen these links (*persuasion*);

☐ involving stakeholders in the diagnosis, planning and implementation of the change. This might reassure them that the change will be managed in a way that will strengthen links between performance and valued outcomes (*participation*).

Anticipate stakeholder perceptions of their net benefits (or losses) compared to those enjoyed by comparable others

There will be less resistance (and more support) in those situations where stakeholders feel that they are being treated equitably relative to others. Where they feel that they are being treated unfairly they may be more likely to resist the change.

Diagnosis

In order to anticipate the effects of perceived equity on the level of resistance or support for change, the change agent needs to:

● Identify those who may regard themselves as being treated inequitably.

Possible action

The change agent may be able to reduce resistance from this source by:

☐ helping people who feel this way recognise all the potential gains available to them and ensuring that they fully understand the possible losses if the change is not implemented (*education and persuasion*);

☐ exploring possibilities for improving the availability of valued outcomes for those who feel they have received inequitable treatment (*planning*);

☐ exploring the possibility of redistributing costs and benefits between those affected by the change in order to produce greater equity (*planning*);

☐ involving stakeholders in the diagnosis, planning and implementation of the change. This might reassure them that the change will be managed in a way that will maximise equity of treatment (*participation*).

RESISTANCE AND THE NEED TO MOTIVATE PEOPLE TO CHANGE

Attempts to introduce change often founder because the new initiative is resisted. Earlier sections of this chapter have considered why resistance might be encountered and presented an expectancy-based model for diagnosing resistance and identifying possible ways of managing it. This section provides a more detailed discussion of how change strategies can be designed to motivate individuals and groups to change.

Kotter and Schlesinger (1979) identify six methods for dealing with resistance to change.

1   **Education and persuasion.** One of the most frequently used ways of minimising resistance is to educate people about the need for change. Zaltman and Duncan (1979) refer to educative strategies as those that provide a relatively unbiased presentation of the facts in order to provide a rational justification for action. This approach is based on the assumption that organisational members and other stakeholders are rational beings capable of discerning fact and adjusting their behaviour accordingly when the facts are presented to them.

A related approach is the *persuasive strategy* that aims to motivate people to change by biasing the message to increase its appeal. Most advertising, for example, is persuasive in nature. When the level of commitment to change is low, persuasive approaches are likely to be more effective than rational educative strategies. Persuasive approaches can increase commitment by stressing (realistically or falsely) either the benefits of changing or the costs of not changing. If the message is so false/biased as to deceive the change target, the approach is better classified as manipulative (see below).

Nadler (1993) builds on Lewin's notion of 'unfreezing' and argues that one of the most effective ways of motivating people to change is to expose or create a feeling of dissatisfaction with the current state. This can be accomplished via education or persuasion, but there is evidence to suggest that focusing attention on the weaknesses of the change target's current practice is less effective than informing them of the potential benefit associated with the adoption of alternative practices. Confronting people about problems associated with current practice can be interpreted as criticism and blame, and can provoke a defensive reaction. Instead of motivating people to change the effect can be to motivate them to save face by justifying current practice and denying the need to change.

2   **Participation and involvement.** Nadler argues that another effective way of surfacing and creating dissatisfaction with the current state and motivating people to change is to involve them in the collection, analysis and presentation of information. Information that people collect for themselves is more believable than information presented to them by external experts or other advocates of change.

A potential benefit of participation and involvement is that it can *excite, motivate and help create a shared perception of the need for change* within a target group. When change is imposed the change target is likely to experience a lack of control and feels the 'victim' of change. The more people are involved the more likely they are to feel that the change is something that they are helping to create. In addition to increasing motivation, participation and involvement can also produce better decisions because of the wider input, and can help to sustain the change once implemented because of a greater sense of ownership.

The classic study by Coch and French (1948) demonstrated that workers are much more accepting of a change in work practices when they are involved in the planning of the change. Their findings suggested that participation led to the *acceptance of new practices* because it encouraged the group to 'own' them as a group goal. Group ownership offered the bonus that group norms developed that helped to implement and sustain the changes. Acceptance (and the effect of acceptance on productivity) was most marked when the basis of participation was the whole group. When participation was by representation there was an initial decline in productivity. This suggests that when people are not personally involved it can take them longer to understand and accept the new practices.

Involvement can be encouraged at any stage of the change process and can include all of a target group or only a representative sample. Organisational members might be invited to participate in the initial diagnosis of the problem, in the development of solutions and the planning of implementation strategies, in the actual implementation of the change plan and/or in the evaluation of the effectiveness of the change. Some of these possibilities will be discussed in more detail in Chapter 16 when different types of intervention are considered.

Some managers have an ideological commitment to participation and involvement whereas others feel that it threatens their power and authority and is almost always a mistake. Kotter and Schlesinger (1979) maintain that both attitudes can lead to problems because neither is very realistic. They argue that where change initiators do not have all the information they need to design and implement a change, or when they need the wholehearted commitment of the change target, involving others can make very good sense. However, involvement does have some costs. It can be very time-consuming and, if those who are involved have less technical expertise than the change initiators, it can result in a change plan that is not as good as it might be.

3 **Facilitation and support.** Kotter and Schlesinger (1979) suggest that when fear and anxiety lie at the heart of resistance an effective approach to motivating change is to offer facilitation and support. They suggest that this might involve the provision of training in new skills, giving time off after a demanding period or simply listening and providing emotional support.

Nadler (1993) refers to the need to provide time and opportunity for people to disengage from the current state. This can be especially helpful when they feel a sense of loss associated with the letting go of something they value or something they feel is an important part of their individual or group identity. He also refers to the value of group sessions that provide organisational members with the opportunity to share their concerns about the change. However, he acknowledges the possibility that such sessions might also have the effect of increasing rather than reducing resistance.

Ceremonies and rituals that mark transitions can also help people let go of the past and begin to think constructively about the future. In addition, the provision of emotional support can be particularly effective in circumstances where feelings and emotions get in the way and undermine people's ability to think clearly and objectively about a problem. Some examples of facilitation and support will be considered in Chapter 13.

4 **Negotiation and agreement**. People can be motivated to change by rewarding those behaviours that will facilitate the change. The explicit provision of rewards is a useful approach when the change target is unlikely to perceive any obvious gains associated with the original change proposal.

Kotter and Schlesinger (1979) suggest that negotiated agreements can be a relatively easy way to avoid resistance when it is clear that someone, who has sufficient power to resist a change, is going to lose out if the change is implemented. The problem associated with this approach is that others who may have been content to go along with the change may now see the possibility of improving their lot through negotiation. The long-term effect can be to increase the cost of implementing changes and to increase the time required to negotiate the change with all the interested parties.

5 **Manipulation and cooption.** Manipulation is the covert attempt to influence others to change and it can involve the deliberate biasing of messages, as considered above in the discussion of persuasive communications. It can also involve cooption. Kotter and Schlesinger (1979) note that coopting usually involves giving an individual or group leader a desirable role in the design or implementation of the change. The aim is not to seek access to any expertise they may have, rather it is to secure their endorsement.

While this approach may be quicker and cheaper than negotiation, it runs the risk of those who are coopted feeling that they have been 'tricked' into supporting the change. Also, those who are coopted may exercise more influence than anticipated and steer the change in a direction not favoured by the change initiators.

6 **Direction and a reliance on explicit and implicit coercion.** The ability to exercise power exists when one person or group is dependent on another for something they value. Coercive strategies involve change managers using their power to grant or withhold valued outcomes in order to motivate people to change. While the result may be a willingness to comply and go along with the change, the change target's commitment to the change may be low. Consequently, compliance may only be sustained so long as the change manager continues to monitor the situation and maintains the threat of withholding valued outcomes.

In spite of the risks of long-term resentment and the possibility of retaliation that are often associated with coercive change strategies, there may be occasions where their use is appropriate. These may include situations where the target group has a low perceived need for change, where the proposed change is not attractive to the target group and where speed is essential.

SUMMARY

This chapter has considered how the general level of commitment in an organisation can affect the level of support for change. It has also considered the utility of expectancy theory for assessing resistance to change, and has examined six methods for dealing with resistance to change.

References

Coch, L. and French, J.R.P. (1948) 'Overcoming Resistance to Change', *Human Relations*, 1, pp. 512–32.

Doherty, N. and Horsted, J. (1995) 'Helping Survivors Stay on Board', *People Management*, 1, pp. 26–31.

Guest, D., Conway, N., Briner, R. and Dickman, M. (1996) *The State of The Psychological Contract in Employment*, London: Institute of Personnel and Development.

Kotter, J.P. and Schlesinger, L.A. (1979) 'Choosing Strategies for Change, *Harvard Business Review*, March/April.

Nadler, D. (1993) 'Concepts for the Management of Organisational Change', in C. Mabey and B. Mayon-White (eds), *Managing Change*, 2nd edn, London: Paul Chapman, pp. 85–98.

Pugh, D. (1993) 'Understanding and Managing Organisational Change', in C. Mabey and B. Mayon-White (eds) *Managing Change*, 2nd edn, London: Paul Chapman, pp.108–12.

Vroom, V.H. (1964) *Work and Motivation*, London: Wiley.

Zaltman, G. and Duncan, R. (1977) *Strategies for Planned Change*, Ch. 3, Resistance to Change, London: John Wiley.

Other useful references:

Arnold, J. (1996) 'The Psychological Contract, a Concept in Need of Closer Scrutiny', *European Journal of Work and Organisational Psychology*, 5(4), pp. 511–20.

Herriot, P., Manning, W. and Kidd, J. (1997) 'The Content of the Psychological Contract', *British Journal of Management*, 8, pp. 151–62.

13

Managing personal transitions

Chapter 12 considered some of the factors that determine whether stakeholders will view a change as an opportunity that promises personal benefit, or a threat that could reduce access to valued outcomes. It also considered some of the steps that change managers can take to motivate stakeholders to support a change.

This chapter addresses the way organisational members experience change, irrespective of whether they view it as an opportunity or threat. It examines the individual's response to change as a progression through a number of stages of psychological reaction, and it also considers how an understanding of the way individuals react to change can help managers plan and implement organisational change in ways that will maximise benefit and minimise cost for both the organisation and individual stakeholders.

Organisational change involves a change in contextual or situational factors (such as technology, structures, systems and required competencies) *and* a series of personal transitions for all those affected. Bridges (1980) suggests that while many managers are wise about the mechanics of change, they are often unaware of the dynamics of transition. Personal transitions are important because, even though some situational factors can be changed relatively quickly, the new organisational arrangements may not work as planned until the people involved let go of the way things used to be and adjust to the new situation. Commenting on the factors that can undermine the successful implementation of change, Bridges (1991) claims that 'It isn't the changes that do you in, it's the transitions'.

THE NATURE OF PERSONAL TRANSITIONS

Individuals, like organisations, can be confronted with incremental or discontinuous change. It was noted in Chapter 4 that a feature of discontinuous change is that it challenges taken-for-granted assumptions about how the organisation relates with the environment. It calls for a rethink about what business the organisation is in and what needs to be done in order to ensure that it survives and grows.

Individuals can also be confronted with incremental and discontinuous types of change. Some changes are very gradual, for example ageing, and individuals can adjust to them without experiencing any sudden personal disruption. Where the process of change is continuous and incremental it rarely presents any abrupt challenges to the assumptions individuals make about how they relate to the world around them. But this is not the case for all types of change. A sudden merger, and the announcement that key personnel will have to compete for senior posts in the new organisation, will raise many questions in the minds of those affected about what the future will hold for them. This is an example of a change that poses a serious challenge to an individual's *assumptive world*.

Parkes (1971) argues that this assumptive world is the only world we are aware of. It includes everything we know or think we know. It affects our interpretation of the past and our expectations of the future, our plans and our prejudices. Any or all of these may need to change as a result of an organisational change, whether or not these changes are perceived as gains or losses.

When changes are lasting in their effects, take place over a relatively short period of time and affect large areas of the assumptive world they are experienced as personal transitions. The change manager might perceive the promotion of a team member to team leader as a simple and quickly accomplished organisational change. However, from the perspective of the individual who is promoted, the personal transition associated with this organisational change might be a much more protracted process. It might be difficult for the newly promoted team leader to let go of his or her former role as team member, and the close friendships this involved with some colleagues and the distant, business-like relationships it involved with others. The newly promoted team leader might feel isolated in the new role and might be unsure about how to behave towards others, especially subordinates who used to be both colleagues and close friends. It might take some time and quite a lot of experimenting to discover a style of managing that works. In some cases the individual may be so unhappy with the new role that he or she might give up the struggle and resign, leaving the change manager with the job of finding a new team leader.

Loss of employment, whether through redundancy or early retirement, is another example of a personal transition. Parkes suggests that loss of a job deprives a person of a place of work, the company of workmates and a source of income. It also removes a familiar source of identity, self-esteem and sense of purpose. Adjustment to this change will require, for example, new assumptions about the way each day will be spent and about sources of income. It might also affect the individual's faith in his or her capacity to work effectively and to earn a living. This kind of disruption to the assumptive world will cause an individual to set up a cycle of internal and external changes aimed at finding a new fit between self and the changed environment.

Even the loss of a job that was wanted but not secured can be difficult to cope with because a person's assumptive world contains models of the world as it is and also as it might be. People who might be promoted to works manager rehearse in their mind the world they hope to create. They engage in a kind of anticipatory socialisation aided by the rich imagery of their new comfortable office, efficient secretary, challenging assignments and respectful subordinates. It may be almost as hard to give up such expectations and fantasies as it is to give up objects that actually exist. Thus the people who are not promoted may actually lose something very important and they may have to make new assumptions about how things will be in the future.

THE PERSONAL COST OF COPING WITH TRANSITIONS

Personal transitions require those affected to engage in some form of coping behaviour. Holmes and Rahe (1967) developed a Social Readjustment Rating Scale that attributed mean values to the degree of adjustment required after individuals experience a series of life events. The scale was originally constructed by telling 394 subjects that marriage had been given an arbitrary value of 50 and asking them to attribute a score to 42 other life events, indicating whether each life event would require more or less adjustment than marriage. The mean values attributed to the 43 events included in the Social Readjustment Rating Scale ranged from 100 for death of spouse to 11 for a minor infringement of the law (Table 13.1). Social readjustment was defined in terms of the amount and duration of change in one's accustomed pattern of life following a life event, irrespective of the desirability of the event.

Various retrospective and prospective studies using the Social Readjustment Rating Scale, reported by Holmes and Masuda (1973), found that magnitude of life change is highly significantly related to the time of onset of illness. An example of a prospective study of this relationship is one that involved recording the life changes experienced by 2500 officers and enlisted men aboard three US Navy cruisers. It was found that there was a clear correlation between life changes experienced in a given period before the cruisers put to sea, and the onset of illness during the period at sea.

It is possible to assess the magnitude of any life crisis that an individual may have had by clustering the values of life-change events experienced over a 12-month period. A life crisis is defined as any clustering of life-change events whose individual values sum to 150 or more life-change units in any one year:

- A mild life crisis is defined as 150 to 199 life-change units.
- A moderate crisis is 200 to 299 life-change units.
- A major life crisis is defined as more than 300 life-change units.

The studies reported by Holmes and Masuda indicate that the higher the score over the last 12 months the greater the likelihood of onset of illness over the next 12 months.

This relationship may be moderated by individual differences in the ability to cope with personal transitions. People may perceive the same event and/or assess their ability to cope with it in different ways. This can be influenced by many factors, including past experience of the event and personality variables such as hardiness, self-esteem and self-reliance, and so forth. You might find it interesting to use the Social Readjustment Rating Scale (Table 13.1) to assess the amount of life change that you have experienced in the last 12 months.

Table 13.1   The Social Readjustment Rating Scale

Rank	Life event	Mean value
1	Death of spouse	100
2	Divorce	73
3	Marital separation	65
4	Jail term	63
5	Death of close family member	63
6	Personal injury or illness	53
7	Marriage	50
8	Sacked from work	47
9	Marital reconciliation	45
10	Retirement	45
11	Change in health of family member	44
12	Pregnancy	40
13	Sexual difficulties	39
14	Gain of a new family member (child or 'oldster' moving in)	39
15	Business readjustment	39
16	Change in financial state	39
17	Death of close friend	37
18	Change to a different line of work	36
19	Change in number of arguments with spouse	35
20	Taking on a large mortgage (e.g. for house purchase)	31
21	Foreclosure of mortgage or loan	30
22	Change in responsibilities at work	29
23	Son or daughter leaves home	29
24	Trouble with in-laws	29
25	Outstanding personal achievement	28
26	Spouse beginning or ceasing work	26
27	Begin or end school (formal education)	26
28	Change in living conditions	25
29	Revision of personal habits (dress, manners, associations etc.)	24
30	Trouble with boss	23
31	Change in work hours or conditions	20
32	Change in residence	20
33	Change in schools/college	20
34	Change in recreation	19
35	Change in church (mosque) activities	19
36	Change in social activities	18
37	Taking on medium level loan (for TV, computer etc.)	17
38	Change in sleeping habits (amount, time of day etc.)	16
39	Change in number of family get-togethers	15
40	Change in eating habits	15
41	Holidays	13
42	Christmas	12
43	Minor violations of the law	11

Source: Adapted from Holmes, T. and Rahe, R. 'The Social Readjustment Rating Scale', *Journal of Psychosomatic Research*, 1967, vol. 11, table 3, p. 215.

The relationship between life change and illness susceptibility highlights the personal cost associated with adjusting to change, irrespective of whether the change is viewed as desirable or undesirable. It also points to the possibility that different people may react to the same organisational change in different ways because for some it is an isolated event whereas for others it is one of a number of changes, at work and elsewhere, that push them towards a major life crisis.

ADJUSTING TO ORGANISATIONAL CHANGE

When individuals adjust to organisational changes that:

- are lasting in their effects,
- take place over a relatively short period of time and
- affect large areas of the assumptive world,

they experience a process of personal transition. Exercise 13.1 invites you to reflect on how you have reacted to a change that involved a personal transition. The information generated by this exercise will enable you to compare your reactions with the typical pattern of reaction described by the stage model of transition that is presented later in this chapter.

Exercise 13.1 Your experience of a transition

Think of a change that was lasting in its effects, took place over a relatively short period of time and affected the assumptions you made about how you related to the world around you. Examples of this kind of change could be redundancy, job change, promotion, relocation, bereavement, illness or accident that affected your mobility or some other aspect of your functioning, marriage, or birth of first child.

For the purpose of this exercise the change need not be an organisational change. Now answer the following questions:

Entry into the change:

- When did you realise that the transition was to take place?

- How did you know?

- What did you feel at the time?

- What did you do/how did you behave?

During the transition:

- Did your feelings and/or behaviour change during the transition? Are you able to identify any stages that highlighted differences in the way you reacted to the change? If so, what were these stages?

Exit:

- When did you realise that your transition had ended? How did you know?

Think about your answers to the questions posed in Exercise 13.1 when the stages of psychological reaction to a change are considered below.

ORGANISATIONAL CHANGE AND PERSONAL TRANSITION

Organisational change involves the ending of something and the beginning of something else. For example, it might involve the introduction of a new organisational structure, a more automated production process, revised procedures, the merger of two units, the closure of a plant, a redundancy programme, job transfers, a new project or a promotion. While these changes might be carefully planned and happen on a predetermined date it might be some time before those involved have adapted to these external events. Managers need to develop an understanding of how people respond to change. They need to know the course of events associated with the process of transition and the kinds of action they can engage in to facilitate adaptation.

A model of change as a transition

The model presented below is based on the work of William Bridges (1980, 1991). It conceptualises transition as beginning with an ending and then going on to a new beginning via a neutral zone. These three phases are not separate stages divided by clear boundaries; phases can overlap and an individual can be in more than one phase at any one time. Bridges sees the movement through a transition as being marked by a change in the dominance of one phase as it gives way to the next.

Endings involve letting go of the old situation and the identity that went with it. It is impossible to fully engage in a new role or have a new purpose until those involved have let go of the old role or old purpose. For example, as noted above, a promotion, especially when it is in the same work group, involves letting go of the role of group member and internalising the new role of group leader. Fink *et al.* (1971), drawing on the work of Lewin, argue that every human system has within it forces for maintenance of the *status quo* and forces for growth. While these forces tend to operate counter to each other, the balance between maintenance and growth is constantly shifting. Endings are often associated with a predominance of maintenance forces that manifest themselves in a resistance to change and a reluctance to let go.

The neutral zone is the in-between state. It involves a recognition of the need to change and uncertainty about the nature of more desirable end states. It is a period of disorientation, self-doubt and anxiety, but it can also be a period of growth and creativity in which new opportunities are identified. However, there is a danger that people may be so uncomfortable with the ambiguity and disorientation associated with this stage of transition that they push prematurely for certainty and closure. Consequently they may lock on to the first opportunity that offers any promise of a more satisfactory state of affairs and, in so doing, lock out the possibility of a creative search for better alternatives.

Beginnings involve reorientation to a new situation and the development of a new identity. Initially the forces for growth predominate but eventually, as the new situation is more clearly defined and a new identity is internalised, the forces for maintenance and growth achieve a new balance.

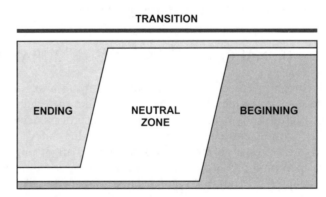

Figure 13.1   Bridges' (1991) model of transition

Source: Bridges, W., *Managing Transitions*, Addison-Wesley, 1991, p. 70.

THE STAGES OF PSYCHOLOGICAL REACTION

People going through change experience a variety of emotional and cognitive states, and transitions typically progress through a cycle of reasonably predictable phases described below. This applies to all kinds of transition: voluntary and imposed, desirable and undesirable. There is a widely held view that in each case the person experiencing the transition will have to work through all of the stages if the transition is to be successfully completed. Understanding this process can help both individuals and managers.

The model presented below has been developed by John Hayes and Peter Hyde from an earlier version which originally appeared in *Transitions: Understanding and Managing Personal Change* by John Adams, John Hayes and Barrie Hopson (1976). The cycle reflects variations in the degree to which people feel able to exercise control over the situation.

- **Awareness/shock**. Often people have little warning of changes and they experience the initial phase of a transition as a shock. They feel overwhelmed, frozen, paralysed. Feelings of anxiety and panic can undermine their ability to take in new information, think constructively and plan, which leads to a state of immobilisation. People behave as though they are on 'auto-pilot' and show little response to new developments. While their mood may be more positive if the transition is perceived as a desirable gain (e.g. first prize on the lottery) they may still experience a state of immobilisation and have difficulty planning and taking constructive action. In those circumstances where people develop a gradual awareness of a pending change they often focus on what they might lose and engage in 'worry work' that diverts their attention from other matters that might require their attention. The intensity of this phase will be influenced by the degree of preparedness and the consequences will be influenced by the desirability of the transition – immobilisation will be greater when the transition is unexpected and unwanted.
- **Denial**. This phase is characterised by a retreat from the reality of change. Negative changes may be denied or trivialised and attention may be displaced onto other more immediate but less important matters. Energy and activity are devoted to the known and the familiar and any perceived threat to the

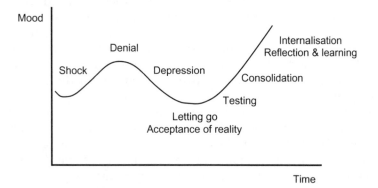

Figure 13.2 Transition phases

status quo is managed by behaving in habitual ways. Clinging to the past and refusing to consider the need to change can lead to a reduction in anxiety, and anything or anyone who challenges this false sense of security is likely to provoke an angry response. Resistance to change is at its highest at this point. Positive changes may induce euphoria together with an unwillingness to consider any possible negative consequences. In some cases denial may be functional if it provides the opportunity to recharge 'emotional batteries' and helps a person face up to the need to change.

● **Depression**. Eventually the reality of the change becomes apparent and the individual acknowledges that things cannot continue as they are. In terms of Bridge's model this corresponds to the start of the neutral zone. This provokes a feeling of depression which is often associated with a feeling that the situation is beyond one's control; the phase may be characterised by anger, sadness, withdrawal and confusion. This depressed mood occurs even in changes which were initially embraced enthusiastically whenever practical difficulties are encountered. It is in the depression phase, therefore, that the change really starts to be experienced as stressful. If the change was a voluntary one, this may be the point at which the person gives up. In involuntary changes, the person may seek to leave the situation.

● **Letting go**. This phase involves accepting reality for what it is; it implies a clear letting go of the past. This may be experienced as a 'little death' and often entails a process of mourning. It can help at this point to remember that the lowest ebb is the turn of the tide.

● **Testing**. A more active, creative, experimental involvement in the new situation starts to take place. New ways of behaving and being are tried out; more energy is available but anger and irritability may be easily aroused if the new behaviour is not successful. This phase may involve trial-and-error behaviour or a more active cycle of experience–review–conclude–plan may be employed. As some patterns are found which seem to work, this phase gradually gives way to the next.

● **Consolidation**. Out of the testing process come some new ways of being and behaving which are gradually adopted as new norms. This corresponds to the Beginning stage in Bridges' model. This stage progresses in parallel with testing, but to begin with there is more testing than consolidation. It involves reflecting on new experiences and assessing whether they offer a basis for a constructive way forward. (Sometimes there is little consolidation. Early experiments with new roles and relationships are rejected and the person experiencing the transition learns little from the experience.) When consolidation occurs it involves reflecting on the new experience and using any learning to build on this experience and inform the choice of further 'testing' experiences.

● **Internalisation, reflection and learning**. The transition is complete when the changed behaviour is normal and unthinking and is the new natural order of things. Ideally the past has been left behind and little or no 'unfinished business' remains. Reflection and learning is a cognitive process involving reflecting on what all the activity and emotion has really meant. It is at this point that learning and personal growth, which may benefit future transitions, is recognised.

Validation of the model

You might find it interesting, at this point, to reflect on the answers you provided to the questions posed in Exercise 13.1. Does the stage model of psychological reaction presented above provide a useful conceptual framework for understanding the process of adjustment you went through?

SOME OBSERVATIONS ON THE STAGE MODEL OF TRANSITIONS

Each individual's experience of a transition will be influenced by a number of factors. These include the importance of the transition, whether it is perceived as a gain or loss, the intensity of its impact, the existence of other simultaneous transitions (and the magnitude of any associated life crisis), personal resilience and so on. It follows therefore that there can be no absolutely standard pattern of reaction. Some possible variations are noted below:

- The wave can be shallower or deeper and the overall shape of the curve may be skewed one way or the other. For example, if the change is perceived as a desirable opportunity the individual might find it easier to let go of the past whereas if it is perceived as a threat or loss the individual might be reluctant to let go and resist the change for as long as possible.
- The time taken to pass through all the phases can vary greatly. Just as some people take longer than others to come to terms with the loss of a loved one, so organisational members can vary in terms of the time it takes for them to adjust to a work related transition.
- Although presented as a purely linear process, people may regress and slip back to an earlier stage in the process.
- People can get stuck at any phase and not complete the cycle. They may, for example, continue to deny the need to change or fail to recognise new opportunities associated with the change.

Where multiple transitions are involved, people handle the situation in different ways. Some people keep the transitions firmly compartmentalised and deal with one at a time; others throw their energy into one as a displacement activity to get away from another (which is therefore held in denial); in other cases, one major transition predominates and swamps the others.

Implications for individuals and change managers

Hayes and Hyde (1996) summarise some of the implications for individuals and change managers.

For individuals

- It takes time for people to make the adjustments required in transitions.
- It can help them to know that their own experience is normal, that it will involve ups and downs and that it will eventually come to an end.
- The process can be managed: there are things that they can do to facilitate their own transitions.

For change managers

- It is important to recognise that there will often be a time lag between the announcement of a change and an emotional reaction to it: it is easy to mistake the apparent calm of the immobilisation and minimisation phases for acceptance of the change.
- Because any given change will have different implications for different individuals or groups, different parts of the organisation will progress through the cycle at different rates and in different ways.
- Change managers need to beware of getting out of phase with their staff. They tend to know about the change before others and, therefore, it is not unusual for them to have reached an acceptance of change long before other organisation members. This can create great potential for ineffective communication.
- The cycle cannot be avoided, but there is much that change managers can do to facilitate people's passage through it.

FACILITATING PROGRESS THROUGH A TRANSITION

This final section outlines, briefly, some of the interventions that change managers can make to help facilitate the progress of other people through a transition. This kind of facilitation is particularly important where people have become stuck at a particular stage in the process. The interventions are presented in relation to each stage of the process of transition.

What follows is not meant to be a prescriptive list of what the change manager should do. It is a set of suggestions, based on observations and anecdotal evidence of what seems to have worked in practice, supplemented by managers' reports (during workshops with John Hayes and Peter Hyde) about what they have done that appeared to help others manage their personal transitions. These suggestions might alert you to some of the issues that have to be managed and to possible ways of intervening that might be appropriate in a particular set of circumstances.

1 Shock associated with the announcement/discovery of a change that affects an individual's assumptive world

Sometimes the shock reaction can be minimised by:

- Preparing the ground and creating a climate of receptivity to change.
- Consulting and involving people in the decision-making.

If this is not possible, the change manager might consider possible ways of announcing the change. Anecdotal evidence suggests that the following points might be worth considering:

- *Who should make the announcement.* This might be a senior manager in order to signal the importance of the change and the organisation's concern for the people involved. Alternatively, it might be decided that a relatively junior manager should make the announcement because s/he has a better relationship with those affected.

- *Timing.* When should an announcement be made?

  □ Should the announcement be made simultaneously to all staff or should some be told before others?
  □ Should people be told as soon as possible or should the announcement be delayed?

- *Method.* Should it be done face to face, via a video link or by letter?

  □ In face-to-face encounters it is important to keep calm and avoid becoming defensive or aggressive in the face of questions.

- *Content.* Should a consistent message be given to all?

  □ How much information should be communicated? Should the message be kept as simple as possible?
  □ Should explanations be given about why the change is necessary?
  □ It often helps to show empathy and understanding for how people will feel (for example, 'I know this will be upsetting for you and I feel very sad about it myself, but ...')

- *Dialogue.* Should questions be encouraged?

It is important to allow time for people to digest the information and share their feelings with others. When people are in shock the change manager needs to recognise that:

- Performance might be temporarily impaired and that in some circumstances this might lead to dangerous or costly consequences. This might influence the timing of the announcement.
- Some people might need more support than others.

2   Denial

The change manager needs to diagnose what it is that is being denied (for example, the change isn't necessary, is not real, does not affect me, etc.) and then consider whether it would be helpful to:

- Confront what is being denied gently and supportively.
- Repeat the message.
- Draw people's attention to relevant examples, evidence and experience.
- Arrange demonstrations of what the change will involve, if possible.
- Establish and keep to a timetable to provide milestones and evidence of change.
- Find ways to ensure that they have to engage with the reality of the change.
- Take early action if at all possible. The longer the gap between the announcement of a change and the change taking effect the easier it is for an individual to ignore that the change is for real.
- Get people to do practical things related to the change.

3 Depression

The change manager can intervene in order to help others understand and accept the situation by:

- Providing support.
- Listening.
- Adopting an accepting and non-critical reaction to their expression of feelings.

The change manager can also help others to work on their feelings about the situation by:

- Helping them get it off their chest.
- Providing space to grieve.
- Providing appropriate opportunities to vent emotion.

They can also help them identify opportunities to move on by:

- Not letting them wallow in feeling bad: gently confronting and challenging.
- Helping them identify other things they are good at.
- Providing further information about the change to help people envisage what the future will be like.
- Helping them identify options and possible benefits.
- Helping them focus their attention on the things they can do or can influence.
- Where possible, providing opportunities for the exercise of influence (e.g. consultation and involvement).

4 Letting go

The change manager can help people let go of the past by:

- Explaining the need for change in terms of benefits rather than problems associated with past practice. Rubbishing the past can provoke a defensive reaction.
- Providing challenging targets associated with the movement towards a more desirable state.
- Drawing attention to deadlines.
- Eliminating the symbols of the past.
- Reminiscing in a way that leads to a process of taking the best forward from the past.
- Marking the ending by rituals and ceremonies, wakes and leaving parties.
- Letting people take souvenirs and mementoes.

5 Testing

Some of the ways in which the change manager can encourage testing include:

- Creating the space, time and resources required to test.
- Promoting creative thinking.

- Helping people identify options.
- Encouraging risk taking and experimentation.
- Discouraging premature closure.
- Avoiding punishing those who make mistakes.
- Injecting new processes, tools and competencies that will help people help themselves.
- Eliminating the drivers of old behaviours.
- Acting as a mentor.
- Praising and supporting successes.
- Encourage networking and cross fertilisation.
- Providing feedback.

6 Consolidation

This can be facilitated by:

- Reviewing performance and learning.
- Helping others identify the characteristics of a more desirable state.
- Recognising and rewarding achievement.
- Getting them to help others and share their experience.
- Helping them to build on successes.
- Broadcasting their successes.

7 Reflecting, learning and internalisation

This can be facilitated by:

- Helping individuals review the experience of change – asking questions, running review workshops, etc.
- Conducting formal post-implementation reviews.
- Getting them to help others and share their experience.

SUMMARY

This chapter has addressed the way organisational members experience change. Attention has been focused on those changes that are perceived to be relatively lasting in their effects, take place over a relatively short period of time and affect large areas of the assumptive world.

When confronted with this kind of change, people experience a process of personal transition that involves a number of stages of psychological reaction. These stages are awareness/shock, denial, depression, letting go, testing, consolidation, reflection and learning and internalisation. The implications of this process of adjustment have been considered from the perspective of the individuals experiencing a transition and the change managers. Attention has also been given to ways in which change managers can intervene to facilitate this process of adjustment.

References

Adams, J., Hayes, J. and Hopson, B. (1976) *Transitions: Understanding and Managing Personal Change*, London: Martin Robertson.

Bridges, W. (1980) *Transitions*, Reading, Mass.: Addison-Wesley.

Bridges, W. (1991) *Managing Transitions: Making the Most of Change*, Reading, Mass.: Addison-Wesley.

Fink, S.L., Beak, J. and Taddeo, K. (1971) 'Organisational Crisis and Change', *Journal of Applied Behavioral Science*, 7(1), pp. 15–37.

Hayes, J. and Hyde, P. (1996) *Transitions Workshop*, unpublished manual, Hyde Management Consulting, Woodvale House, Basingstoke Road, Reading RG7 1AE.

Holmes, T.H. and Masuda, M. (1973) 'Life Change and Illness Susceptibility', *Separation and Depression*, AAAS, pp. 161–86.

Holmes, T.H. and Rahe, R.H. (1967) 'The Social Readjustment Rating Scale', *Journal of Psychometric Research*, 11, pp. 213–18.

Parkes, C.M. (1971) 'Psycho-social Transitions: a Field for Study', *Social Science and Medicine*, 5, pp. 101–15.

Additional reading:

Stuart, R. (1995) 'Experiencing Organisational Change: Triggers, Processes and Outcomes of Change Journeys', *Personnel Review*, 24(2), pp. 1–87.

Part IV

Shaping implementation strategies and managing the transition

Here we deal with some of the issues that need to be considered when deciding how to manage the change process and how to maintain control during the transition phase.

Chapter 14   Shaping the implementation strategy

This chapter identifies some of the key situational variables that can influence the shaping of an implementation strategy, considers how and why this strategy may need to change over time, and reviews some possible start points for a change initiative. After reading this chapter you will be invited to critically assess the strategy used to manage a recent change within your organisation.

Chapter 15   Maintaining control during the change

It is not unusual for change programmes to disrupt normal work practice and undermine existing management systems. This chapter looks at issues of control and considers some of the steps change mangers can take to maintain control during the period between the identification of a need for change and the achievement of a desired future state. After reading this chapter you will be invited to reflect on an occasion when you were involved in the management of a change and to consider what you or others might have done differently to maintain better control.

14

Shaping the implementation strategy

This chapter presents a model that provides a brief overview of the situational variables that can influence choice of implementation strategy. The need to vary an implementation strategy over time, and the advantages and disadvantages of different start points are also discussed.

A CONTINUUM OF INTERVENTION STRATEGIES

Kotter and Schlesinger (1979) argue that successful change strategies are those that are internally consistent and are compatible with key situational variables. The continuum of implementation strategies presented in this chapter is based on Kotter and Schlesinger's model, but attempts to specify more clearly some of the situational variables that need to be considered when shaping a strategy.

The approach to implementation represented by the left-hand end of the continuum presented in Figure 14.1 is very directive and involves imposing a plan for change without any discussion or consultation. Change managers who adopt a directive approach behave as if they assume that they:

- are sufficiently expert and well-informed to be able to diagnose the need for change and develop an implementation plan that will move the organisation to a more desirable future state; and
- have sufficient power to ensure that others will comply with the requirements of the implementation plan.

At the other end of the continuum the approach to implementation is very collaborative and involves working with others to diagnose the need for change and develop a plan for implementation. Change managers who adopt this approach behave as if they need to draw on the experience and expertise of others and/or assume that by involving others they will generate a sense of ownership and a level of commitment that will increase the likelihood of the change plan being implemented successfully.

DIRECTIVE	COLLABORATIVE
Urgent requirement for change	Non-urgent requirement for change
Desired end state clearly specified from the start	Problem/opportunity recognised but what needs to be done to resolve problem or exploit opportunity not clear from the start
Little resistance anticipated	Great resistance anticipated
Change managers have access to all the information they need to diagnose the need for change, develop a change plan and monitor its implementation	Change managers need information from other stakeholders
Others have high trust in change managers	Others have low trust in change managers
Change managers do not have to rely on the commitment and effort of others to implement the change plan	Successful implementation of the change plan is highly dependent on the commitment and effort of others

Figure 14.1   A continuum of intervention strategies

In practice, change managers may vary their approach at different stages of the change process. For example, some may decide not to involve others in the preliminary diagnostic phase but might draw more people into the latter stages of problem definition and the specification of a more desirable future state. They may then move on to involve many more in the details of implementing the plan for change. Factors that might lead to a variation in approach over time will receive more attention below. Some of the main factors that can influence the choice of an implementation strategy are illustrated in Figure 14.1.

SITUATIONAL VARIABLES

Six important situational variables are:

1   *Urgency and stakes involved.* The greater the short-run risks to the organisation if the current situation is not changed quickly the more the change managers may have to adopt a directive strategy towards the left-hand side of the continuum. Involvement and participation take time, and this time might not be available if the need for change is urgent.

2   *Clarity of desired future state.* Reference has already been made to two very different types of change; blueprint change and evolutionary change (see Chapter 5 on process models of change). Blueprint changes are those where the desired end state can be clearly specified from the start, whereas evolutionary changes are those where the need for change is recognised but it is impossible to anticipate what a more desirable future state will look like.

Depending on other factors, such as the power of the change managers relative to other stakeholders, it may be easier to adopt a more directive approach to implementation when confronted with a blueprint-type change than when the change involves an incremental process of action learning. Implementing an evolutionary change involves hypothesising about what might be a useful next step, planning how to achieve it, taking action to implement the plan, reflecting on what happened, and then hypothesising about what needs to be done next. This process is more likely to be successful when change managers involves others and adopt a more collaborative approach.

3   *The amount and type of resistance that is anticipated.* All other factors being equal, the greater the anticipated resistance the more the change manager will have to work at persuading others to accept the need for change. This might require the adoption of a more collaborative approach towards implementation.

4   *The extent to which change managers have the required data for designing and implementing the change.* The more the change managers anticipate that they will need information from others to help design and implement the change, the more they will have to adopt a collaborative approach and move towards the right-hand side of the continuum.

5   *Degree to which other stakeholders trust the change managers.* The more the other stakeholders trust the change managers the more likely they are to be prepared to follow their direction. The lower the level of trust the more the change managers may have to involve others in order to win their trust and build their commitment to the change plan.

6   *Degree to which the change managers have to rely on the commitment and energy of others to implement the plan.* The more the change managers have to rely on the energy and commitment of others to make the change plan work, the more they may have to adopt a collaborative approach and involve them in the change process.

Kotter and Schlesinger argue that one of the most common mistakes made by change agents is that they often rely on a single approach to implementing change regardless of the situation. They refer to:

- The autocratic manager whose only approach is to coerce people.
- The people-oriented manager who typically tries to involve and support people.
- The cynical manager who always tries to manipulate others.
- The intellectual manager who relies too much on education as an influence strategy.
- The lawyer-type boss who typically tries to negotiate and bargain.

The model presented here emphasises the need for change managers to adopt a contingent approach to the choice of implementation strategy that accommodates and balances a number of interdependent factors.

VARIATIONS OVER TIME

Balogun and Hailey (1999) suggest that the focus of the change strategy may need to change over time. For example, in the short term the critical requirement might be to secure the organisation's survival, and in order to do this it might be necessary to impose radical cuts and closures and to redefine the purpose of the organisation. (This kind of change was referred to in Chapter 1 as re-creation.) Over the longer term the focus may switch to a more incremental strategy of tuning and the major concern may become continuous improvement. Associated with this change in focus may be a move towards a more collaborative approach to implementation.

Zaltman and Duncan (1977) cite complexity, communicability, compatibility, relative advantage and divisibility as factors that might influence the way change managers attempt to influence others. These factors might also affect the styles of influence that will be most effective at different stages of the transition phase.

Complexity and communicability. If the required change is very complex and difficult to communicate, the initial style of influence might involve a high level of explanation and education. However, once people understand the problem and what is required, other means of influence might be more effective.

Compatibility and relative advantage. Similarly, a change that is compatible with the change target preferences and offers relative advantage over current practice might lend itself to a persuasive strategy. In other cases negotiation or high levels of involvement might be the most effective way forward.

Divisibility. Where the change is divisible and where quick action is required it might be decided to direct a part of the organisation to adopt a small-scale trial before making a decision about how to proceed. If it is decided to go ahead, speed may be less of an issue and commitment might be more important. Consequently, at this stage, a less directive approach may be adopted.

ALTERNATIVE START POINTS

Balogun and Hailey (1999) consider the advantages and disadvantages of different start points for change:

- *Pilot sites.* A small-scale change might be introduced into a pilot site that might be a single unit or a completely new site. New sites, with new staff, can provide effective test beds for initiatives that might be resisted elsewhere because of ingrained traditional attitudes and practices. Once a change initiative has been proven on the pilot site, other parts of the organisation might find it more difficult to resist the change.
- *Pockets of good practice.* Another type of small-scale change is the kind of development that is led by an individual or group who takes an initiative and promotes a pocket of good practice that, eventually, might be copied by others.
- *Top-down versus bottom-up.* The first of the small-scale changes just mentioned is an example of top-down change where the initiative is taken by senior management. Most of the literature on change management adopts a top-down perspective. An alternative approach (which can include pockets of good practice) is bottom-up change.

An advantage of a bottom-up approach is that organisational members who are in a position to recognise problems long before they are obvious to top management can take the initiative and introduce needed change at an early stage. A bottom-up strategy also encourages the commitment of organisational members.

However, while bottom-up change can help ensure that needed change is recognised early, where rapid adjustment is required it may not be able to produce widespread action fast enough. As mentioned above, imposed change from above may be more effective in times of crisis. Also, coordination may become a problem if a number of separate and incompatible change initiatives begin to emerge at different points across the organisation. In some cases the coordination that can be provided by senior management may be an essential ingredient of an effective change strategy, thus swinging the balance back towards a more top-down approach.

SUMMARY

This chapter has considered how situational variables can affect the choice of an implementation strategy. It has also considered some of the factors that might lead to the strategy being modified over time. Finally, the advantages and disadvantages of alternative start points for change have been discussed.

Exercise 14.1

Identify a recent change in your organisation and critically assess the effectiveness of the strategy used to implement it.

References

Balogun, J. and Hailey, V.H. (1999) *Exploring Strategic Change*, London: Prentice-Hall.
Kotter, J. and Schlesinger, L.A. (1979) 'Choosing Strategies for Change', *Harvard Business Review*, March/April.
Zaltman G. and Duncan R. (1977) *Strategies for Planned Change*, London: Wiley.

15

Maintaining control during the change

Every stage of the change process raises issues of control, and one of the reasons why managers are sometimes reluctant to call in external consultants is the fear that they may be difficult to control. This chapter focuses attention on the issues of control associated with the implementation stage of the change process.

Beckhard and Harris (1987) define the period of time between the identification of the need for change and the achievement of a desired future state as the *transition state*. Often key phases of this state are unique and different from either the state that exists before the change or the state that will exist after the change. For example, if an organisation recognises that it needs to improve the way it manages information and, after exploring a number of possibilities, decides to move to a new information management system it will experience a period of transition. There will come a point when the organisation continues to rely on the old system while the new one is being developed, installed and debugged. During this period people affected by the change will have to (a) keep the old system going while learning how to work with the new system, and (b) develop the work roles and relationships that will have to be in place when the new system is up and running.

It is not unusual for many types of change to disrupt normal work practices and undermine existing systems of management. Nadler (1993) argues that during this period one of the major challenges facing management is one of *control*. To abandon previous management systems before new ones have been developed can frustrate any attempt to manage the change unless some form of temporary management system is put in place. Nadler refers to the need for 'transition devices'. These include the appointment of a transition manager; the development of a plan for the period of transition between the old state and the proposed future state; the allocation of specific transition resources such as budgets, time and staff, and the development of feedback mechanisms to facilitate monitoring and control.

This chapter highlights seven steps that the change manager can take to help maintain control during the transition state.

1 Develop and communicate a clear vision of the future state

The first step in managing a transition is to provide a sense of direction. Nadler make the obvious point that it is difficult to manage towards something when people do not know what that something is. People need a vision in order to recognise what kind of behaviour will be appropriate, helpful and constructive. This was identified as a key leadership task in Chapter 9.

With the 'blueprint' type of change, referred to in Chapter 5, this kind of vision is relatively easy to establish and communicate. However, it can be much more difficult to achieve in situations that involve more of an evolutionary process of change. In these circumstances, Nadler proposes an incremental approach that involves presenting change in terms of a *series* of short transitions, the first being defined in relatively concrete terms and subsequent steps towards the uncertain future being envisioned in less concrete and more flexible terms.

2 Appoint a transition manager

Should the person in charge of the pre-change state continue to be in charge during the transition, or should management responsibility pass to the person who will be in charge post-transition? Beckhard and Harris (1987) suggest that there is no cut and dried answer to this question. Typically the transition state is one which is characterised by high levels of ambiguity and conflict, and the individual (or group) tasked with managing the transition needs:

- The 'clout' to mobilise the resources necessary to keep the change moving. (In situations where resources are scarce those responsible for keeping the old system going may resist giving up the staff time and other resources required to develop the new system. The transition manager needs the power and authority to ensure that resources are allocated as required.)
- The respect of both the existing operational leadership and those who are working on the development of the new system.
- The ability to get things done in ways that will win support and commitment rather than resistance and compliance.

Depending on the nature of the change, there may be several possible candidates for the transition management role. A very senior person in the organisation may step in and take control. A project manager may be appointed on a temporary basis. The person in charge of the pre-change state may be given responsibility for the transition in addition to his or her current operating role. A task force or temporary team may be established. Where a team approach is adopted consideration needs to be given to team composition. It might include representatives from the constituencies affected by the change; a diagonal slice of staff representing different levels of the organisation, 'natural leaders' (people who have the confidence and trust of large numbers of their colleagues), or a group who are drawn together because of their technical skills.

3 Develop a transition plan

Mention has already been made of the need to diagnose sources of resistance, identify who needs to be involved in the change, develop a critical mass of political support, and establish temporary transition structures. There is also a need to develop a plan of how activities will be managed through the transition state. Beckhard and Harris (1987) identify seven characteristics of effective transition plans. Effective plans are:

- *Purposeful* – the planned activities are clearly linked to the change goals and priorities.
- *Task-specific* – the types of activities involved are clearly identified rather than broadly generalised.
- *Integrated* – the discrete activities are linked.
- *Temporal* – events and activities are time-tabled.
- *Adaptable* – there are contingency plans and ways of adapting to unanticipated opportunities and problems.
- *Agreed* by top management (and other key stakeholders, as required).
- *Cost-effective* – avoid unnecessary waste.

This list might be extended to include some of the issues considered below, for example, the provision of adequate resources, and rewards for desired behaviours.

4 Provide the resources for the transition

There is always a cost associated with change. For example, there may be a need for training, new equipment, the development of software, the design of new structures, and staff time for all of this. When the need to change is anticipated it is more likely that the resource requirements will have been foreseen. However, when change is imposed as an urgent response to a pressing problem the organisation may find itself stretched. In some circumstances it may be so stretched that it cannot resource the change and has no option but to go out of business. In less pressing circumstances it is not unusual for management to assume that much of the staff burden of change will be borne by employees working longer and harder. While people often rise to the challenge in the short term, goodwill cannot be relied on for ever. In situations where change is a constant feature of organisational life this needs to be recognised and the required resources made available.

5 Reward transition behaviours

In those situations where people are required to continue working in accordance with the pre-change system in order to 'keep the show on the road' and maintain operations while simultaneously developing the new system, they might give insufficient attention to the change. This can happen because existing control systems reward current practice and offer little incentive for development work.

Consequently people are discouraged from investing their time in this work and from experimenting with new behaviours that might be required in the future. Steps need to be taken to ensure that transition behaviour is not penalised and every opportunity to reward this kind of behaviour needs to be explored.

6 Use multiple and consistent leverage points for change

It was noted in Chapter 11 that organisations are equilibrium-seeking systems. If only one component of the system is changed this can trigger forces that seek to realign all the components of the system by reestablishing the status quo. One way of avoiding this is to use multiple and consistent leverage points for achieving change. For example, if it is decided to change the product or service provided by a unit, it might be necessary to modify the technology used, develop new work practices, and train people in order to develop new competencies.

Example

The consequences of attempting to change the *structure* of an organisation without paying attention to other components of the system offers another example of the need to develop a transition plan that incorporates multiple and consistent leverage points for change. In response to environmental pressures, a company may decide to develop formal organisational arrangements that focus on the complex technical issues associated with production at the same time as focusing on the unique project requirements of the customer (see Figure 14.1). This kind of dual focus has long been recognised as a requirement in the aerospace industry where products are technically complex and customers are very demanding. A solution to this kind of problem might be to move from a functional to a matrix structure.

However, the success of such a matrix structure might be dependent on the appropriate adjustment of a range of other components of the wider organisation, such as systems, culture and individual attitudes and behaviour. For example, the matrix will need to be supported by organisational systems concerned with planning, controlling, appraising and rewarding that serve the needs of both the functional and project dimensions of the new structure. If appraising and rewarding are left in the hands of functional managers (such as the heads of engineering and production), the managers responsible for the customer-related projects might find that they have little influence over the members of their project teams who also report to a functional manager. Team members will give priority to the demands of the manager who can exercise most influence over their career and reward package. New systems need to accommodate this dual focus. The pre-change organisation culture might also need to be modified if it is not compatible with matrix management. For example, a rigid bureaucratic tradition, a belief in the sanctity of unity of command and a commitment to immediate departmental objectives at the expense of wider organisational goals may undermine attempts to develop an effective organisation that has the dual strength of technical competence and customer focus. A matrix organisation requires members who are aware of and are willing to work towards these broad goals and who have the skills and competence to expand their contribution to embrace responsibility for managing the relationship between their sub-task and the broader organisational purpose.

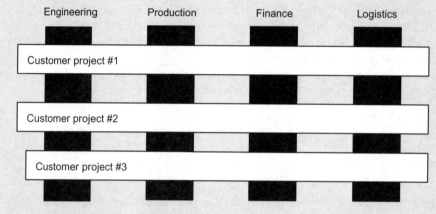

Figure 15.1 A matrix organisation structure

7   Develop feedback mechanisms

A key requirement for maintaining control is the development and installation of new feedback devices and control systems that will facilitate the monitoring of progress towards the desired future state. Nadler is a particularly strong advocate of customised feedback mechanisms during the transition phase because the feedback processes that managers normally use to collect information about how the organisation is functioning might be less appropriate during this period. Additional sources of feedback might include organisation wide surveys, focus group discussions and feedback from individual organisational members.

Exercise 15.1   Maintaining control during the transition stage

Reflect on some of the changes that you have been responsible for managing at work or elsewhere.

- Did you lose control or fear that you might lose control during the transition stage?
- If so, why was this?
- What could you have done differently that might have helped you to maintain better control?

If you cannot identify an occasion when maintaining control was a problem for you, reflect on an occasion when you were aware of somebody else who had lost control of a change that they were responsible for managing. Identify what this other change manager might have done to maintain better control. Make notes of what you/they might have done to maintain better control in the space provided below.

SUMMARY

This chapter has considered some of the steps that can be taken to maintain control of the change process. These include:

- Developing and communicating a clear vision.
- Identifying an individual or group who can lead the change and promote a vision of the desired future state.
- Producing an implementation plan, with clear targets and goals, that can indicate progress and signal any need for remedial action.
- Ensuring that adequate resources are allocated to the change and that an appropriate balance is maintained between keeping the organisation running and implementing the changes necessary to move to the desired future state.
- Implementing reward systems that encourage experimentation and change.
- Using multiple and consistent leverage points for change.
- Developing feedback mechanisms that provide the information required to ensure that the change programme moves forward in a co-ordinated manner, especially where the plan calls for consistent change in a number of related areas.

References

Beckhard, R. and Harris, R.T. (1987) *Organizational Transitions: Managing Complex Change*, Reading, Mass.: Addison-Wesley.

Nadler, D.A. (1993) 'Concepts for the Management of Organisational Change', in C. Mabey and B. Mayon-White (eds) *Managing Change*, London: Paul Chapman.

Part V

Interventions

This part considers some of the interventions that change managers can use to help secure a desired outcome and some of the issues that need to be considered when deciding which interventions to use in particular circumstances.

Chapter 16   Types of intervention

In this chapter we first consider how different theoretical perspectives on change have influenced the development of interventions over the course of the last 100 years. We then introduce a typology that classifies interventions according to the focal issues they are designed to address. The main types of intervention are human process, techno-structural, strategic and human resource interventions.

After reading this chapter you will be invited to review some of the change programmes in your organisation (that you have witnessed or been involved in) and classify the types of interventions used.

Chapter 17   Selecting interventions

This chapter examines the factors that need to be considered when selecting which type of intervention to use. Consideration is also given to the factors that can affect decisions regarding the sequencing of interventions in those circumstances where it might be necessary to use more than one type of intervention. This is important because sometimes an inappropriate sequence can undermine the effectiveness of a change programme.

After reading this chapter you will be invited to critically assess the choice and sequencing of interventions in one or more of the change programmes that you have been involved in.

16

Types of intervention

Change efforts can be less successful than they might be because those responsible for managing the change are unaware of the full range of interventions that are available. This chapter reviews some of the main types of intervention. The first section considers how the development of interventions over the last century has been influenced by theoretical perspectives on who should do what. Four main types of intervention involve:

- Experts applying scientific principles to solve specific problems.
- Groups working collaboratively to solve their own problems.
- Experts working to solve system-wide problems.
- Everybody working to improve the capability of the whole system for future performance.

We then introduce an alternative typology that classifies type of intervention in terms of the issues they address. Again, four main types of intervention are identified, focusing on:

- Human process issues.
- Technology/structural issues.
- Strategic issues.
- Human resource issues.

A number of specific interventions are briefly considered under each of these headings.

A CLASSIFICATION OF INTERVENTIONS
BASED ON WHO DOES WHAT

Weisbord (1989) observes that there has been a continuous development of new types of intervention over the last century and suggests that this has been a response to environmental changes, particularly the trend towards greater turbulence and uncertainty.

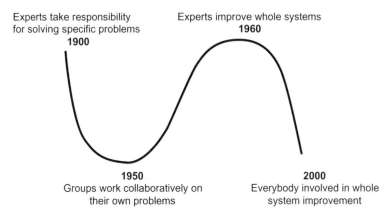

Experts take responsibility
for solving specific problems
1900

Experts improve whole systems
1960

1950
Groups work collaboratively on
their own problems

2000
Everybody involved in whole
system improvement

Figure 16.1   Developments in type of intervention over the last century

Source: Adapted from Weisbord (1987).

He classifies the range of interventions available to change agents into four categories according to criteria relating to *who* does the intervening and *what* it is that they do to bring about improvement. In terms of who does the intervening, he notes that 100 years ago the typical intervention relied on an expert to solve a problem, whereas today interventions often involve the whole system (including experts). In terms of what it is that the interventions focus on, he notes that there has been a shift from problem-solving past mistakes in particular parts of the system to improving the capability of the whole system for future performance. This evolution in interventions is illustrated in Figure 16.1.

The use of technical experts to solve problems

Frederick W. Taylor published his *Principles of Scientific Management* in 1911 in which he advocated a systematic experimental approach to problem-solving. His principles involved a careful analysis of tasks and experimentation to determine, from the perspective of efficiency, how the task should be divided into segments and how the work in each segment should be done. One of the most frequently quoted examples of Taylor's work involved an assignment at the Bethlehem steel plant designed to find the most efficient way of moving 100lb pigs of iron from a loading dock into a railroad truck. He enlisted the help of a pig-iron handler called Schmidt and studied him while, on instruction, he moved the pigs in different ways. The outcome was an ideal approach to doing the job that also specified rest periods and included an incentive system that rewarded the jobholder for working efficiently. The new approach increased productivity by 280 per cent.

Taylor's approach led to the widespread use of experts to solve problems, such as methods engineers to identify the most efficient way of accomplishing a task, and time-and-motion analysts to set standard times for the completion of each segment of the work.

Today many organisations still employ experts to solve specific problems, for example to develop a new payments system or to design a new information management system. Experts are often used when a unit (or the organisation) only has occasional need for a specific kind of expertise, when the need is for 'cutting-edge' expertise which might only be obtained from specialist departments or external consultants, or when a solution has to be found urgently and the quickest approach is to buy in external help. A potential problem associated with the use of experts is that members of the system may not share the expert's diagnosis of the problem and therefore may not be committed to implementing the prescribed solution. Also, members of the system may not learn how to solve the problem for themselves, so should it reoccur they will continue to be dependent on the expert for the solution.

Interventions which involve groups working on their own problems

Half a century later the work of Kurt Lewin and associates at the Research Centre for Group Dynamics began to produce evidence that supported the proposition that the behaviour, attitudes, beliefs and values of individuals are all based in the groups to which they belong. This led to the view that groups will exert a strong influence over whether individuals will accept or resist a change. A consequence was the development of new kinds of intervention that involved all members of a workgroup working together to solve problems.

Cartwright (1951) summarised eight principles (that emerged from the early research on group dynamics) that influenced the design of interventions. The first five are concerned with the group as a medium of change and with how the group is able to exert influence over its members. The final three focus on the potential benefits of making the group the target of change, even when the prime aim is to change individual behaviour. Evidence suggests that by changing the standards, style of leadership and structure of a group it is possible to change the behaviour of individual group members. The eight principles are:

1   *If the group is to be used as a medium of change, those people who are to be changed and those who are to exert influence for change must have a strong sense of belonging to the same group.*

This implies that in situations where the change agents are regarded as part of the group, and when a strong 'we' as opposed to 'us and them' feeling exists, those trying to bring about change will have more influence over others. Cartwright cites research findings that show that there is greater change in members' opinions when discussion groups operate with participatory rather than supervisory leadership.

2   *The more attractive a group is to its members the greater the influence it will exert over its members.*

When individuals find a group attractive and want to be members of the group they are more ready to be influenced by other members of the group. Attractiveness promotes cohesiveness and a willingness, on the part of members, to conform with others when conformity is a relevant matter for the group.

A group is more attractive to members the more it satisfies their needs. Some of the ways that group attractiveness can be increased include:

- Increasing the liking of members for each other;
- Increasing the perceived importance of the group goal; and
- Increasing the prestige of the group in the eyes of others.

3   *A group has most influence over those matters that attract members to it.*

Research evidence suggests that in attempts to change attitudes, values or behaviour, the more relevant they are to the basis of attraction to the group, the greater is the influence that the group is able to exert upon them. This helps to explain, for example, why a member of a local branch of a trades union might be willing to follow a union recommendation to engage in industrial action to influence the outcome of a pay negotiation but refuse to join a wider political protest targeted at government policies. While some members might be attracted by the union's political agenda others might not share the union's political affiliation. However, all may be attracted by the role the union can play in protecting their interests in the workplace.

4   *The greater the prestige of a member in the eyes of other group members, the greater the influence that member can exert.*

The relevance of this principle, in the context of change management, is that the person who has greatest prestige and who exerts most influence may not be the manager or formal leader designated by the organisation. Also, in peer groups the most influential person may not be the person who behaves in ways that are valued by superiors. For example, in a classroom situation the teacher's pet may have low prestige in the eyes of other members of the class and therefore will have low influence over them.

5   *Efforts to change individual members or sub-parts of a group which, if successful, would have the effect of making them deviate from the norms of the group will encounter strong resistance.*

In many groups the price of deviation is rejection. Consequently (especially where group membership is valued) there is pressure to conform to the norms of the group. This principle helps to explain why training interventions that involve taking individuals from different groups and training (changing) them often have a poor record in terms of transfer of learning when compared with training interventions which are directed at all members of a natural work group. Where the focus is on changing an individual that individual may be reluctant to continue to behave differently after training for fear of rejection. Where the intervention is targeted at the whole group this problem is less likely to arise.

6   *It is possible to create strong pressures for change in a group by establishing a shared perception of the need for change, thus making the source of pressure for change lie within the group.*

When groups are presented with 'facts' by an outsider (for example, by a manager, an internal or an external consultant) even where the facts 'prove' the case for change, in the eyes of the outsider, the facts may not be accepted by the group. The group may reject the facts because it does not own them.

When groups collect and test their own facts they are more likely to accept the evidence. Cartwright notes that there appears to be all the difference in the world between those cases where external consultants are hired to do a study and present a report and those in which a technical expert collaborates with the group in doing its own study. Often external reports are not acted on, they are left to gather dust rather than stimulate lasting change.

7   *Information relating to the need for change and the consequences of change (or no change) must be shared by all relevant people in the group.*

This principle is about getting people talking about the need for change. Changes can be blocked unless action is taken to improve communication. Evidence suggests that where the prospect of change creates feelings of threat, mistrust or hostility people avoid communicating openly and freely about the issues that concern them. Just at the point when the need for communication is at its highest people act defensively and communicate less.

8   *Changes in one part of the group (or system) produce strain in other parts of the group (or system) that can be reduced only by eliminating the initial change or by bringing about readjustments in the related parts.*

This principle is about alignment. For example, a training programme that has produced changes in one sub-group (nurses working on a hospital ward) will have implications for other sub-groups working above, below and around them as part of the total group of people dealing with patients on that ward.

The use of experts to solve systemic problems

Following the impact of von Bertalanfy's (1950) seminal paper on 'The Theory of Open Systems in Physics and Biology' (see von Bertalanfy, 1971), social scientists began to pay more attention to organisations as systems of interrelated units that transact with a larger environment (some of the main implications of systems thinking for organisations are summarised in Chapter 3). This interest led to the development of a new class of intervention. Attention shifted from solving isolated problems to looking at more systemic issues. Organisations began to employ experts, such as operations researchers and systems analysts, to guide this approach to problem-solving and in the UK social scientists at the Tavistock Institute of Human Relations began to develop interventions based on socio-technical theory. Much of their work was based on the principle that, in any situation, there is rarely only one single social system (work relationship structure) that can be used to accomplish a given task. Usually there are a number of such systems that can be used to operate the same technology and therefore there exists an element of choice in designing the work organisation (see Trist, 1969). This gives rise to the question of which social system will provide the optimum conditions and contribute most to the outcomes valued by various stakeholders.

These developments gave rise to a proliferation of other interventions that were directed towards systemic issues such as managing the organisation's relationship with its environment and helping to promote a better alignment of the elements within the organisation. While most early systemic interventions were led by experts, many of those that were developed later integrated representatives of the target system into the process of managing change. This development has been taken a stage further in whole systems interventions.

Whole system interventions to improve capability for future performance

The most recent development has been whole systems interventions in which *everybody* is involved in whole system improvement. Many examples of this type of intervention, such as Weisbord's Strategic Search Conference, adopt a 'whole system in the room' or conference model format. Some of the principles that underpin the whole system approach are summarised below.

- *Parallel organisation versus whole system in the room approaches.* The effectiveness of attempts to introduce change, especially at the strategic level, is dependent on the actions and behaviours of *everybody* affected by the change. Therefore, wherever practicable, everybody should be involved in the change process.

  A typical intervention used to develop a shared vision and an agreed strategic plan is to set up a temporary parallel organisation involving representatives from different groups (and levels) across the regular organisation to work together in various committees and task forces to produce the desired output. It is assumed that this kind of approach creates a wide feeling of involvement and gains the commitment of all organisational members. Often, however, only the representatives and those close to them feel involved. While this minority may become excited and passionate about the changes, others may feel left out and unable to influence developments. This can undermine their commitment to the vision and strategic plan produced by this process.

  An alternative approach, embedded in the whole system in the room or conference model, involves a significant part of the whole system rather than a parallel organisation of representatives. This permits everybody to contribute, and it is not uncommon to accommodate 500 or more members of the organisation in a single conference. In large organisations several conferences may be required, with some mechanism for integrating the findings from the different meetings at key stages.

- *Problem-solving versus preferred future approaches.* Lippitt (1983) argues that trying to 'fix the past' by problem-solving depletes energy whereas focusing attention on planning for a new future releases energy. Dannemiller and Jacobs (1992) report that when Lippitt compared a problem-solving group and a group using a 'preferred futures' approach to planning, the latter group envisioned the future they preferred and developed plans to achieve it whereas the former group restricted itself to problem identification and action planning. He also found that the 'preferred futures' approach was associated with higher levels of energy, greater ownership of the situation and more innovative and future-oriented goals and plans. The focus of whole systems approaches tends to be on what the organisation might become, rather than the current problems that need to be solved.

● *Organisational biographies: understanding the past and the present as a basis for exploring a preferred future.* All too often organisational members are unaware of the assumptions and consistent patterns that guide how they interpret and respond to situations, yet these assumptions and consistent patterns may blind them to threats and opportunities and may lead them to develop unrealistic strategic plans.

What an organisation is today has been influenced by the way organisational members have interpreted and responded to opportunities and threats in the past. But organisations are not victims of the past. It is possible to learn from past experience and to use this learning to challenge and modify assumptions, identify new possibilities and identify what needs to happen if these possibilities are to become reality. An element of many interventions, therefore, is the development of a better understanding of where the organisation has come from, where it is today and how it moved from where it was to where it is.

● *Overcoming resistance to change.* Change occurs when organisational members experience a tension that results from a discrepancy between their awareness of current reality and their desired future state (Fritz, 1984). They are motivated to reduce the tension by acting in ways that will help the organisation move towards the more desired future state. The conference method is designed to create this necessary tension across the whole organisation. Dannemiller and Jacobs (1992) advance this view and adapt Gleicher's change formula to argue that change (C) will occur when the product of dissatisfaction with the present situation (D), a vision of what is possible (V), and practical first steps towards reaching the vision (F) are greater than the cost of change/resistance (R):

$$C = (DVF) > R$$

The conference method involves a process that openly explores organisational members' satisfaction with the status quo, develops a clear vision of the future possibilities and identifies practical first steps in order to motivate people to change.

● *Open-systems planning.* Jayaram (1977) and others strongly advocate open-systems planning. In the conference method external stakeholders, such as suppliers and customers, are invited to contribute their views about the organisation's current performance and the opportunities and threats it will have to respond to in the future. This kind of input enriches the database available to organisational members.

The last 100 years has seen many developments in the types of intervention available to change agents, but all four types considered so far can be used to good effect in appropriate circumstances. The next section will review interventions from a different perspective.

A CLASSIFICATION OF INTERVENTIONS BASED ON FOCAL ISSUES

Cummings and Worley (2001) offer an alternative typology for classifying interventions based on the kinds of issues that they are designed to resolve, and Figure 16.2 shows the four main types of intervention. Systemic interdependencies are indicated by the double-headed arrows. Specific interventions within each of the four types can differ in terms of their intended target: individual, group or whole organisation. For example, under the heading of human resource

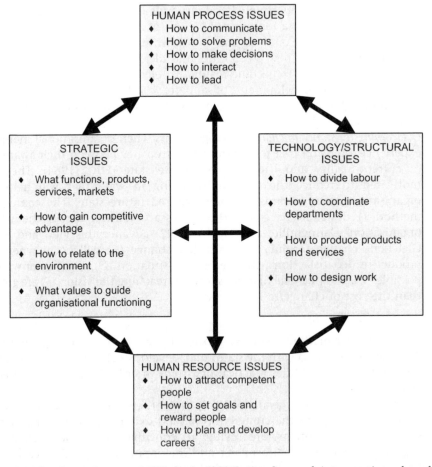

Figure 16.2 Cummings and Worley's (2001) typology of interventions based on focal issue

management interventions, there might be some interventions, such as those concerned with reward systems, that could be targeted at all three levels, whereas other interventions, such as those concerned with performance appraisal, might only be targeted at the individual and group levels.

Human-process interventions

These focus on people and the processes through which they accomplish organisational goals, such as communication, problem-solving, decision-making and leadership. Cummings and Worley (2001) provide a good overview of this type of intervention. Interpersonal and group process approaches include interventions such as T-groups, process consultation, third-party interventions and team-building.

- T-groups, sometimes referred to as sensitivity training, involves trainees exploring group dynamics and providing each other with feedback about the impact of their behaviour on others.
- Process consultation typically involves a consultant helping group members diagnose what is going on in their group as they work on real issues, and helping them devise solutions to problems that undermine group effectiveness.
- Third-party interventions involve an outsider helping organisational members resolve conflicts.
- Team-building interventions are designed to improve team working, often by reexamining the group's task, members' roles and the strategies they use for completing the task.

Human-process interventions can be applied at the organisational level to deal with more systemic issues. These include organisational confrontation meetings, intergroup relations interventions designed to help groups work with and through other groups, and large group interventions such as the whole system in the room interventions discussed above, and Grid interventions.

- Confrontation meetings are interventions designed to mobilise organisation-wide resources to identify problems, set priorities and targets and devise plans for action. They are often employed to bridge the gap between senior management and the rest of the organisation.
- Intergroup relations interventions can take a number of forms such as microcosm groups with members representing different interests coming together to work on issues relating to diversity, and interventions designed to help two or more groups work to resolve dysfunctional conflicts.
- Large group interventions go under a number of labels, such as whole system in the room conferences, search conferences, open-space meetings and future searches, and are designed to involve many people, including external stakeholders, in the management of issues that affect the whole organisation.
- Grid interventions, like Likert's System 4 (Likert, 1961), are normative in the sense that they specify a single best way to manage organisations and involve processes that help organisations to move to this ideal.

Techno-structural interventions

These are the second broad type of intervention referred to by Cummings and Worley (2001). They focus on structure, task methods and job design. Interventions relating to the design of organisations include the grouping of activities, downsizing and reengineering.

- Structural design encompasses interventions that aim to identify and move towards more effective ways of structuring activities. It often involves moving towards more process-based and network-based structures in order to provide the flexibility to cope with increasing turbulence and uncertainty.
- Interventions aimed at reducing the size of the organisation are referred to as 'downsizing'.
- Business process reengineering (BPR) involves a fundamental rethink and radical redesign of business processes to achieve a step change in performance. It often involves the use of IT systems to help organisational members control and coordinate work processes more effectively.

Interventions designed to increase employee involvement in order to enhance their commitment and performance often involve moving decision-making downwards in the organisation, closer to where the work is done. To achieve this, employees at all levels have to be provided with the power, information, knowledge and skills required to act effectively. Interventions of this type include:

- General interventions designed to improve the quality of worklife such as job enrichment, self-managed teams and labour-management committees.
- Interventions of various types that involve the creation of a parallel structure that operate in tandem with the formal organisation to provide alternative settings (such as awaydays, project groups or quality circles) in which organisational members can address problems and search for solutions.
- Other broadbased interventions designed to increase employee involvement are high-involvement organisations which entail a joint manager–worker redesign of the organisation to promote high levels of involvement and performance (rather that the addition of parallel structures), and total quality management (TQM) which is a long-term effort designed to focus all the organisation's activities around the concept of quality.

Work/job design interventions include engineering, motivational and socio-technical systems approaches to designing work for groups and individuals.

- Engineering approaches to work design focus on efficiency and job simplification.
- Motivational approaches focus on enriching the work experience and are designed to motivate employees to work more effectively.
- Socio-technical approaches to work design focus on integrating the technical and social aspects of work. They often involve the introduction of self-managed work groups.

Human-resource management interventions

This third broad type of intervention referred to by Cummings and Worley (2001) focuses on personnel practices and how they can be used to integrate people into the organisation. Performance management interventions focus on how goal-setting, performance appraisal and reward systems can contribute to organisational effectiveness by aligning members' work behaviour with business strategy and workplace technology.

Interventions designed to develop and assist organisational members can be grouped under three headings: career planning and development, managing workforce diversity and employee wellness.

- Interventions designed to promote career planning and development are often introduced to help employees manage their own careers and prepare themselves to respond to the uncertainties and lack of job security that are increasingly becoming a feature of organisational life.
- Workforce diversity interventions are designed to respond to the different needs, preferences and expectations of the various groups of employees who bring different resources and perspectives to the organisation. A key aim of these interventions is to help the organisation retain a diverse workforce and use it to gain competitive advantage.
- Employee wellness interventions are designed to promote the well being of organisational members and to contribute to the development of a productive workforce. They include employee assistance and stress management programmes.

Strategic interventions

This fourth broad type of intervention referred to by Cummings and Worley links the internal functioning of the organisation with the wider environment. They aim to align business strategy with organisational culture and the external environment. Cummings and Worley (2001) highlight three interventions designed to improve the organisation–environment fit: open-systems planning; integrated strategic change; and trans-organisational development.

- Open-systems planning is an intervention designed to help an organisation systematically assess its environment and develop strategic responses to it.
- Integrated strategic change interventions are directed towards integrating strategic planning and operational and tactical actions.
- Trans-organisational development is an intervention that focuses on the creation of beneficial partnerships with other organisations to perform tasks or solve problems that are beyond the capability of a single organisation.

Another sub-category of strategic interventions are those that focus more directly on changing the organisation's culture and mental models. They involve diagnosing the existing culture and assessing the cultural risks associated with planned changes.

Exercise 16.1

Review some of the change programmes that have been pursued within your organisation and consider the types of intervention used. Do they all tend to fall within one or two of the categories reviewed in this chapter or have a wide range of different types of intervention been employed?

SUMMARY

This chapter has adopted two contrasting typologies to provide a brief overview of the wide range of interventions available to change agents.

References

Bertalanfy, L. von (1971) *General Systems Theory*, Harmondsworth: Penguin.

Cartwright, D. (1951) 'Achieving Change in People: Some Applications of Group Dynamics Theory', *Human Relations*, 4(2), pp. 381–92.

Cummings, T.G. and Worley, C.G. (2001) *Organisational Development and Change*, 6th edn, Cincinnati, Ohio: South-Western.

Dannemiller, K.D. and Jacobs, R.W. (1992) 'Changing the Way Organizations Change: A Revolution of Common Sense', *Journal of Applied Behavioural Science*, 28(3), pp. 480–98.

Fritz, R. (1984) *The Path of Least Resistance*, Salem, Mass.: DMA Inc.

Jacobs, R. (1994) *Real Time Strategic Change*, San Francisco: Berrett-Koehler.

Jayaram, G. (1977) 'Open Systems Planning', in T. Cummings and S. Srivastra (eds), *Management at Work; A Socio-Technical Systems Approach*, San Diego: University Associates.

Likert, R. (1961) *New Patterns of Management*, New York: McGraw-Hill.

Lippitt, R. (1983) 'Future Before You Plan', in R.A. Ritvo and A.G. Sargent (eds), *The NTL Managers' Handbook*, Arlington, Va.: NTL Institute.

Trist, E.L. (1969) 'On Socio-Technical Systems', in W.G. Bennis, K.D. Benne and R. Chin (eds), *The Planning of Change*, New York: Holt, Rinehart & Winston, pp. 269–82.

Weisbord, M. (1987) *Productive Workplaces: Organising and Managing for Dignity, Meaning and Community*, San Francisco: Jossey-Bass.

Weisbord, M. (1989) *Building Productive Workplaces: Change Strategies for the 21st Century*. Blue Sky Videos.

17

Selecting interventions

This chapter examines the factors that need to be considered when selecting which type of intervention to use. Consideration is also given to the factors that can affect decisions regarding the sequencing of interventions in those circumstances where it might be necessary to use more that one type of intervention. This is important because sometimes an inappropriate sequence can undermine the effectiveness of a change programme.

FACTORS INDICATING WHICH INTERVENTIONS TO USE

Consideration is given first to those factors that need to be taken into account when deciding which interventions are likely to contribute most to achieving the goals of a change programme. Attention is given to three main factors: the nature of the problem or opportunity that the intervention has to address (diagnosed issue), the level of change target (individual, group and so forth) that is to be the focus for change, and the depth of intervention required. Two additional factors are also considered: the time available for the change, and the efficacy of different types of interventions.

Diagnosed issue

A key determinant of the appropriate intervention is the nature of the diagnosed problem or opportunity. This underpins the aim of the change programme and indicates the issues that have to be attended to in order to move an organisation or unit from the current position to a more desirable future state.

At a *macro level* the issue might be defined in terms of either transformational or incremental change. Where the issue is defined in terms of a need for *transformational change*, Burke and Litwin (1992) suggest that the most effective interventions will be those that are targeted at changing system-wide elements such as mission and strategy, leadership and culture. Interventions that successfully change these elements will have knock-on effects that will affect just about every other element in the system.

On the other hand, where the issue is defined in terms of *incremental change* (or fine-tuning) the most effective interventions may be those that address elements that, if changed, might have a more localised impact in terms of units or levels affected. These include interventions targeted at elements such as structure, systems, climate, tasks and roles. For example, the focal issue might be to improve task performance in a particular department. The intervention selected to address this issue might be work redesign. Redesigning the work to improve task performance may affect other elements of the departmental organisation (such as the competencies required of those who do the work or departmental structure if redesigning the work involves reducing the number of levels in the hierarchy). However, this kind of intervention may have relatively little impact on how the entire organisation functions, even if it does have some implications for how the target unit interacts with related units.

At a *micro level*, issues might simply be defined in terms of the organisational elements that are most closely associated with the diagnosed problem or opportunity. The 12 elements of the Burke–Litwin model could provide a basis for classifying issues in this way. An alternative, used in the three-dimensional model presented below, is the typology used by Cummings and Worley (2001) to classify interventions. This model points to four broad types of diagnosed issue:

- Human-process issues which include communicating, problem-solving, decision-making, interpersonal and intergroup interactions, and leadership.
- Technology and structural issues which include horizontal and vertical differentiation, coordination, technology and production processes, and work design.
- Human-resource issues which include attracting, selecting, developing, motivating and retaining competent people.
- Strategic issues which include managing the interface between the organisation and its environment, and deciding which markets to engage in, what products and services to produce, how to gain competitive advantage and what values should guide the organisation's development.

Level of change target

Schmuck and Miles (1971), Blake and Mouton (1986), Pugh (1986) and others all include the individual, group, intergroup and organisation in their classifications of units that can be the target for change. Blake and Mouton also include the larger social system as the potential client or target for change and Schmuck and Miles include dyads/triads as a separate unit.

In the three-dimensional model for selecting interventions presented below the four *levels* are individual, group, intergroup and organisation. A diagnostic analysis might indicate that the critical issue has to do with a mismatch between task demands and individual competencies, suggesting that the target for change is at the individual level. Alternatively, the diagnosis might point to poor working relationships within a group, indicating that the group should be the target for change. Another possibility is that the diagnosis focuses on poor relationships between groups, suggesting that intergroup relations should be the target. At the level of the organisation the diagnosis may suggest that organisational strategy is not matched to market conditions or is not properly appreciated by organisational members at all levels, indicating that the target for change is the whole organisation.

Depth of intervention required

Harrison (1970) argues that the depth of individual emotional involvement can be a key factor in determining whether an intervention will be effective. This factor is concerned with the extent to which core areas of personality or self are the focus of change events. He posits a dimension running from surface to deep levels. Interventions that focus on external aspects of an individual and deal with the more public and observable aspects of behaviour are located at the surface end of the continuum. Interventions that touch on personal and private perceptions, attitudes or feelings and attempt to affect them are located at the deep end.

Operations research is an example of an intervention that can be classified at the surface end of the continuum because it is a process of rational analysis that deals with roles and functions without paying much attention to the individual characteristics of the persons occupying these roles. An example of a deeper intervention is management by objectives. This involves a boss and subordinate establishing mutually agreed goals for performance, and monitoring performance against these goals. Typically the exchange of information is limited to that which is observable. Further along the continuum are interventions such as management counselling that, for example, involve a consultant working with managers to increase their awareness of how their personality, role relationships and previous experience affect their management style. Deeper interventions might involve members of a group discussing with peers the interpersonal processes that affect their contribution to group performance. This kind of intervention can involve group members sharing very personal information about themselves, how they perceive their own behaviour and the behaviour of others and exploring with them how they and others might modify their attitudes, roles and behaviour to improve group performance.

Harrison argues that as the level of intervention becomes deeper, the information needed to intervene becomes less available. For example, the information needed by the operations researcher is easily obtained because it is often a matter of record, and the information required by those engaged in management by objectives can often be observed. However, people may not be prepared to freely discuss their attitudes and feeling towards others, or to be open to feedback from others about their own interpersonal style. These considerations led Harrison to suggest that *change agents should intervene at a level no deeper than that required to produce an enduring solution to the problem at hand.*

However, this criterion, while necessary, is not sufficient for determining the depth of intervention. While the change agent may have a view about the nature of the information required and the depth of intervention necessary to produce this information, the change target (individual, group or system) may not be comfortable working at this level. Harrison argues that any intervention, if it is to be successful, must be legitimised in the norms of the group or organisation and must be seen to relate to the felt needs of organisational members. This led him to suggest a second criterion; *intervene at a level no deeper than that at which the energy and resources of the client can be committed to problem-solving and change.*

Harrison suggests that in those circumstances where the change agents suspect that the required information is located at a depth greater than that at which the client is comfortable working, they should resolve the dilemma by selecting an intervention on the basis of the second criterion. Once the client has gained confidence they may be prepared to engage in an intervention that will involve the sharing of information such as attitudes and feelings that they would normally regard as private and confidential.

A three-dimensional model to aid choice

The factors considered so far can be combined to produce a three dimensional model that can be used as a rough guide to the type of intervention that might be most effective in a given situation. This is presented in Figure 17.1. Figures 17.2–17.5 provide examples for each of the four types of diagnosed issue.

Some cells in Figures 17.2–17.5 are blank because they represent situations that are unlikely to call for an intervention that complies with all three criteria. For example, there may not be many (any?) situations that call for a deep-level techno-structural intervention targeted at the individual.

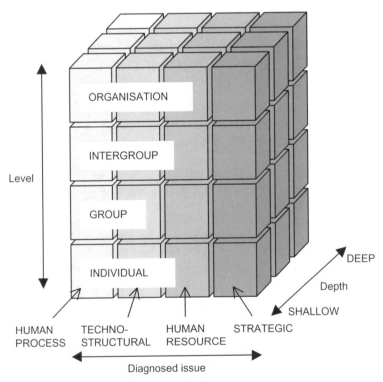

Figure 17.1 A three-dimensional model to aid choice of interventions

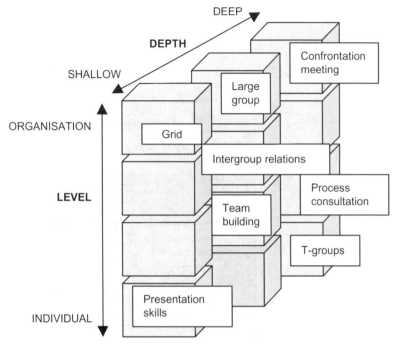

Figure 17.2 Examples of human-process interventions

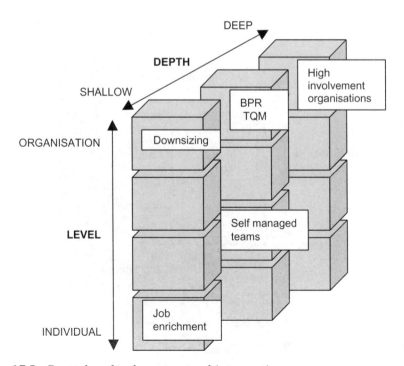

Figure 17.3 Examples of techno-structural interventions

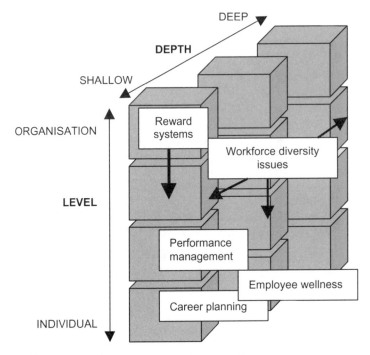

Figure 17.4 Examples of human-resource interventions

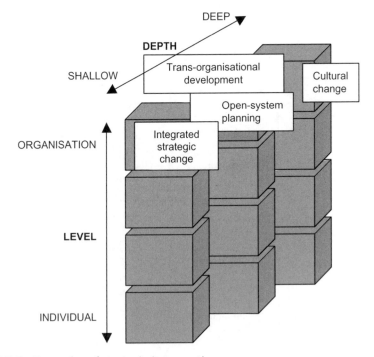

Figure 17.5 Examples of strategic interventions

On the other hand, some interventions could appear in more than one cell. Team-building, for example, is a human-process intervention that is targeted at the group. In terms of depth, however, some team building interventions are shallow and others rather deep. At the shallow end, interventions might only be concerned with agreeing the purpose of the group, indicators of effective performance and performance strategies that could contribute to achieving this level of performance. On the other hand, at the deep end interventions could involve an exploration of interpersonal relationships and how these promote or undermine performance.

Figures 17.2–17.5 only contain a sample of the interventions that are available to change agents. The literature on the management of change is a rich source of other possibilities.

Two additional factors might also influence choice of intervention.

Time available to implement change

Where the need for change is urgent and the stakes are high, there may be insufficient time to employ some of the more time-consuming interventions that offer organisational members the opportunity to be involved in deciding what needs to be changed or how the change will be achieved. It might be necessary to restrict choice to those interventions that can be implemented quickly and this might, for example, involve the use of experts who can rapidly prescribe solutions. Prescriptive/directive interventions can be effective, especially over the short term and where organisational members recognise the need for this kind of action. However, there is always the possibility that organisational members may resent the way the change was managed, experience little sense of ownership of the process or the outcome and therefore may only go along with the change so long as their behaviour is being closely supervised and there is a perceived threat of sanctions for non-compliance. Where the need for change is less pressing the change agent may be able to consider a much wider range of interventions.

Efficacy of interventions

A basic question that needs to be addressed when considering whether or not to choose a particular intervention is 'will it produce the intended result?' Some very popular interventions are not always as effective as many would like to believe. There are frequent reports in academic journals and the business press indicating disappointment with the outcome of major change programmes that have involved interventions such as business process reengineering (BPR), total quality management (TQM), job design or interpersonal skills training.

Sometimes the problem is that the change agents select an ineffective intervention. This kind of problem can be avoided by seeking evidence about the efficacy of interventions from reports, colleagues and elsewhere. Often, however, the problem is not that the intervention is ineffective, but that its success is dependent on a number of contingent factors. In these circumstances it is important to take account of these factors when selecting interventions. There are many examples of interventions that are affected by contingent variables.

T-group training is a form of social skills training which provides participants with an opportunity to increase their awareness about themselves and their impact on others in order to learn how to function more effectively in groups. Some of the early evidence on the effectiveness of T-groups indicated that they can be very effective. Cooper and Mangham (1971), for example, report that they can improve skills in diagnosing individual and group behaviour, lead to clearer communication, greater tolerance and consideration and greater action skill and flexibility. However, other reports suggest that while there is evidence of learning and behaviour change, this may not always be transferred to the work situation. Transfer is dependent on a number of factors, one of which is the match between the structures and norms that characterise the work and training situations. The closer the match the greater the transfer, and vice versa.

Job design is another example. It is often presented as the universal answer to low commitment and poor performance in situations where people are required to perform repetitive, sort-cycle, simple tasks. Motivation theory suggests that people will be more committed and will perform best when they are engaged in varied and challenging work that (a) provides feedback about how well they are doing, (b) allows them to feel personally responsible for outcomes, and (c) offers them the possibility of producing outcomes that are perceived to be worthwhile and meaningful. In practice, job design has been found to be very effective in some circumstances and not in others. One of the most important contingent variables related to the success of this intervention is the level of need that employees are seeking to satisfy at work. Job design appears to be most effective where employees are seeking to satisfy higher-order needs for personal growth and development at work.

Total quality management (TQM) is an organisation-wide, long-term change effort designed to orient all of an organisation's activities around the concept of quality. Cummings and Worley (2001) report that in the USA a survey of Fortune 1000 companies showed that about 75 per cent of them have implemented some form of TQM. They also report that the overwhelming majority (83 per cent) rate their experience with TQM as either positive or very positive. However, other reports of the success of TQM initiatives are less optimistic. Crosby (1979), for example, asserts that over 90 per cent of TQM interventions by US companies fail, and Burnes (1996) lists a number of studies that suggest that European companies have experienced a similar rate of failure. It is not immediately obvious why TQM interventions are very successful in some settings and less so in others, but one possibility relates to the attitude of top management. In those settings where TQM is viewed in instrumental terms, for example as a way of gaining a kitemark such as ISO 9000 that will provide competitive advantage, it may be less successful than where there is a genuine commitment to routinely meeting or exceeding customer expectations. Where the aim is merely to gain a kitemark, organisational members may experience the intervention as a requirement to comply with a new set of rules. This may have little long-term affect on their values and attitudes towards customers. Also, once the kitemark has been secured, top management may shift attention elsewhere, and any movement towards a more customer-focused culture may be short-lived.

Occasions where there is a need to use more than one type of intervention

Often because of the nature of the problem or opportunity, systemic interdependencies and the need to maintain alignment it may not be possible to think in terms of selecting a single intervention to respond to an isolated issue. For example, the recognition of a new opportunity and the decision, by senior management, to intervene in order to develop a strategy to exploit it might require a range of further interventions. The organisation may have to introduce a new technology, adapt its structures and systems, introduce new management practices, redesign tasks, reallocate employees to new roles and provide training to equip people to perform as required. The change agent has to decide whether to pursue all of them simultaneously or to sequence them in some way.

SEQUENCING INTERVENTIONS

The organisation's capacity to cope with change is often limited, and consequently decisions have to be made about priorities and the sequencing of interventions. Several factors can influence these decisions, including the overall purpose or intention of the change, organisational politics, the need for an early success, the stakes involved, and the dynamics of change.

1 *Intent.* Where the intention is to transform the organisation, interventions that address the transformational variables, such as mission and strategy, leadership and culture, need to be given priority (see above and Chapter 7 on diagnostic models). Where, on the other hand, the intention is to seek an incremental change, the focus of attention might be on the transactional variables identified by Burke and Litwin, such as structure, management practices, systems, work climate and so on.

2 *Politics.* The change agent needs to be aware of how political factors can affect who is prepared to support different kinds of intervention. Some of the issues that relate to this have been considered elsewhere (for example, Chapter 9 on power, leadership and stake holder management, Chapter 11 on motivating others to change, and earlier in this chapter when factors influencing the depth of intervention were considered). Other issues include:

   ● *Professional orientation.* Many managers have been socialised over the course of their training and work experience to focus attention on certain variables rather than others. For example, many managers are more comfortable with and give priority to interventions that focus on changing structures, technology, and manufacturing and information systems rather than with interventions that focus on 'softer' people issues.

   ● *Fashion and fad* can influence choice of intervention. In the 1990s many managers were keen to adopt certain interventions, such as performance-related pay, in order to be seen as progressive and attuned to the latest developments. Change agents who propose favoured interventions might receive more encouragement than those who propose an intervention that has 'gone out of fashion', even if is the most appropriate intervention to deal with the issue at hand.

● *Past experience with certain interventions.* Change agents who have a track record of success with certain interventions may be more inclined to recommend their use than interventions they are less familiar with. While it may be wise to take account of a change agent's skills and experience, other factors also need to be considered. Just because a change agent is skilled at hammering does not mean that nails are the only means of 'fixing things'. There may well be occasions when 'screws or glue' may be much more effective.

3 *Need for an early success.* It has already been noted in Chapter 9 that long-term change efforts can slow down if people lose their initial sense of urgency. One way of countering this is to select problems and interventions that offer the promise of some early successes.

4 *Stakes involved.* Priority needs to be given to those interventions that can resolve issues that threaten the survival of the organisation. Where survival is not an issue, priority might still be given to issues where the potential gains and losses are relatively high.

5 *Dynamics of change.* In some circumstances the dynamics of change may suggest that the best way to proceed is to adopt an indirect approach rather than addressing the prime issue or change target first.

● *Causal links.* Consideration needs to be given to causal links and the relative strength of the interrelationships between the elements of the organisational system. The Burke–Litwin model points to the relative strength of high-level elements such as strategy, leadership and culture, over lower-level elements such as structure, systems and management practices. While culture and systems can affect one another, culture is seen to have a stronger influence over systems than vice versa. This kind of consideration can influence which elements are selected as the initial targets for change, thereby influencing the sequencing of interventions.

● *The effect of groups on individuals.* A related dynamic relationship that can affect the sequencing of interventions is the effect that the group can exert over individual behaviour (this was discussed in Chapter 16). Research evidence suggests that there may be occasions when the most effective way of changing individual behaviour is to intervene at the level of the group. Group-level interventions, such as team-building activities designed to produce a more cohesive group that has high prestige in the eyes of other organisational members, might *motivate* individuals to change their behaviour to support group goals. A follow-up intervention might involve training selected individuals to provide them with the *competencies* they might need to make a more effective contribution to group performance. If individual training had been the first intervention it might only have had limited success because of low member motivation. After a group-level intervention, individual members might be much more highly motivated to acquire the competencies that will enable them to play a full and active part in the work of the group.

● *The effect of attitudes on behaviour and vice versa.* There have been many debates about whether the most effective route to lasting change is to target attitudes and values first or behaviour first. While there is support for the view that strongly held values and attitudes influence behaviour, the evidence that interventions targeted at values and attitudes can change behaviour is more equivocal. An alternative view is that the most effective route to lasting change is to intervene to create conditions that require people to behave differently because over the longer term attitudes and values will be realigned with the new behaviour.

Porter, Lawler and Hackman (1975) offer a third way. They suggest that an effective route to change is to intervene in ways that simultaneously modify structures (in order to create the conditions that will elicit new and desired behaviours) *and* modify interpersonal processes (to address issues of managerial style, attitudes and the social climate of the organisation). This approach employs structural interventions to support intrapersonal and interpersonal learning. They suggest that structural interventions might include:

- □ modifying work structures in order to change how individual employees actually spend most of their time;
- □ modifying control structures in order to determine what individuals attend to; and
- □ modifying reward structures in order to influence what individuals will do when they have choice.

While there are no hard and fast rules about whether interventions should address interpersonal processes or structures first, there is a growing body of opinion that intervening to change one without the other is less effective than intervening to change both.

Exercise 17.1 Choice of interventions

Review some of the change programmes that have been pursued within your organisation and, with reference to the content of this chapter, critically assess the choice of interventions. Are you able to identify occasions when inappropriate interventions have been used? Give reasons and suggest interventions that might have been more effective.

SUMMARY

There is no easy formula that can be used to identify the most effective intervention for all types of situation. However, there are some useful principles that can be applied to aid the selection of appropriate interventions and assist with decisions about how they should be sequenced.

This chapter has reviewed some of the factors that need to be considered when selecting interventions. The main factors (diagnosed problem, level of change target and depth of intervention) have been integrated into a three-dimensional model to aid choice. Attention has also been given to the factors that can affect the sequencing of interventions. These include intent or purpose of the change, organisational politics and how they affect the support for different interventions, the need for an early success to maintain motivation, the stakes involved and causal links that affect the dynamics of change.

References

Blake, R.R. and Mouton, J.S. (1986) *Consultation, A Handbook for Individual and Organization Development*, 2nd edn, Reading, Mass.: Addison-Wesley.

Burke, W.W. and Litwin, G.H. (1992) 'A Causal Model of Organizational Performance and Change', *Journal of Management*, 18(3), pp. 523–45.

Burnes, B. (1996) *Managing Change: A Strategic Approach to Organisational Dynamics*, 2nd edn, London: Pitman.

Cooper, C.L. and Mangham, I.L. (1971) *T-groups: A Survey of Research*, London: Wiley.

Crosby, P.B. (1979) *Quality is Free*, New York: McGraw-Hill.

Cummings, T.G. and Worley, C.G. (2001) *Organisational Development and Change*, 7th edn, Cincinnati, Ohio: South-Western.

Harrison, R. (1970) 'Choosing the Depth of Organizational Interventions', *Journal of Applied Behavioral Science*, 6(2), pp.182–202.

Porter, L.W., Lawler, E.E. and Hackman, J.R. (1975) *Behavior in Organizations*, London: McGraw-Hill.

Pugh, D. (1986) *Planning and Managing Change*, Milton Keynes: The Open University Business School.

Schmuck, R.A. and Miles, M.B. (1971), *Organization Development in Schools*, Palo Alto, Cal.: National Press Books.

Part VI

Keeping the change on track

Managing change involves implementing and, where necessary, modifying plans to move the organisation towards a more desirable state. Issues associated with maintaining control during the implementation phase have already been highlighted in Chapter 15, and other issues that need to be addressed if change plans are to be successfully implemented have been considered in Chapters 9 to 17.

Chapter 18 addresses some other issues associated with managing, reviewing and sustaining change.

18

Managing, reviewing and sustaining change

This chapter focuses special attention on how the process of reviewing progress can provide change managers with feedback that they can use to assess whether interventions are being implemented as intended, whether the chosen interventions are having the desired effect and whether the change plan continues to be valid. The utility of the Balanced Scorecard as a template for designing a system for managing change is also discussed.

MANAGING THE IMPLEMENTATION STAGE OF THE CHANGE PROCESS

It was noted in Chapter 5 that there are two main approaches to implementation:

- *Implementing blueprint change.* In the case of blueprint change the desired end state is known in advance and change managers are in a position to formulate a clear plan of action to achieve this vision. Implementation involves rolling out this plan, monitoring the effect of interventions and taking corrective action as and when required in order to ensure that the desired end state is achieved. Change managers do not typically think in terms of reexamining the validity of the blueprint or the assumptions that underpin the change plan designed to achieve the desired end state.

  The learning associated with this kind of change tends to be restricted to single-loop learning. Assumptions about what needs to be changed and assumptions about how the change will be achieved tend to go unchallenged unless the feedback from implementation is so unexpected that it shocks the change managers into making a radical reassessment.
- *Implementing evolutionary change.* In the case of evolutionary change it may be difficult or impossible to specify an end point in advance. Change managers

have to develop an implementation plan on the basis of broadly defined goals and a general direction for change. Sometimes, because of a high rate of change in the operating environment, ideas about the desired future state have to be constantly revised, even in those cases where the original vision has only been defined in the broadest of terms.

In such circumstances change managers have to adopt a very open-ended approach to planning and implementation. Managing evolutionary change involves taking tentative incremental steps and, after each step, reviewing the intervention(s) that constituted that step (did it/they work as planned?) and the general direction of change (does it still hold good or does it need to be revised?). This questioning of the validity of the desired future state and the plan for achieving it calls for double-loop learning.

MONITORING THE IMPLEMENTATION OF THE CHANGE PLAN

A plan for change reflects a set of hypotheses about cause and effect. Kaplan and Norton (1996) view the measurement and review process as a means of making these hypothesised relationships explicit. They argue that once they are more clearly articulated and widely understood the change process can be more easily managed. The process of managing change involves validating or, where necessary, revising the assumptions and hypotheses that underpin the change plan. The desired future state (vision) is reflected in the outcome measures embedded in the change plan. Performance drivers are the variables that determine whether the desired outcome will be achieved. Specifying these in the change plan signals to organisational members what they need to do in order to contribute to the achievement of the desired future state.

Some of the questions that need to be addressed when managing change and validating the hypothesised cause and effect relationships that underpin the change plan are considered below.

Are interventions being implemented as intended?

Sometimes it is more difficult than anticipated to roll out a plan for change. The change manager may respond by reviewing the situation and identifying those factors that have hindered implementation first time round. These might include a lack of commitment and motivation on the part of those immediately affected by a proposed intervention, a lack of political support from those in a position to champion or sabotage the change, or insufficient resources to ensure that the change initiative gets the attention it requires. The content of previous chapters points to ways of addressing these kinds of problem.

Are interventions producing the desired effect?

Change managers need to be alert to the possibility that while the intervention might have been implemented as intended, it might not be producing the effect that was anticipated. An example might illustrate this possibility and indicate ways in which the change manager might address the situation:

- A company might be losing market share because it is lagging behind competitors in the time it takes to bring new products to market.
- A factor contributing to this predicament might be diagnosed as the high level of conflict between members of the product engineering department (responsible for developing new products) and members of the production engineering department (responsible for developing the manufacturing system required to produce a new product).
- Informed by this diagnosis, the change manager might send members of both departments on a variety of external courses to learn about intergroup dynamics and the management of conflict.
- After monitoring the effect of this intervention, the change manager might discover that while members of both departments are much more aware of constructive ways of behaving in conflict situations, this awareness has had little effect on the level of manifest conflict between the two departments.

An initial response might be to explore ways of modifying the original intervention in order to make it more effective. In this example, attempts to modify the intervention to improve its efficacy might involve finding ways of improving the transfer of learning from the training activity to the work situation:

- Rather than sending people on external courses the change manager might decide to facilitate an in-house confrontation meeting that involves members of both departments working together to identify ways of managing their differences in a more constructive way.

If modifying the original intervention in this way still fails to produce the desired effect on the targeted performance driver (the quality of interdepartmental relationships), the change manager might begin to question the assumed cause and effect relationship between poor conflict management skills and high levels of interdepartmental conflict.

As a result of this questioning the change manager might identify other possible causes of the immediate problem (high levels of interdepartmental conflict) and consider ways of modifying the change plan to include interventions that target them.

- It might be found that the original diagnosis was valid in so far as it identified the level of inter-departmental conflict as a major cause of delay in getting new products to market (and, therefore, of loss of market share). However, it may have been flawed when it focused on poor conflict management skills as the root cause of this damaging behaviour. It may be that the conflict management skills of departmental members have little or no effect on the level of conflict and the quality of interdepartmental relationships.
- A re-examination of the situation might suggest that the main source of conflict is rooted in the way the company is structured. This broad heading could include a number of possible causal factors. One might be the siting of

departments in locations that make it difficult for members of one department to communicate on a face-to-face basis with members of the other. Another might be mis-aligned performance criteria that results in competing sets of priorities in the two departments.

This questioning of the taken-for-granted cause and effect assumptions involves a process of double-loop learning.

Is the change plan still valid?

There may be occasions when the interventions have been implemented as intended and they have produced the desired effect. However, this chain of events may have had little or no impact on overall organisational performance. This kind of outcome poses another challenge to the validity of the change plan and the hypothesised cause and effect relationships on which it is based. Faced with this kind of outcome, the change manager may decide to embark on a further reexamination of the original diagnosis and the causal models that were used to inform the design of the change plan.

- This further reexamination might reveal that, despite what many managers in the company accept as given wisdom, the time it takes to get new products to market has had little effect on the gradual decline in market share. Further investigations might suggest that customers are more concerned about other value propositions such as product reliability, price and so on, and might feel that competitors are better able to satisfy their needs in these areas.
- It may be, on the other hand, that the further investigations reveal that the original diagnosis was correct at the time, but has been overtaken by new developments (for example, changes in customer requirements) that challenge its validity, with obvious implications for the change plan.

There may also be (hopefully many) occasions when the interventions have been implemented as intended, where they have produced the desired effect and where this has had a positive impact on organisational performance. This kind of positive outcome signals a need to consolidate this achievement and use it, as appropriate, as a basis for achieving further improvements in performance.

THE ROLE OF PERFORMANCE MEASURES IN THE MANAGEMENT OF CHANGE

Some of the issues that encourage or inhibit learning have been considered in Chapter 4; this chapter focuses attention on how the cycle of monitoring, reviewing, planning, acting and further reviewing can facilitate double-loop learning during the process of managing change. Central to this process is the collecting and feeding back of information about how interventions affect performance.

Attention has already been given to some of the different ways in which performance can be measured (Chapter 2), and it is essential that performance measures should be related to the outcomes that are important to key stakeholders and to the hypotheses about cause and effect relationships that are embedded in the change plan. Without the feedback that such measures can provide, change managers will be unable to monitor what is going on and determine what further action may be required to successfully implement the change plan.

Approaches to measuring performance

It was noted in Chapter 15 that many control systems are designed to reward current practice and offer little incentive for people to invest effort in changing the organisation to promote long-term effectiveness. Even in those organisations where change is given a high priority, the monitoring and feedback process may only focus attention on a limited set of performance measures. Many organisations direct most of their attention to financial measures, and often too little attention is given to other performance indicators that relate to important outcomes and key cause and effect relationships that are central to the change plan.

One of the early attempts to widen the base of performance monitoring on an organisation-wide and systematic basis was the development, by Analog Devices, of a 'Corporate Scorecard'; this included, alongside a number of traditional financial measures, measures of customer delivery time, quality and cycle times of manufacturing processes, and effectiveness of new product development. This, and other similar experiments, encouraged Kaplan and Norton (1996) to develop what is now referred to as the 'Balanced Scorecard'.

THE BALANCED SCORECARD

The Balanced Scorecard integrates financial measures of past performance with measures of the 'drivers' of future performance. It provides a template that can be adapted to provide the information that change managers need to monitor and review the effects of their interventions and to plan what they might do next to move the organisation towards a more desirable future state. The scorecard includes four categories of measure: financial, customer, internal business process, and innovation and learning.

- *Financial measures*, such as return on investment, economic value added, sales growth and generation of cash flow, summarise the economic consequences of past actions. This financial perspective considers how the organisation needs to appear to its shareholders if it is to achieve its vision.
- *Customer-related measures* include indicators of business performance that relate to the customer and market segments that are important to the organisation. Examples include measures of satisfaction, retention, new customer acquisition, customer profitability, account share and market share. They might also include measures of those performance drivers that affect the value propositions that influence customer loyalty, such as on-time delivery and product innovation. This customer perspective considers how the organisation needs to appear to its customers if it is to achieve its vision.

● *Internal business process measures* such as quality, response time and cost relate to the internal business processes that make a critical contribution to the organisation's current and future performance. They might measure the performance of the processes that enable the organisation to deliver value propositions that attract and retain important customers, that satisfy shareholders by contributing to the delivery of excellent financial returns or that deliver other important outcomes to key stakeholders.

● *Measures of the infrastructure that facilitates long-term growth and improvement.* Kaplan and Norton (1996) argue that organisational learning and growth comes from three principle sources: people, systems and organisational procedures. They suggest that the financial, customer and internal-business-process objectives on the Balanced Scorecard typically reveal large gaps between the existing capabilities of people, systems and procedures and the capability that is required to achieve a performance breakthrough. In order to transform an organisation (or even to achieve a more modest level of change) these gaps have to be addressed. This can involve intervening in the normal process of organisational functioning to enhance this infrastructure and improve the organisation's capacity for innovation and learning.

Figure 18.1 illustrates how the Balanced Scorecard can be used as a framework to translate a change strategy into operational terms.

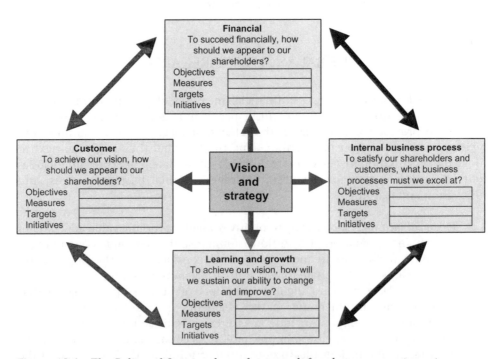

Figure 18.1   The Balanced Scorecard as a framework for change management

Source: Adapted from Kaplan, P. and Norton, D.P., 'Using the Balanced Scorecard as a Strategic Management System', *Harvard Business Review*, Jan.–Feb. 1996, p. 76.

DEVELOPING TOOLS TO HELP WITH IMPLEMENTATION

The Balanced Scorecard can be used as a change management tool to clarify and gain consensus about the change strategy. Translating the vision and change strategy into an agreed set of operational goals is likely to stimulate a debate that will ensure that the change management team develop a shared understanding of what they are seeking to achieve. Specifying operational goals can also help the change management team think about their plan for change in systemic terms and it can assist them develop a shared view of how and why the various change goals are related in terms of cause and effect.

The feedback that this kind of tool can provide on how the organisation (or unit of an organisation) is performing will enable change managers to test the validity of the cause and effect relationships embedded in the change plan. Kaplan and Norton (1996) cite the example of Echo Engineering where change managers were able to test and validate their assumption that employee morale was a key performance driver. They found that employee morale correlated with a number of important performance indicators; for example, the most satisfied customers were those who were served by the employees with highest morale. They also found that the most satisfied customers were the ones who settled their accounts in the shortest period.

Haskett, Jones and Loveman (1994) report a whole sequence of linkages that they found highlighted key performance drivers that contributed to important financial outcomes such as profitability and revenue growth. These are summarised in Figure 18.2.

Management tools such as the Balanced Scorecard can also help change managers communicate the plan for change throughout the organisation and can provide a framework for consultation and debate about what a more desirable future state will look like and what needs to happen if it is to be achieved. This kind of management tool can also help to ensure that the range of change initiatives that might be started in different units and at different levels in the organisation will be aligned to contribute to the strategic goals of the change programme.

The Balanced Scorecard is presented here as one example of a tool that can help change managers manage the change process. In any change programme plans have to be operationalised and communicated widely, and furthermore, targets for change have to be specified as clearly as possible if progress is to be monitored and if the change plan is to be kept under review and adjusted as circumstances require.

SUSTAINING THE CHANGE

Managing change rarely involves moving from one steady state to another, and the goal of 're-freezing' in Lewin's three-stage model (see Chapter 5) should not be regarded as establishing/ossifying the organisation in a new steady state that will last indefinitely. However, the goal of the change normally involves more than just *reaching* a desired future state. The intention is usually to sustain the change, at least for a while.

If change managers fail to give sufficient attention to sustaining the change, at least until they are ready to lead the organisation into a phase of further change, the new situation may be short-lived and the organisation may drift back towards its

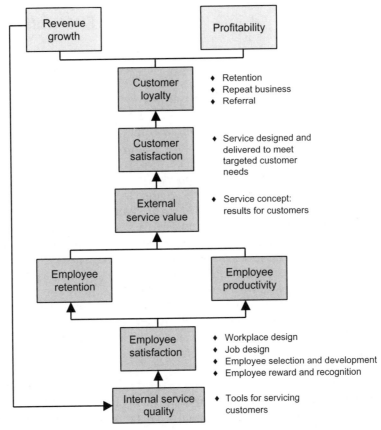

Figure 18.2 Cause and effect relationships in the service–profit chain

Source: Adapted from Heskett, J.L., Jones, T.O. and Loveman, G.W., 'Putting the Service–Profit Chain to Work', *Harvard Business Review*, March–April 1994, p. 166.

previous condition. Change managers can help to sustain a change by helping the operational managers (who will have ongoing responsibility for day-to-day management) design and introduce feedback mechanisms that they can use for themselves to monitor and manage the situation over the longer term.

SUMMARY

This chapter has considered how monitoring and reviewing the implementation of the change plan can help managers adjust and adapt the plan for change to help ensure that the organisation moves towards a more desirable future state. Attention has been given to the kind of information change managers need in order to, at one level, determine whether interventions are being implemented as intended and assess whether they are having the anticipated effect and, at a higher level, to assess whether the change plan continues to be valid. Assessing the continued validity of the change plan, and updating it as required, is especially important when managing evolutionary-type change.

It has been argued that change managers need to identify measures of organisational effectiveness that relate to those outcomes that are important to the organisation's long-term survival and growth. This might involve attending to more than just the short-term interests of shareholders.

It has also been argued that, when monitoring the effectiveness of interventions, attention needs to be paid to the hypotheses of cause and effect that have influenced the design of the change plan. Where feedback raises questions about the validity of these hypothesised relationships the change manager needs to review the change plan and consider whether alternative ways of intervening to move the organisation towards a more desirable future state might be more effective. The Balanced Scorecard has been considered as an example of a management tool that can help the manager attend to these points when managing change.

References

Heskett, J.L., Jones, T.O. and Loveman, G.W. (1994) 'Putting the Service–Profit Chain to Work', *Harvard Business Review*, March–April.

Kaplan, P. and Norton, D.P. (1996) *The Balanced Scorecard*, Boston, Mass.: Harvard Business School Press.

Author index

Adams, J. 151, (158)
Argyris, C. 40, (46), 128
Arnold, J. (143)
Athos, A. 78, 80, (88)

Bales, R.F. 94, (100)
Balogun, J. 163, 164–5, (165)
Barrington, H. 124, (127)
Beak, J. (158)
Beckhard, R. 52, (58), 166, 167, 168, (171)
Beer, M. 16, (22)
Bertalanfy, L. von 179, (186)
Blake, R.R. 188, (198)
Bridges, W. 150, (158)
Briner, R. (143)
Brown, S.L. 7, (10)
Buchanan, D.A. 56, (58)
Burke, W.W. 7, (10), 78, 84–6, (87), 90, 97, (100), 187, 194, (198)
Burnes, B. 18, (22), 25, (35), (198)
Burnes, T. 24–5, (35)

Carnall, C.A. 15, (22)
Cartwright, D. 177–9, (186)
Clarkson, M.B.E. 106, (113)
Coch, L. 141, (143)
Conway, N. (143)
Cooper, C.L. 194, (198)

Covey, S.R. 43–4, (46)
Crosby P.B. 194, (198)
Cummings, T.G. 68, (70), 92, 95, (100), 182–5, (186), 187, 194, (198)

Daft, R.L 39, 41, (46)
Dannemiller, K.D. 181, (186)
Dawson, P. 52, (58)
De Geus, A. 36, (46)
Devanna, M.A. 7, (10), 108, (113)
Dickman, M. (143)
Dixon, N. 43, (46)
Doherty, N. 130, (143)
Douglas, M. 41, (46)
Duncan R. 130–1, (143), 164, (165)

Egan, G. 43, (46), 52, (58)
Eisenhardt, K.M. 7, (10)

Farr, R. 119, (121)
Fink, S.L. 150, (158)
Fiol, C.M. 41, (46)
Ford, D.J. 51, (58)
Ford, L.W. 51, (58)
Fordyce, J.K 93, (100)
Freeman, R.E. 106, (113)
French, J.R.P. 141, (143)

Fritz, R.   181, (186)
Frombrun, C.   (22)

Goffman, E.   117, (121)
Goldstein, I.L   123, (127)
Goodman P.S.   15, (22)
Grundy, T.   107, (113)
Guest, D.   128–9, (143)

Hackman, J.R.   99, (100), 197, (198)
Hailey, V.H.   163, 164–5, (165)
Harris, R.T.   52, (58), 166, 167, 168, (171)
Harrison, R.   189–90, (198)
Hatvany, N.G.   (22)
Hayes, J.   19, (22), 50, 52, (58), 151, 153–4, (158)
Hendry, C.   52, (58)
Herriot, P.   (143)
Heskett, J.L.   207–8, (209)
Holmes, T.H.   146–7, 148, (158)
Hopson, B.   151, (158)
Hornstein, H.A.   72, (88)
Horsted, J.   130, (143)
Hyde, P.   50, 52, (58), 151, 153–4, (158)

Jacobs, R.W.   181, (186)
Janis, I.L.   43, (46)
Jawahar, I.M.   106, (113)
Jayaram, G.   181, (186)
Jick, T.D.   (58)
Johnson, G.   38, 42, (46)
Jones, T.O.   207–8, (209)

Kahn, R.L.   31, (35)
Kantor, R.M.   52, (58)
Katz, D.   31, (35)
Kidd, J.   (143)
Kirkpatrick, D.L.   126, (127)
Kottter, J.P.   7, 9, (10), 12, 26–9, (35), 36, 37, 81–3, (87), 108–12, (113). 130–1, 140–2, (143), 161, 163, (165)

Lank, A.G.   36, (46)
Lank, E.A.   36, (46)
Lawler, E.   99, (100), 197, (198)
Lawrence, P.R.   24–5, (35)
Leavitt, H.J.   31, (35)
Leroy F.   41, (46)
Lewin, K.   51–2, (58), 96–7, (100), 140, 177, 207
Likert,   185, (186)
Lippitt, R.   52, (58), 180–1, (186)
Litwin, G.H.   7, (10), 78, 84–6, (87), 90, 97, (100), 187, 194, (198)
Lorch, J.W.   24–5, (35)
Loveman, G.W.   207–8, (209)
Lyles, M.   41, (46)

MacDonald, S.   115, 116, (121)
Maletz, M.C.   107, (113)
Mangham, I.L.   117–8, 119. (121), 194, (198)
Manning. W   (143)
March, J.E.   42, (46)
Marguilies, N   16, (22)
Masuda, M   146, 146, (158)
May, R.   20, (22)
McCall, M.W.   105, (113)
McLoughlin, G.L   106, (113)
Miles, M.B.   36, (46), 188, (198)
Morgan, M.A.   (22)
Mouton, J.S.   188, (198)

Nadler, D.A.   5, 6, 8, (10), 26, 28–31, (35), 36, 63–4, (70), 81–3, (87), 97, (100), 108, (113), 140, (143). 166, (171)
Newman, W.   (10)
Norton, D.P.   202, 205–6, (209)

O'Reilly, C.A.   114–17, (121)

Parkes, C.M.   145, (158)
Pascale, R.   78, 80, (88)
Penning J.M.   15, (22)
Pettigrew, A.   18, (22), 38, (46)
Piecy, N.   107, (113)
Pondy, L.R.   114–7, (121)
Porras, J   16, (22)
Porter, L.W.   26, 99, (100), 197, (198)
Pugh, D.   65, (70), (143), 188, (190)

Quinn, J.B.   37, (46), 51, (58)

Rahe, R.H.   146–7, (158)
Raia, A.P.   16, (22)
Ramanantsoa, B.   41, (46)
Reid, M.   124, (127)
Robertson, P.J.   16, (22)
Romanelli, E.   5, (10)
Rotter, J.R.   20, (22)

Schein, E. H.   39, (40)
Schlesinger, L.A.   130–1, 140–2, (143), 161, 163, (165)
Schmuck, R.A.   188, (198)
Scholes, K.   42, (46)
Schön, D.   40, (46)
Selegman, M.E.P.   21, (22)
Shaw, B.   6, 8, 63–4, (70), 108, (113)
Shaw, B.R.   107, (113)
Smith, M.   124, (127)
Stalker, G.M.   24, (35)
Stein, B.A.   (58)
Storey, J.   56, (58)
Strebel, P.   78, 79–80, (88)

Stuart, R.   (158)
Swieringa, J.   39, 43, (46)

Taddeo, K.   (158)
Tailor, F.W.   176
Tichy, N.M   7, (10), (22), 72, (88), 108, (113)
Toffler, A.   3–5, 7, (10)
Trist, E.L.   180, (186)
Tushman, M.L.   5, 7, 8, (10), 28, 31, (35), 36, 51, 78, 81, 83, (87)

Van de Ven, A.   (22)
Vroom, V.H.   132, (143)

Walsh, J.P.   43, (46)
Watson, J.   52, (58)
Weick, K.E   39, 41, 43, (46), 51, (58)
Weil, R   93, (100)
Weisbord, M.R.   43, 80–1, (88), 175–6, 180, (186)
Wesley, B.   52, (58)
Whipp, R.   18, (22), 38, (46)
Wierdsma, A.   39, 43, (46)
Wilson, D   17, (22), 32, (35)
Worley, C.G.   68, (70), 92, 95, (100), 182–5, (186), 194, (198)

Zaltman, G.   130–1, (143), 164, (165)

Subject index

adaptability 4
adaptive breakdown *see* future shock
alignment 2, 9, 13–14, 23–32, 78–84, 178, 179
analysis 95–7
  qualitative techniques 95–6
  quantitative techniques 97
anticipatory socialisation 145
assumptive world 145
attitudes, effect on behaviour 196–7

balanced scorecard 205–7
BBC staff survey 90–1, 97–8
benchmarking 14
biographies 181
boundaries 24
Bridges' model of transition 150
Burke–Litwin's causal model of organisational performance and change 84–6
business process reengineering (BPR) 184, 193

causal links 85, 196, 202–4
change
  agency 17–21
  intensity of 6
  process models of 2, 47–59
  recognising need for 54, 63–5
  relationships 67–8
  starting the process 63–70
  strategies 161–5
  triggers for 151

  types of: adaptation 8–9;
    anticipatory 8; blueprint 56,
    162–3, 167, 201;
    discontinuous 5–10, 51, 144 (*see also*
    transitions); emergent 57, 201;
    incremental 5–10, 51;
    re-creation 8–9; reactive 8;
    re-orientation 8–9; top-down versus
    bottom-up 164–5;
    transactional 84–5;
    transformational 84–6; tuning 8–9
clients, identification of 68
coalitions 111
  see also stakeholders *and* stakeholder
    management
coercion 142
collective learning *see* learning
communication 114–20
  channels 116
  content 116
  directionality 114–15
  interpersonal factors and 116–19
  networks 114–16
  roles 115–16
competencies 123–4
component models of organisational functioning 23, 89
confrontation meetings 183
congruence model of organisations 28–31
conguency *see* alignment
constituents *see* stakeholders
content analysis 96
contingency theories 25
continuous change *see* incremental change

continuous improvement *see* incremental
    change
control, maintaining 166–71
culture *see* organisational culture

data-collection methods 92–5
    and political considerations 97–9
denial 151–2
determinism 17
    see also change agency
diagnosis 54–6, 71–87
    internal alignment 80–1
    organisation–environment fit 78–80
    characteristics of good diagnostic
        models 86–7
    clarifying information
        requirements 90
    role of conceptual models 71–2, 86–7
    selecting diagnostic models for 89–90
diversity 5
dominant coalition 29
downsizing 184
durational expectancy

effectiveness 1, 11–19
    and conceptualisations of
        organisations 15–17
    and time frame 27–9
efficiency 14
entropy 23
equifinality 24
equity of treatment 133
expectancy theory 132–9
expectations *see* expectancy theory
experts, use of 176–7

fashion and fad 195
feedback mechanisms 170
fit *see* alignment
force field 52
force-field analysis 96–7
future shock 3, 7

Grid interventions 183
groups, influence of 177–9, 196
groupthink 44

helplessness 21
holistic models of organisational
    functioning 23, 89

ideologies *see* learning
implementation 56–7

interaction process analysis 94
interventions
    selection of 187–98: depth of emotional
        involvement 189–90; diagnosed
        issue 187–8; efficacy of
        interventions 193–5; level of change
        target 187–8; sequencing 195–7;
        three-dimensional model 190–3;
        time available 193
    types of 175–86: Cummings and
        Worley's typology 182;
        HRM interventions 185;
        human-process interventions 183;
        strategic interventions 185;
        technostructural interventions 184
interviews 116–19
    see also data-collection methods

job design 184, 194

Kotter's integrative model of organisational
    dynamics 26–8, 82–3

large group interventions 183
    see also whole system interventions
leadership 108–12
learned helplessness *see* helplessness;
    compare with change agency
learning
    collective 2, 38–42
    and collective memories 41
    double-loop 39–41, 202
    and ideologies 2, 38–42
    impediments to 42–4
    individual 39
    organisational 2, 36–46
    single-loop 39–40, 201
    triggers for 41
letting go 151
leverage points 169
Lewin's three-step model of change 51–2,
    96–7
life crisis 146
Likert's system 4, 183
locus of control 20
    see also helplessness
logical incrementalism *see* strategy

manipulation 142
meaning, sharing of 43
mental models 39, 42, 43–5, 185
methods engineering 176
monitoring 202–4
motivation 128–42

Nadler and Tushman's congruence
    model   28–31, 83
negotiation   142
novelty   5, 7
NUDist software tool   96

observation   *see* data collection
open-systems planning   181, 185
open-systems theory   23–32
operations research   189
organisational culture   39
organisational learning   *see* learning
organisations
    goals perspective   15
    OD perspective   16
    political arena perspective   16–17, 105–8
    systems perspective   15

paradigms   *see* mental models
parallel organisations   180
participation   140
Pascal and Athos' 7S model   80
performance drivers   203
performance management   185
performance measurement   204–7
    see also effectiveness
personal transitions   *see* transitions
persuasion   140
PEST   38, 78
pilot sites   164
pockets of good practice   164
political factors   16–17, 57–8, 97–9, 105–8,
    195
    see also stakeholders
power   *see* stakeholders *and* stakeholder
    management
process consultation   183
projective methods of gathering
    information   *see* data collection
psychological contract   128–30
psychological well-being   7
punctuated equilibrium   5–6
purpose   12

quality of work life   184

redundancy   145
resistance   65, 97–9, 130–1, 140–2, 163, 181
rituals   141

sampling   95
self-report bias   93
sensitivity training   183, 194
    see also T-groups

social readjustment rating scale   146–8
socio-technical systems   179–80
stakeholder management   106–8, 134
stakeholders   12, 16
strategic change management   36–8
strategic drift   42, 63
strategy
    emergent approach   37–8
    logical incrementalism   37
    organisational learning and   38
    planning approach   37
    Strebel's cycle of competitive
        behaviour   79–80
success
    need for an early   196
    trap of   63, 4
support   141
survivor syndrome   130
sustaining change   207–8
SWOT   38, 79

task analysis   123
team building   183
T-groups   183, 194
    see also sensitivity training
third-party inteventions   183
time-and-motion analysis   176
time pressure   8
timing   120
total quality management (TQM)   184, 193,
    194
training   122–6
    evaluating effectiveness of   125–6
    methods   124–5
    needs analysis   123–4
transience   4–5, 7
transition manager   167
transition plan   168
transition state   166
transitions   144–57
    states of psychological reaction   151–4
trust   117, 130, 163
    see also change relationships

unobtrusive measures   *see* data collection
urgency   110, 162, 196

vision   55, 111, 167
voluntarism   17, 18
    see also change agency

Weisbord's six-box model   80–1
whole system interventions   180–2